THE X-MEN HAVE WORKED HARD TO PROVE THEIR WORTH AS HEROES, DESPITE THE STRUGGLES THAT CAME WITH BEING DISPLACED IN TIME. THE TEAM HAS [...] OF ALTERNATE-UNIVERSE WOLVERINE, AND BLOODST[...] HIS MERRY GANG OF MISFITS.

BUT DURING ALL OF THE ADVENTURES THE TEAM HAS SHARED, MAGNETO HAS BEEN HIDING A TERRIBLE SECRET...
AND SECRETS CAN'T STAY BURIED [...]

X-MEN BLUE

CROSS TIME CAPERS

Writer/**CULLEN BUNN**

ISSUE #16
Artist/**THONY SILAS**
Color Artist/**RAIN BEREDO**
Cover Art/**ARTHUR ADAMS** & **IAN HERRING**

ISSUES #17-20
Penciler/**R.B. SILVA**
Inker/**ADRIANO DI BENEDETTO**
Color Artist/**RAIN BEREDO**
Cover Art/**ARTHUR ADAMS**
with **PETER STEIGERWALD** (#17, #20),
FEDERICO BLEE (#18) and **RAIN BEREDO** (#19)

Letterer/**VC's JOE CARAMAGNA**

Assistant Editors/**CHRISTINA HARRINGTON** & **CHRIS ROBINSON**
Editors/**MARK PANICCIA** & **DARREN SHAN**

X-MEN CREATED BY **STAN LEE** & **JACK KIRBY**

Collection Editor/**JENNIFER GRÜNWALD** • Assistant Editor/**CAITLIN O'CONNELL**
Associate Managing Editor/**KATERI WOODY** • Editor, Special Projects/**MARK D. BEAZLEY**
VP Production & Special Projects/**JEFF YOUNGQUIST** • SVP Print, Sales & Marketing/**DAVID GABRIEL**
Book Designer/**JAY BOWEN**

Editor in Chief/**C.B. CEBULSKI** • Chief Creative Officer/**JOE QUESADA**
President/**DAN BUCKLEY** • Executive Producer/**ALAN FINE**

16

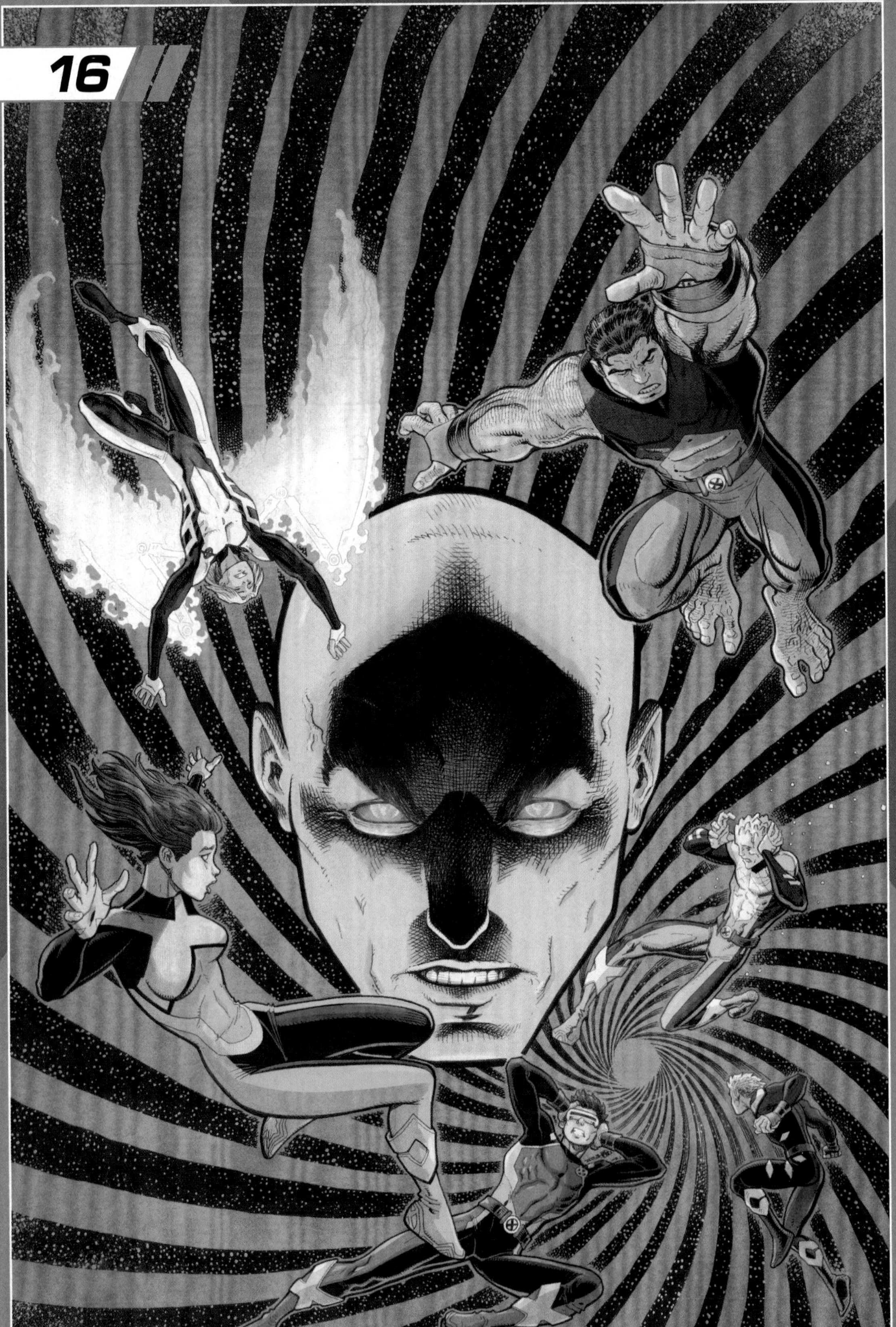
ARTHUR ADAMS
8-9-2017

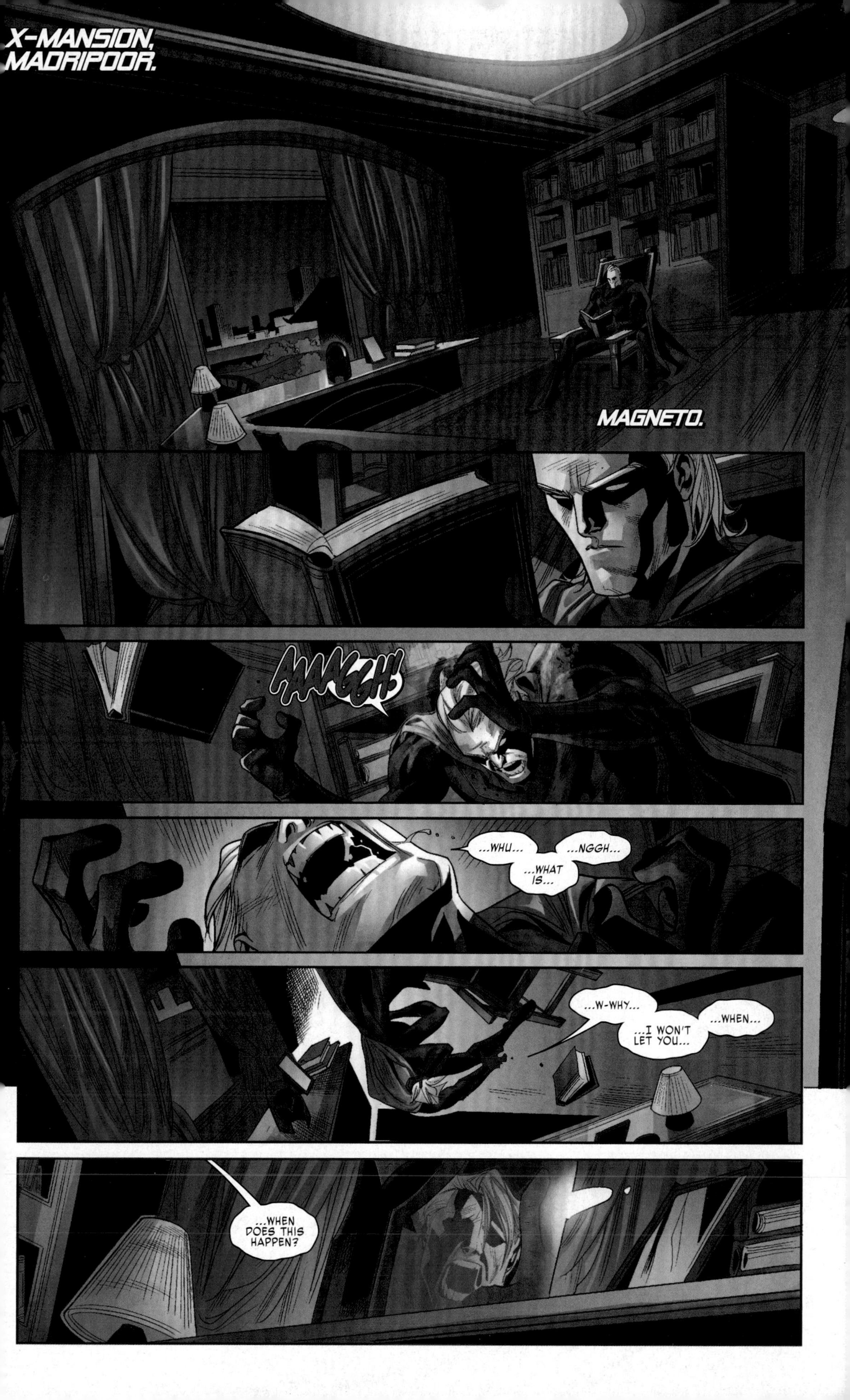
X-MANSION, MADRIPOOR.
MAGNETO.
AAAAGGH!
...WHU...
...WHAT IS...
...NGGH...
...W-WHY...
...I WON'T LET YOU...
...WHEN...
...WHEN DOES THIS HAPPEN?

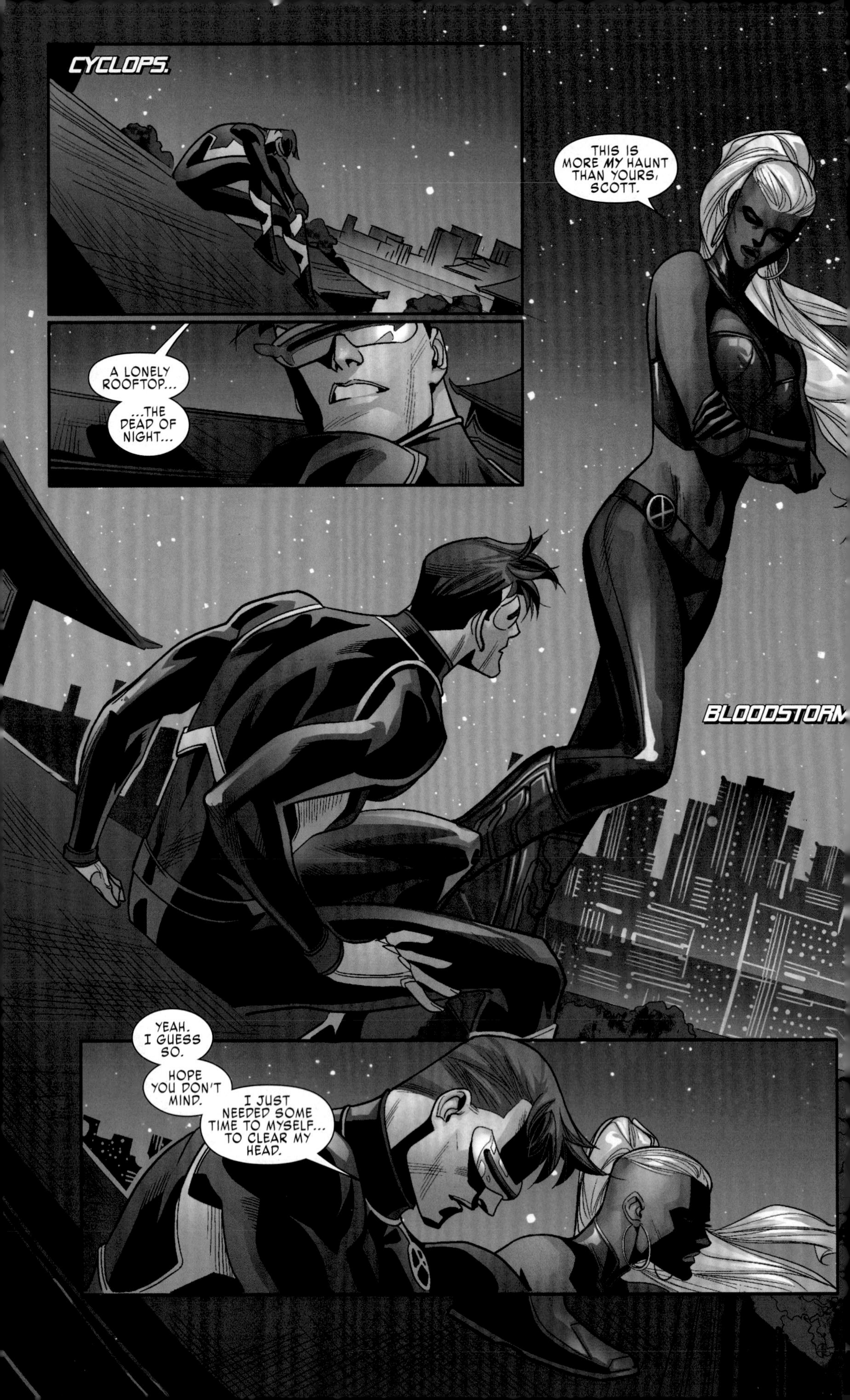
CYCLOPS.
THIS IS MORE MY HAUNT THAN YOURS, SCOTT.
A LONELY ROOFTOP...
...THE DEAD OF NIGHT...
BLOODSTORM
YEAH. I GUESS SO.
HOPE YOU DON'T MIND.
I JUST NEEDED SOME TIME TO MYSELF... TO CLEAR MY HEAD.

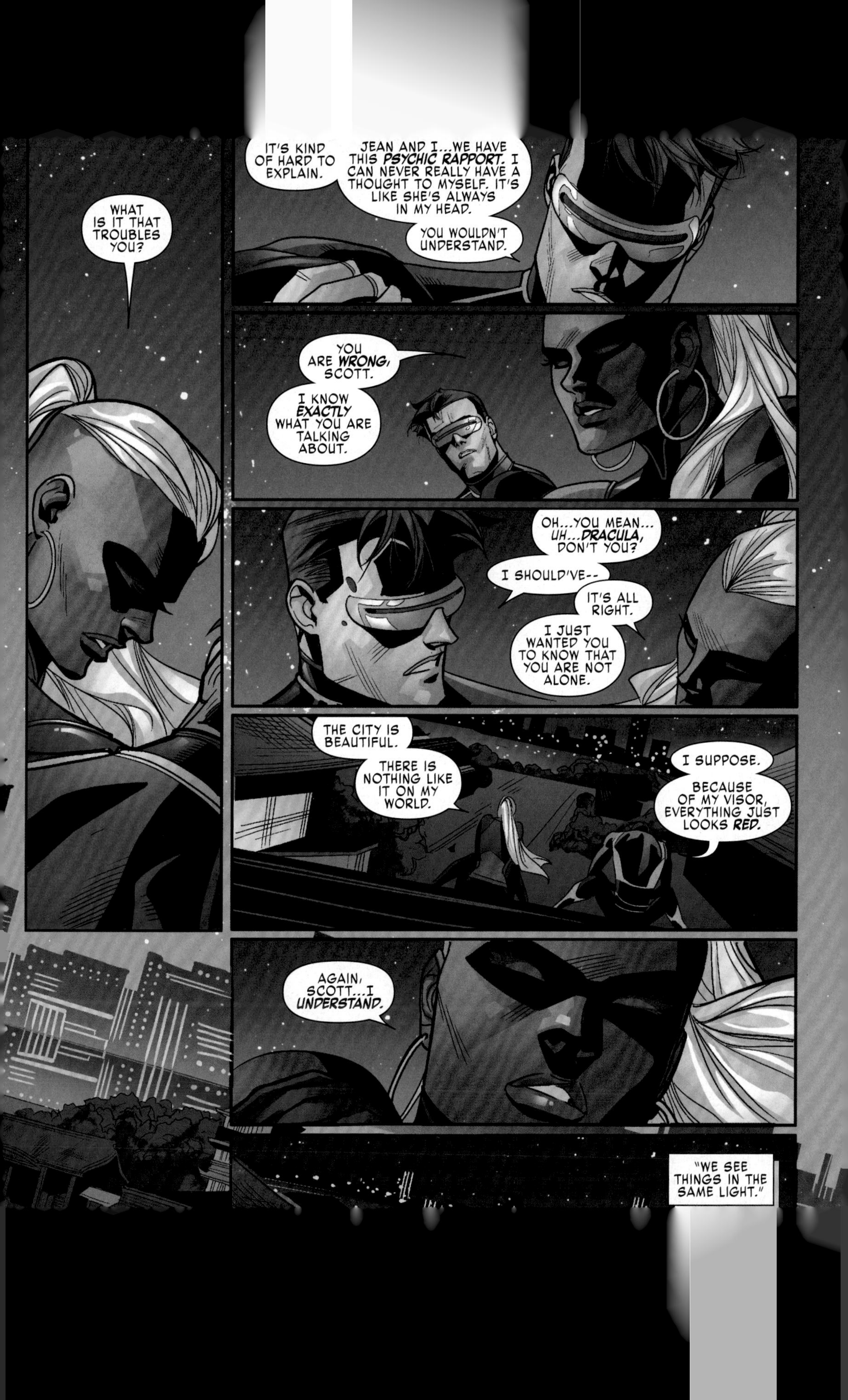
WHAT IS IT THAT TROUBLES YOU?
IT'S KIND OF HARD TO EXPLAIN.
JEAN AND I...WE HAVE THIS PSYCHIC RAPPORT. I CAN NEVER REALLY HAVE A THOUGHT TO MYSELF. IT'S LIKE SHE'S ALWAYS IN MY HEAD.
YOU WOULDN'T UNDERSTAND.
YOU ARE WRONG, SCOTT.
I KNOW EXACTLY WHAT YOU ARE TALKING ABOUT.
OH...YOU MEAN... UH...DRACULA, DON'T YOU?
I SHOULD'VE--
IT'S ALL RIGHT.
I JUST WANTED YOU TO KNOW THAT YOU ARE NOT ALONE.
THE CITY IS BEAUTIFUL.
THERE IS NOTHING LIKE IT ON MY WORLD.
I SUPPOSE.
BECAUSE OF MY VISOR, EVERYTHING JUST LOOKS RED.
AGAIN, SCOTT...I UNDERSTAND.
"WE SEE THINGS IN THE SAME LIGHT."

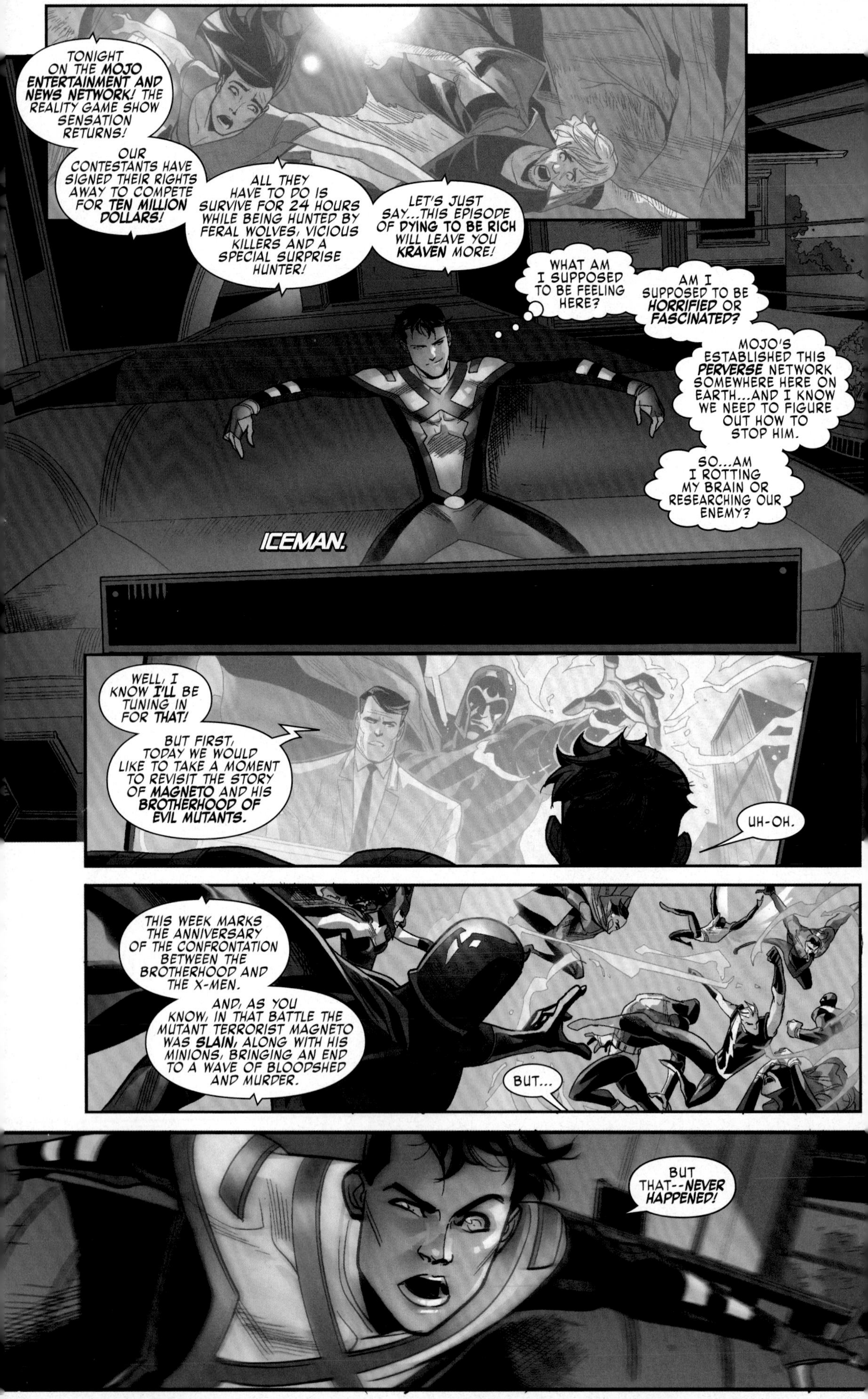
TONIGHT ON THE MOJO ENTERTAINMENT AND NEWS NETWORK! THE REALITY GAME SHOW SENSATION RETURNS!
OUR CONTESTANTS HAVE SIGNED THEIR RIGHTS AWAY TO COMPETE FOR TEN MILLION DOLLARS!
ALL THEY HAVE TO DO IS SURVIVE FOR 24 HOURS WHILE BEING HUNTED BY FERAL WOLVES, VICIOUS KILLERS AND A SPECIAL SURPRISE HUNTER!
LET'S JUST SAY...THIS EPISODE OF DYING TO BE RICH WILL LEAVE YOU KRAVEN MORE!
WHAT AM I SUPPOSED TO BE FEELING HERE?
AM I SUPPOSED TO BE HORRIFIED OR FASCINATED?
MOJO'S ESTABLISHED THIS PERVERSE NETWORK SOMEWHERE HERE ON EARTH...AND I KNOW WE NEED TO FIGURE OUT HOW TO STOP HIM.
SO...AM I ROTTING MY BRAIN OR RESEARCHING OUR ENEMY?
ICEMAN.
WELL, I KNOW I'LL BE TUNING IN FOR THAT!
BUT FIRST, TODAY WE WOULD LIKE TO TAKE A MOMENT TO REVISIT THE STORY OF MAGNETO AND HIS BROTHERHOOD OF EVIL MUTANTS.
UH-OH.
THIS WEEK MARKS THE ANNIVERSARY OF THE CONFRONTATION BETWEEN THE BROTHERHOOD AND THE X-MEN.
AND, AS YOU KNOW, IN THAT BATTLE THE MUTANT TERRORIST MAGNETO WAS SLAIN, ALONG WITH HIS MINIONS, BRINGING AN END TO A WAVE OF BLOODSHED AND MURDER.
BUT...
BUT THAT--NEVER HAPPENED!

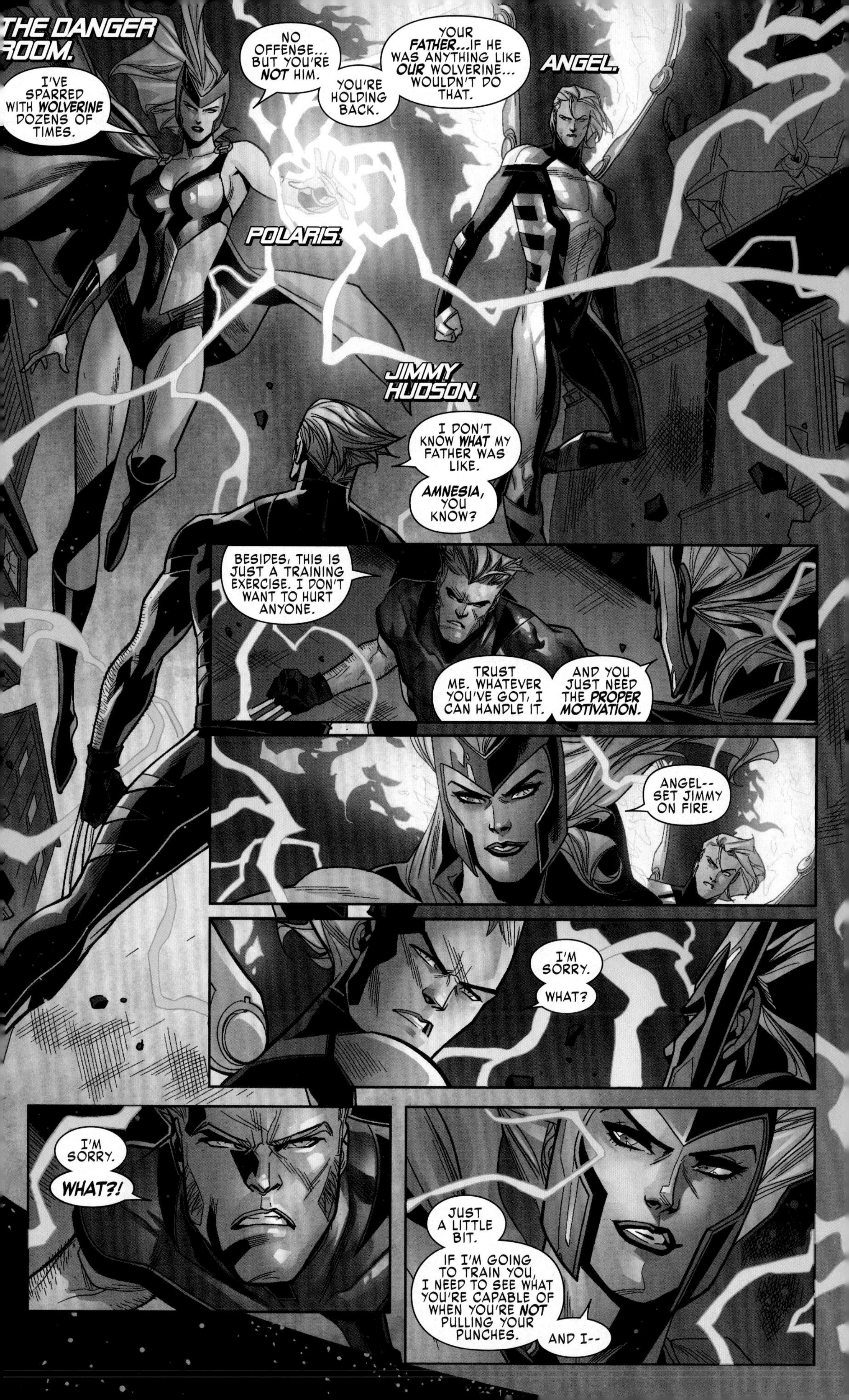
THE DANGER ROOM.
I'VE SPARRED WITH WOLVERINE DOZENS OF TIMES.
NO OFFENSE... BUT YOU'RE NOT HIM.
YOU'RE HOLDING BACK.
YOUR FATHER...IF HE WAS ANYTHING LIKE OUR WOLVERINE... WOULDN'T DO THAT.
ANGEL.
POLARIS.
JIMMY HUDSON.
I DON'T KNOW WHAT MY FATHER WAS LIKE.
AMNESIA, YOU KNOW?
BESIDES, THIS IS JUST A TRAINING EXERCISE. I DON'T WANT TO HURT ANYONE.
TRUST ME. WHATEVER YOU'VE GOT, I CAN HANDLE IT.
AND YOU JUST NEED THE PROPER MOTIVATION.
ANGEL-- SET JIMMY ON FIRE.
I'M SORRY.
WHAT?
I'M SORRY.
WHAT?!
JUST A LITTLE BIT.
IF I'M GOING TO TRAIN YOU, I NEED TO SEE WHAT YOU'RE CAPABLE OF WHEN YOU'RE NOT PULLING YOUR PUNCHES.
AND I--

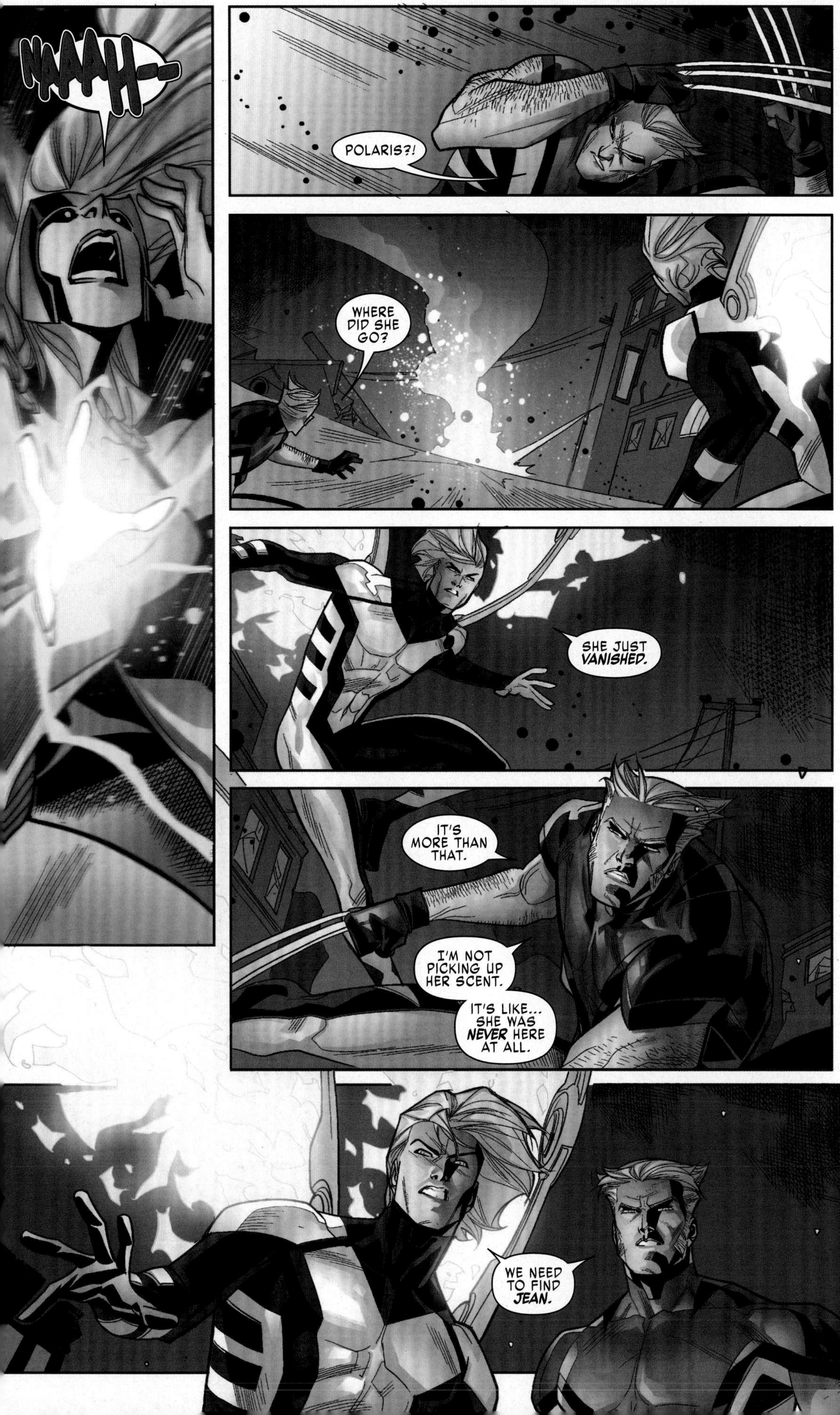
NAAAH--
POLARIS?!
WHERE DID SHE GO?
SHE JUST VANISHED.
IT'S MORE THAN THAT.
I'M NOT PICKING UP HER SCENT.
IT'S LIKE... SHE WAS NEVER HERE AT ALL.
WE NEED TO FIND JEAN.

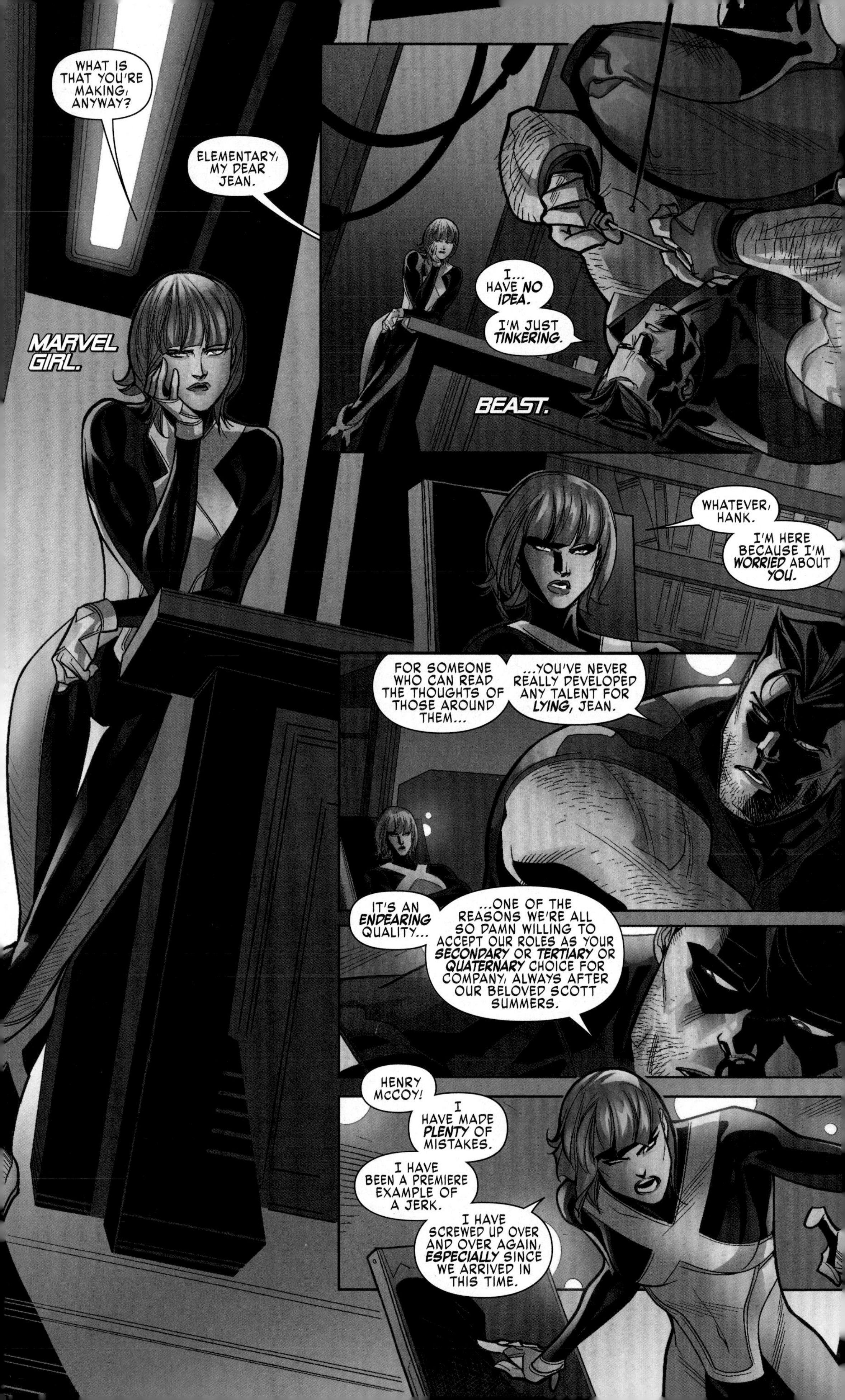
WHAT IS THAT YOU'RE MAKING, ANYWAY?
ELEMENTARY, MY DEAR JEAN.
MARVEL GIRL.
I... HAVE NO IDEA.
I'M JUST TINKERING.
BEAST.
WHATEVER, HANK.
I'M HERE BECAUSE I'M WORRIED ABOUT YOU.
FOR SOMEONE WHO CAN READ THE THOUGHTS OF THOSE AROUND THEM...
...YOU'VE NEVER REALLY DEVELOPED ANY TALENT FOR LYING, JEAN.
IT'S AN ENDEARING QUALITY...
...ONE OF THE REASONS WE'RE ALL SO DAMN WILLING TO ACCEPT OUR ROLES AS YOUR SECONDARY OR TERTIARY OR QUATERNARY CHOICE FOR COMPANY, ALWAYS AFTER OUR BELOVED SCOTT SUMMERS.
HENRY McCOY!
I HAVE MADE PLENTY OF MISTAKES.
I HAVE BEEN A PREMIERE EXAMPLE OF A JERK.
I HAVE SCREWED UP OVER AND OVER AGAIN, ESPECIALLY SINCE WE ARRIVED IN THIS TIME.

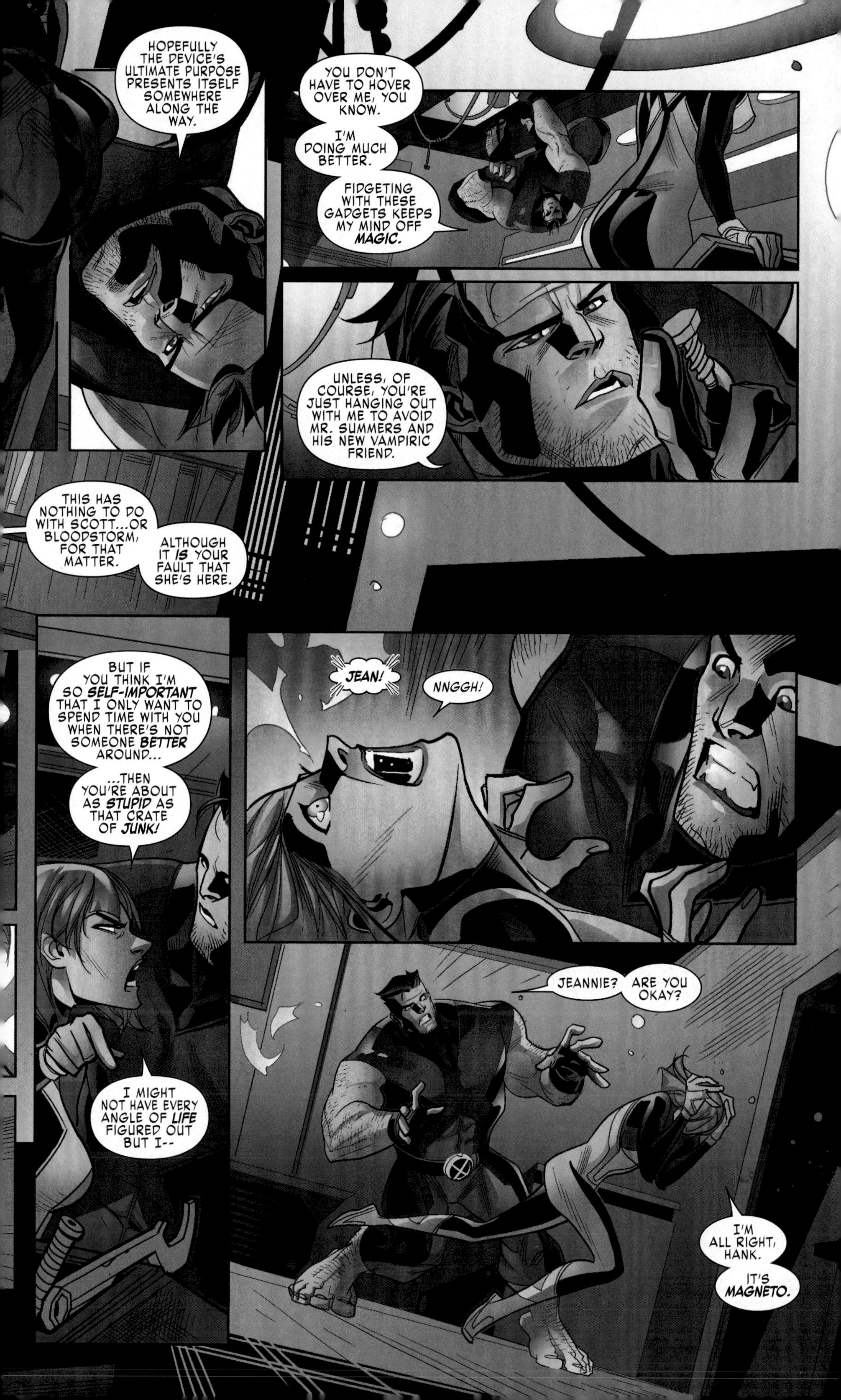

HOPEFULLY THE DEVICE'S ULTIMATE PURPOSE PRESENTS ITSELF SOMEWHERE ALONG THE WAY.
YOU DON'T HAVE TO HOVER OVER ME, YOU KNOW.
I'M DOING MUCH BETTER.
FIDGETING WITH THESE GADGETS KEEPS MY MIND OFF MAGIC.
UNLESS, OF COURSE, YOU'RE JUST HANGING OUT WITH ME TO AVOID MR. SUMMERS AND HIS NEW VAMPIRIC FRIEND.
THIS HAS NOTHING TO DO WITH SCOTT...OR BLOODSTORM, FOR THAT MATTER.
ALTHOUGH IT IS YOUR FAULT THAT SHE'S HERE.
BUT IF YOU THINK I'M SO SELF-IMPORTANT THAT I ONLY WANT TO SPEND TIME WITH YOU WHEN THERE'S NOT SOMEONE BETTER AROUND...
...THEN YOU'RE ABOUT AS STUPID AS THAT CRATE OF JUNK!
I MIGHT NOT HAVE EVERY ANGLE OF LIFE FIGURED OUT BUT I--
JEAN!
NNGGH!
JEANNIE? ARE YOU OKAY?
I'M ALL RIGHT, HANK.
IT'S MAGNETO.

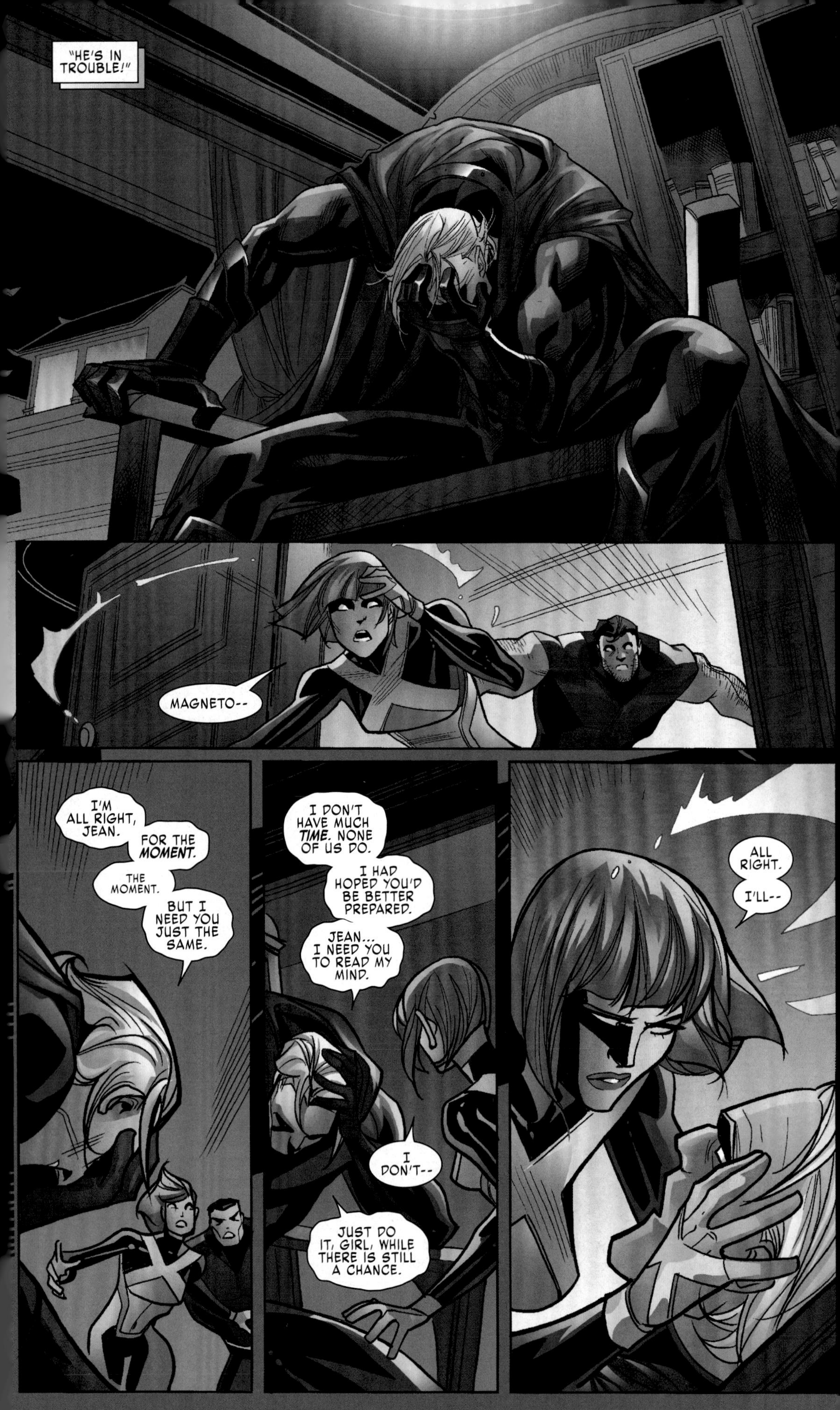
"HE'S IN TROUBLE!"
MAGNETO--
I'M ALL RIGHT, JEAN.
FOR THE *MOMENT*.
THE MOMENT.
BUT I NEED YOU JUST THE SAME.
I DON'T HAVE MUCH *TIME*. NONE OF US DO.
I HAD HOPED YOU'D BE BETTER PREPARED.
JEAN... I NEED YOU TO READ MY MIND.
I DON'T--
JUST DO IT, GIRL, WHILE THERE IS STILL A CHANCE.
ALL RIGHT.
I'LL--

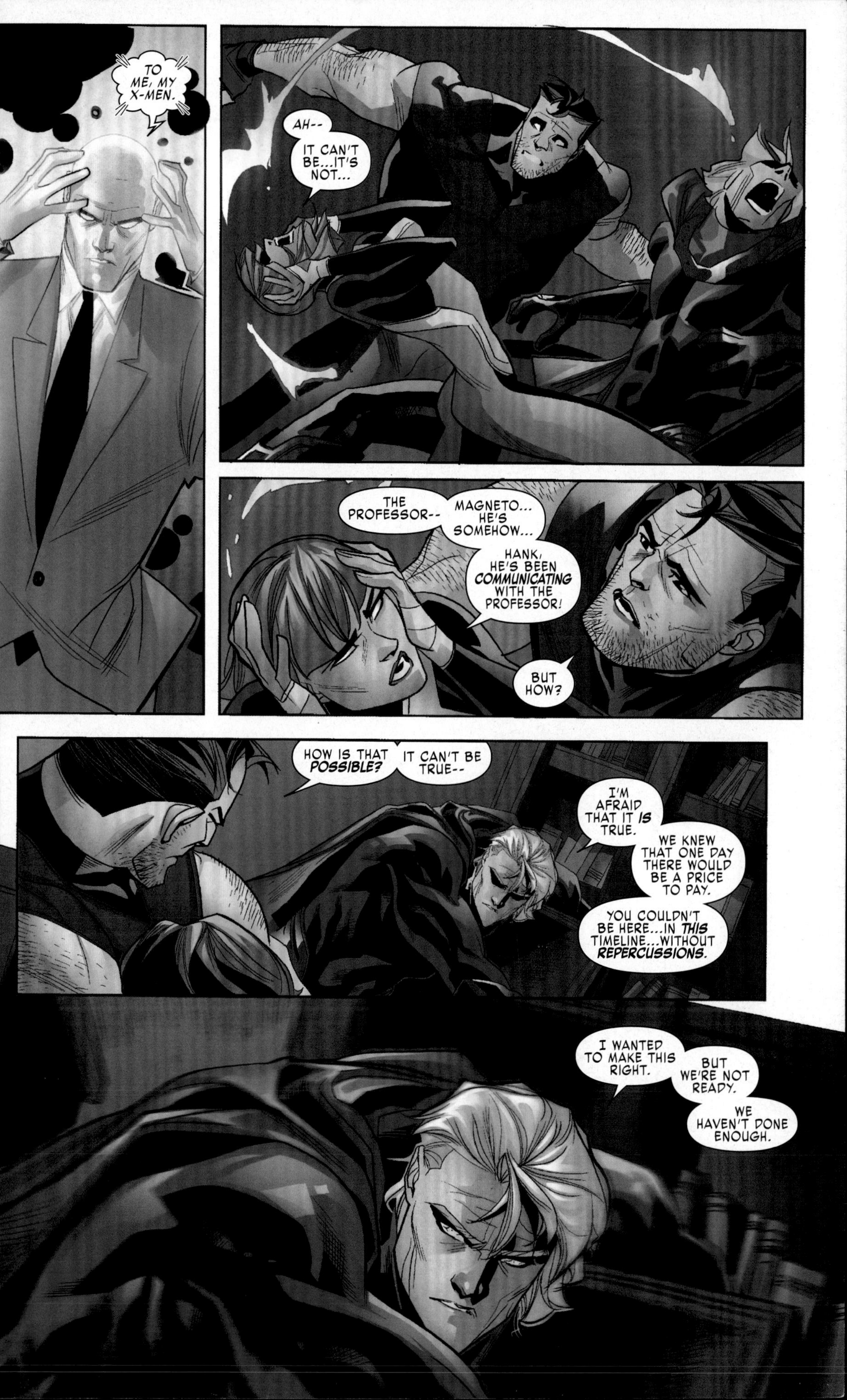
TO ME, MY X-MEN.
AH--
IT CAN'T BE...IT'S NOT...
THE PROFESSOR--
MAGNETO... HE'S SOMEHOW...
HANK, HE'S BEEN **COMMUNICATING** WITH THE PROFESSOR!
BUT HOW?
HOW IS THAT **POSSIBLE?**
IT CAN'T BE TRUE--
I'M AFRAID THAT IT **IS** TRUE.
WE KNEW THAT ONE DAY THERE WOULD BE A PRICE TO PAY.
YOU COULDN'T BE HERE...IN **THIS** TIMELINE...WITHOUT **REPERCUSSIONS.**
I WANTED TO MAKE THIS RIGHT.
BUT WE'RE NOT READY.
WE HAVEN'T DONE ENOUGH.

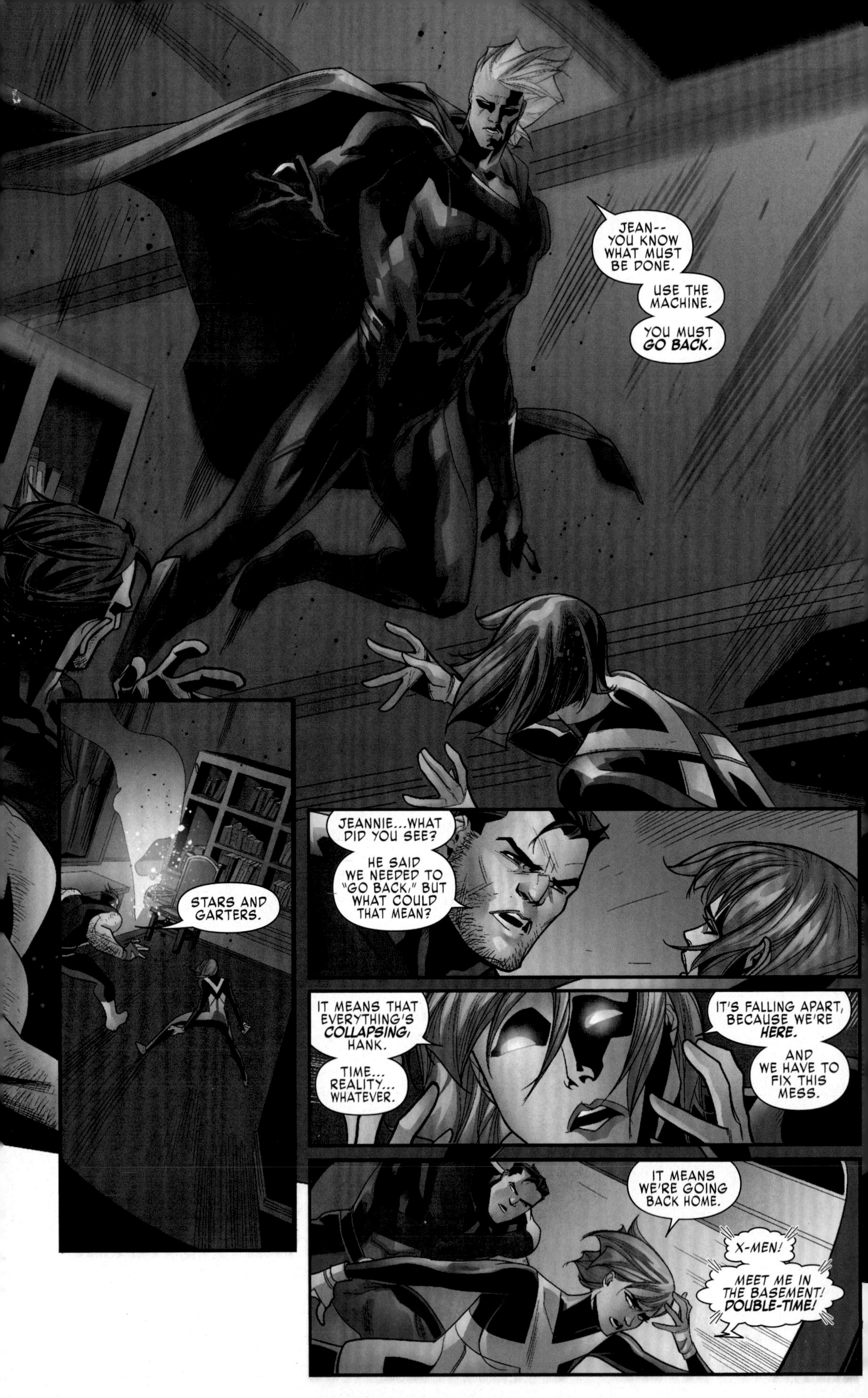

JEAN-- YOU KNOW WHAT MUST BE DONE.
USE THE MACHINE.
YOU MUST *GO BACK.*
STARS AND GARTERS.
JEANNIE...WHAT DID YOU SEE?
HE SAID WE NEEDED TO "GO BACK," BUT WHAT COULD THAT MEAN?
IT MEANS THAT EVERYTHING'S *COLLAPSING,* HANK.
TIME... REALITY... WHATEVER.
IT'S FALLING APART, BECAUSE WE'RE *HERE.*
AND WE HAVE TO FIX THIS MESS.
IT MEANS WE'RE GOING BACK HOME.
X-MEN!
MEET ME IN THE BASEMENT! *DOUBLE-TIME!*

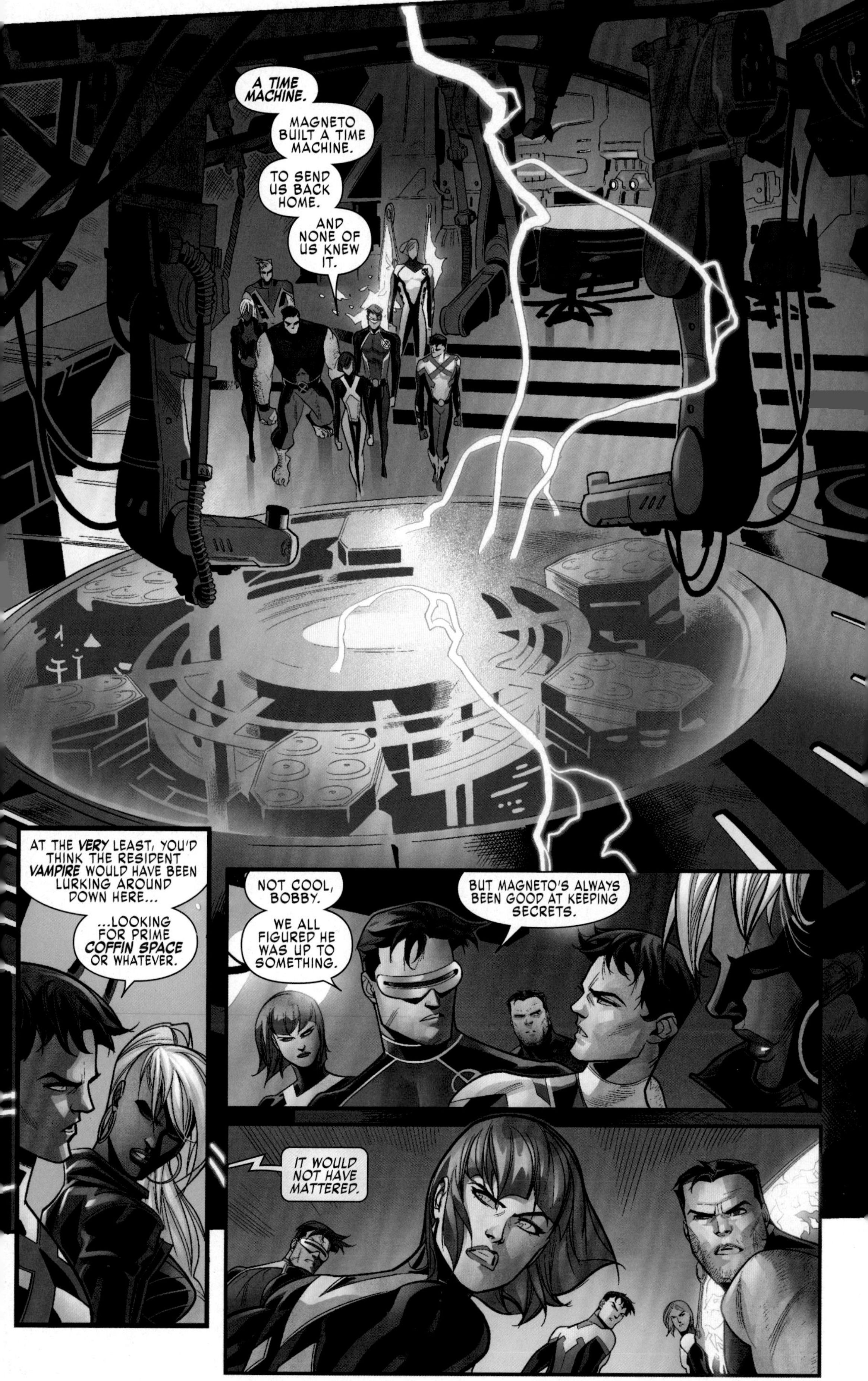

A TIME MACHINE.
MAGNETO BUILT A TIME MACHINE.
TO SEND US BACK HOME.
AND NONE OF US KNEW IT.
AT THE VERY LEAST, YOU'D THINK THE RESIDENT VAMPIRE WOULD HAVE BEEN LURKING AROUND DOWN HERE...
...LOOKING FOR PRIME COFFIN SPACE OR WHATEVER.
NOT COOL, BOBBY.
WE ALL FIGURED HE WAS UP TO SOMETHING.
BUT MAGNETO'S ALWAYS BEEN GOOD AT KEEPING SECRETS.
IT WOULD NOT HAVE MATTERED.

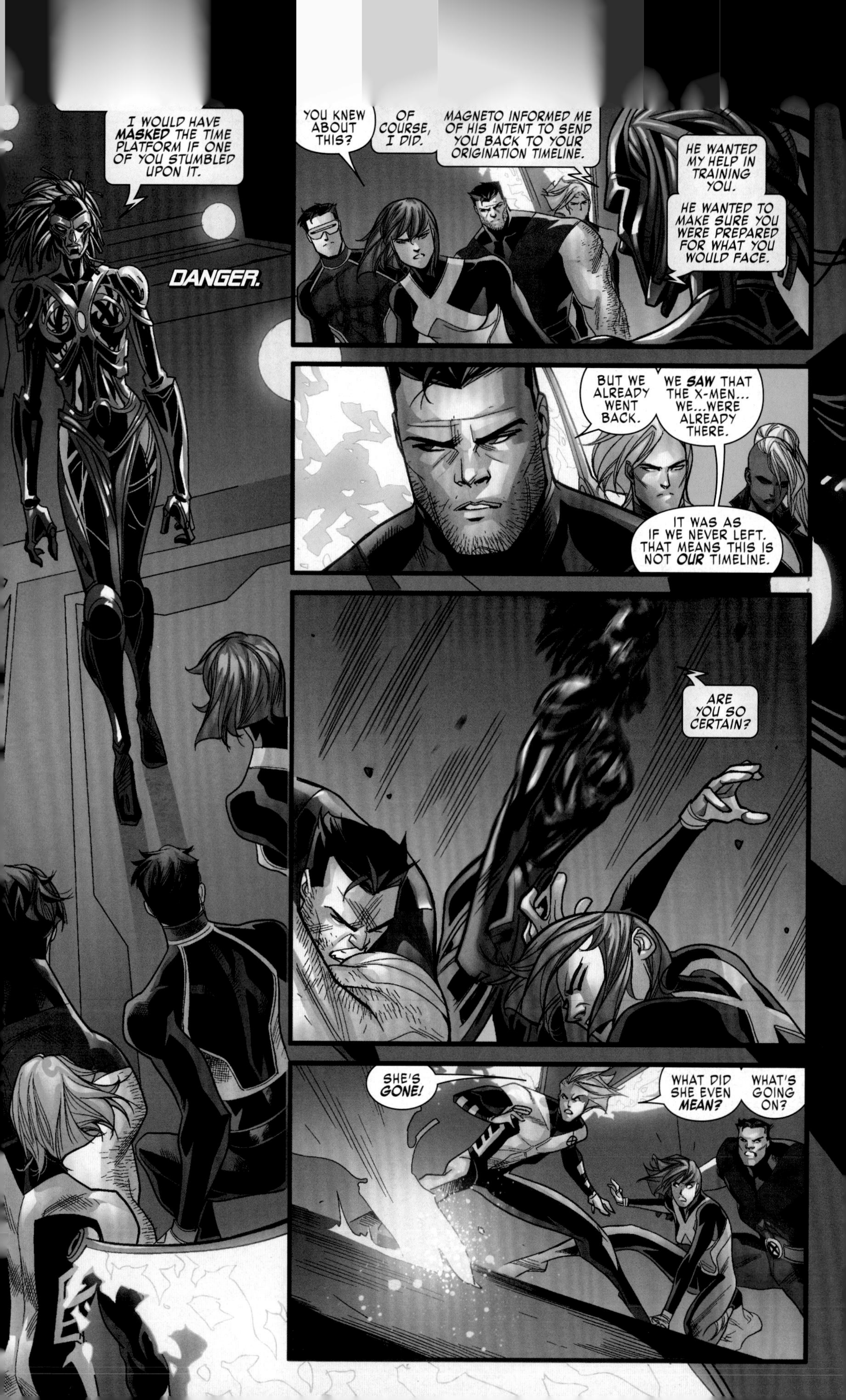

I WOULD HAVE MASKED THE TIME PLATFORM IF ONE OF YOU STUMBLED UPON IT.
DANGER.
YOU KNEW ABOUT THIS?
OF COURSE, I DID.
MAGNETO INFORMED ME OF HIS INTENT TO SEND YOU BACK TO YOUR ORIGINATION TIMELINE.
HE WANTED MY HELP IN TRAINING YOU.
HE WANTED TO MAKE SURE YOU WERE PREPARED FOR WHAT YOU WOULD FACE.
BUT WE ALREADY WENT BACK.
WE SAW THAT THE X-MEN... WE...WERE ALREADY THERE.
IT WAS AS IF WE NEVER LEFT. THAT MEANS THIS IS NOT OUR TIMELINE.
ARE YOU SO CERTAIN?
SHE'S GONE!
WHAT DID SHE EVEN MEAN?
WHAT'S GOING ON?

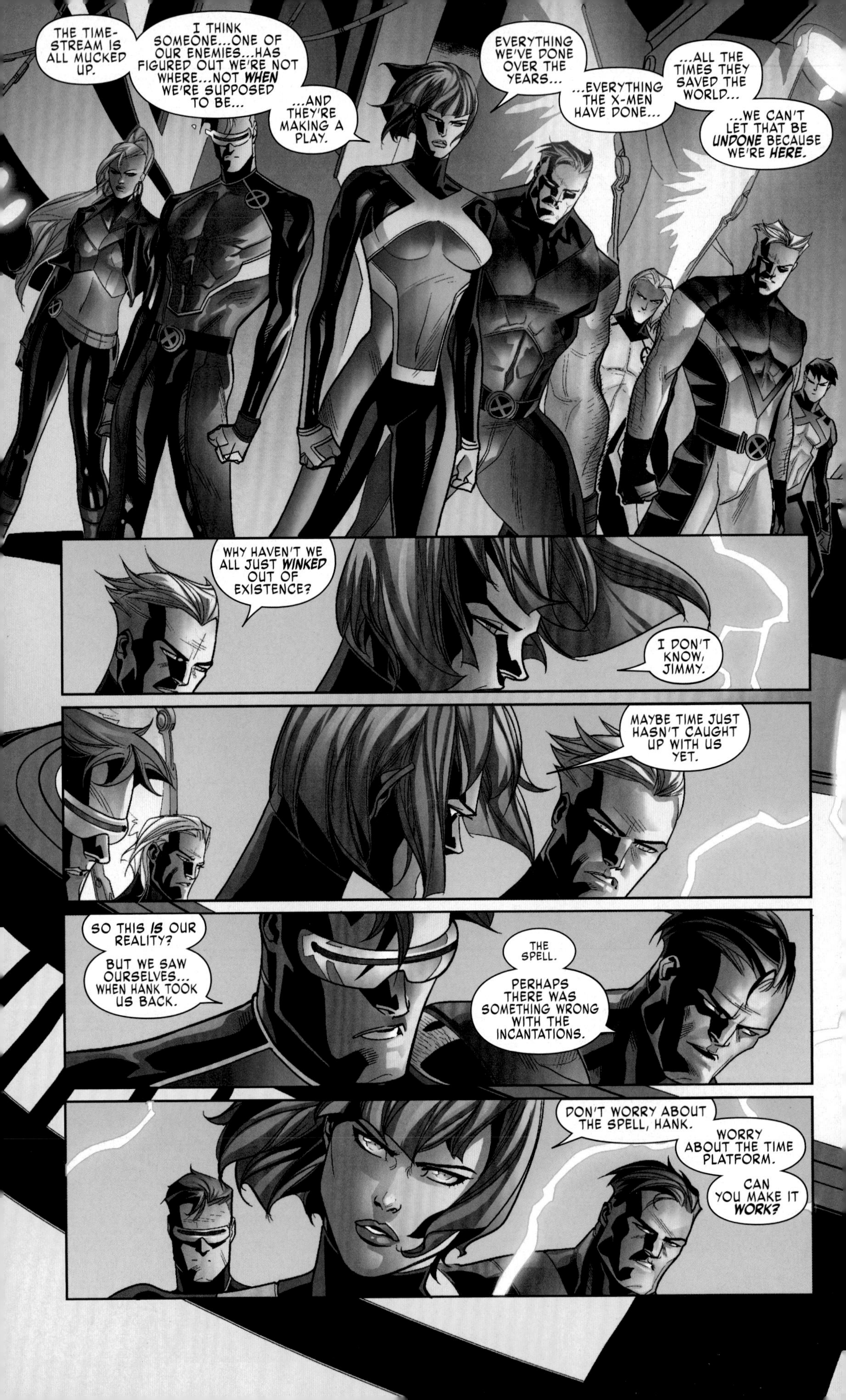
THE TIME-STREAM IS ALL MUCKED UP.
I THINK SOMEONE...ONE OF OUR ENEMIES...HAS FIGURED OUT WE'RE NOT WHERE...NOT WHEN WE'RE SUPPOSED TO BE...
...AND THEY'RE MAKING A PLAY.
EVERYTHING WE'VE DONE OVER THE YEARS...
...EVERYTHING THE X-MEN HAVE DONE...
...ALL THE TIMES THEY SAVED THE WORLD...
...WE CAN'T LET THAT BE UNDONE BECAUSE WE'RE HERE.
WHY HAVEN'T WE ALL JUST WINKED OUT OF EXISTENCE?
I DON'T KNOW, JIMMY.
MAYBE TIME JUST HASN'T CAUGHT UP WITH US YET.
SO THIS IS OUR REALITY?
BUT WE SAW OURSELVES... WHEN HANK TOOK US BACK.
THE SPELL.
PERHAPS THERE WAS SOMETHING WRONG WITH THE INCANTATIONS.
DON'T WORRY ABOUT THE SPELL, HANK.
WORRY ABOUT THE TIME PLATFORM.
CAN YOU MAKE IT WORK?

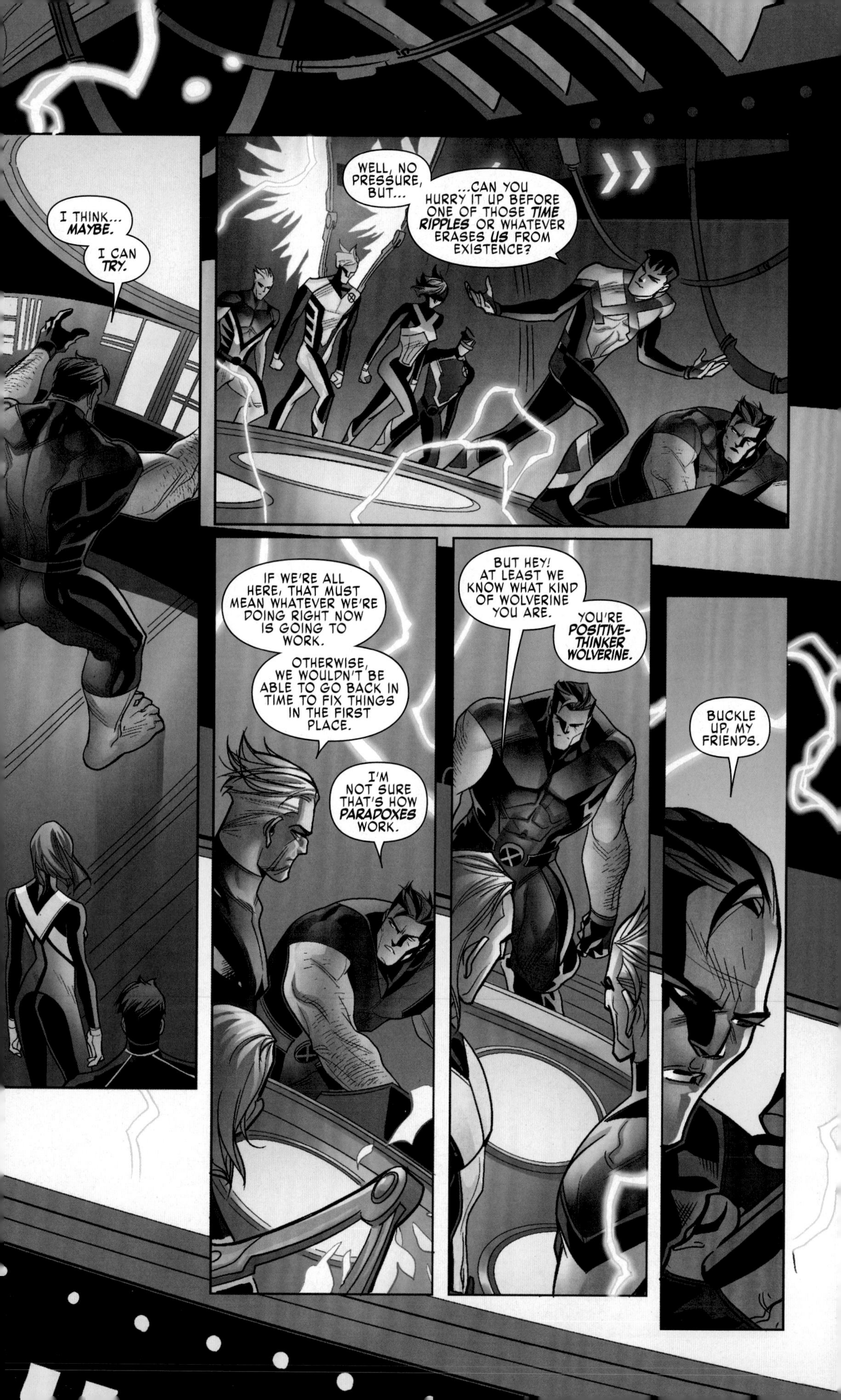
I THINK... MAYBE.
I CAN TRY.
WELL, NO PRESSURE, BUT...
...CAN YOU HURRY IT UP BEFORE ONE OF THOSE TIME RIPPLES OR WHATEVER ERASES US FROM EXISTENCE?
IF WE'RE ALL HERE, THAT MUST MEAN WHATEVER WE'RE DOING RIGHT NOW IS GOING TO WORK.
OTHERWISE, WE WOULDN'T BE ABLE TO GO BACK IN TIME TO FIX THINGS IN THE FIRST PLACE.
I'M NOT SURE THAT'S HOW PARADOXES WORK.
BUT HEY! AT LEAST WE KNOW WHAT KIND OF WOLVERINE YOU ARE.
YOU'RE POSITIVE-THINKER WOLVERINE.
BUCKLE UP, MY FRIENDS.

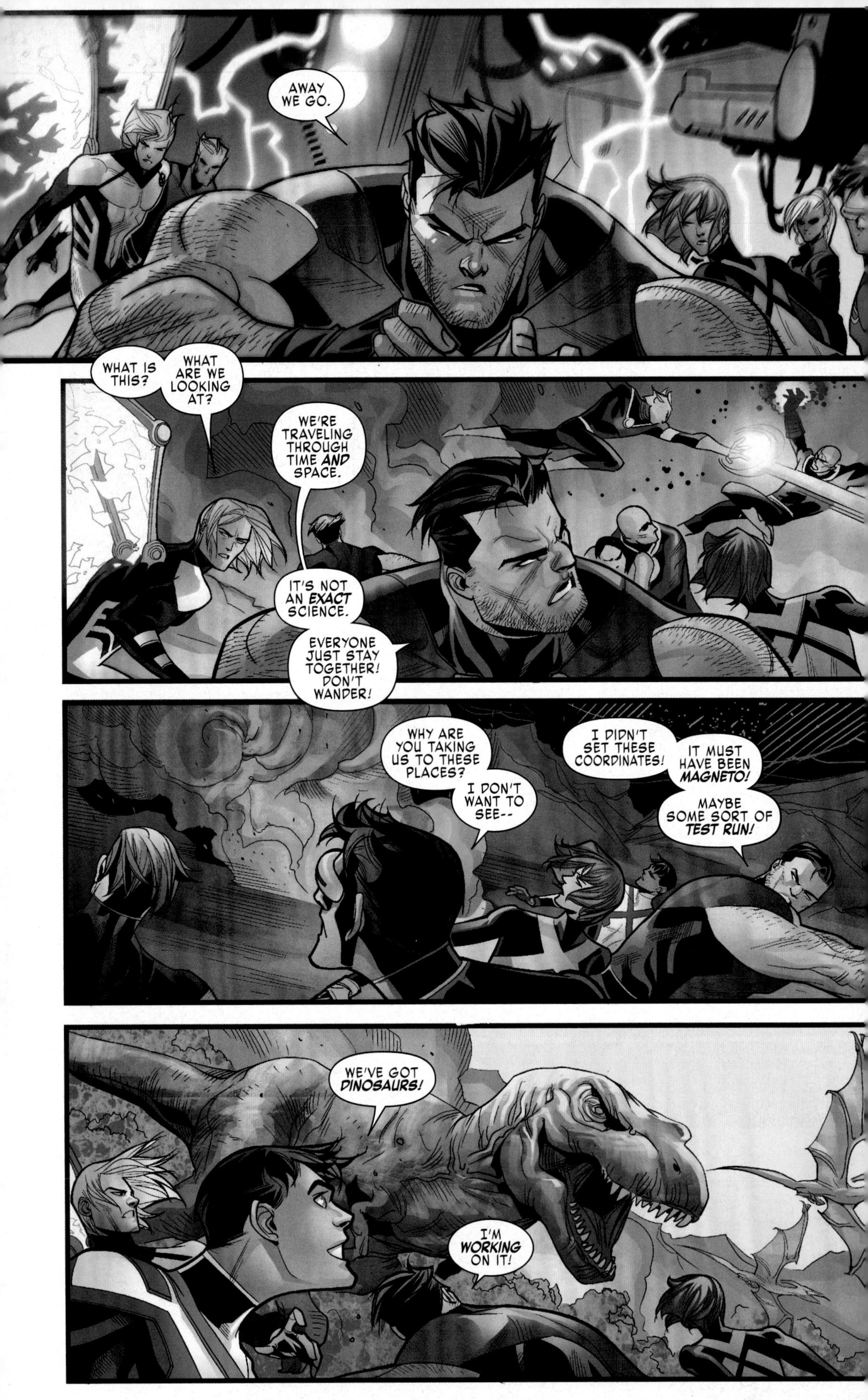

AWAY WE GO.
WHAT IS THIS?
WHAT ARE WE LOOKING AT?
WE'RE TRAVELING THROUGH TIME AND SPACE.
IT'S NOT AN EXACT SCIENCE.
EVERYONE JUST STAY TOGETHER! DON'T WANDER!
WHY ARE YOU TAKING US TO THESE PLACES?
I DON'T WANT TO SEE--
I DIDN'T SET THESE COORDINATES!
IT MUST HAVE BEEN MAGNETO!
MAYBE SOME SORT OF TEST RUN!
WE'VE GOT DINOSAURS!
I'M WORKING ON IT!

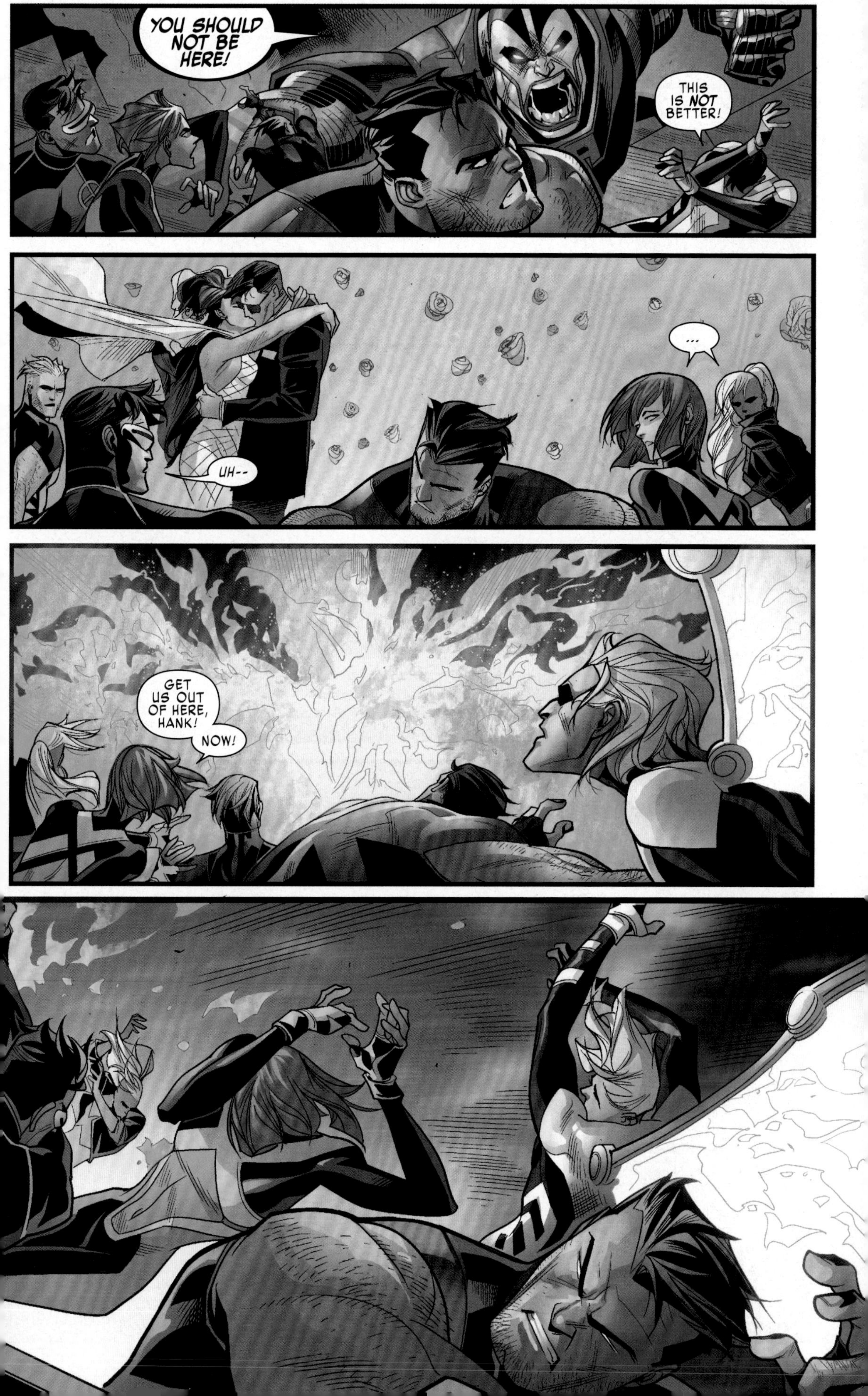
YOU SHOULD NOT BE HERE!
THIS IS NOT BETTER!
...
UH--
GET US OUT OF HERE, HANK!
NOW!

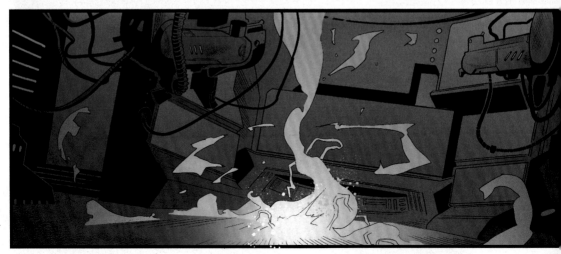

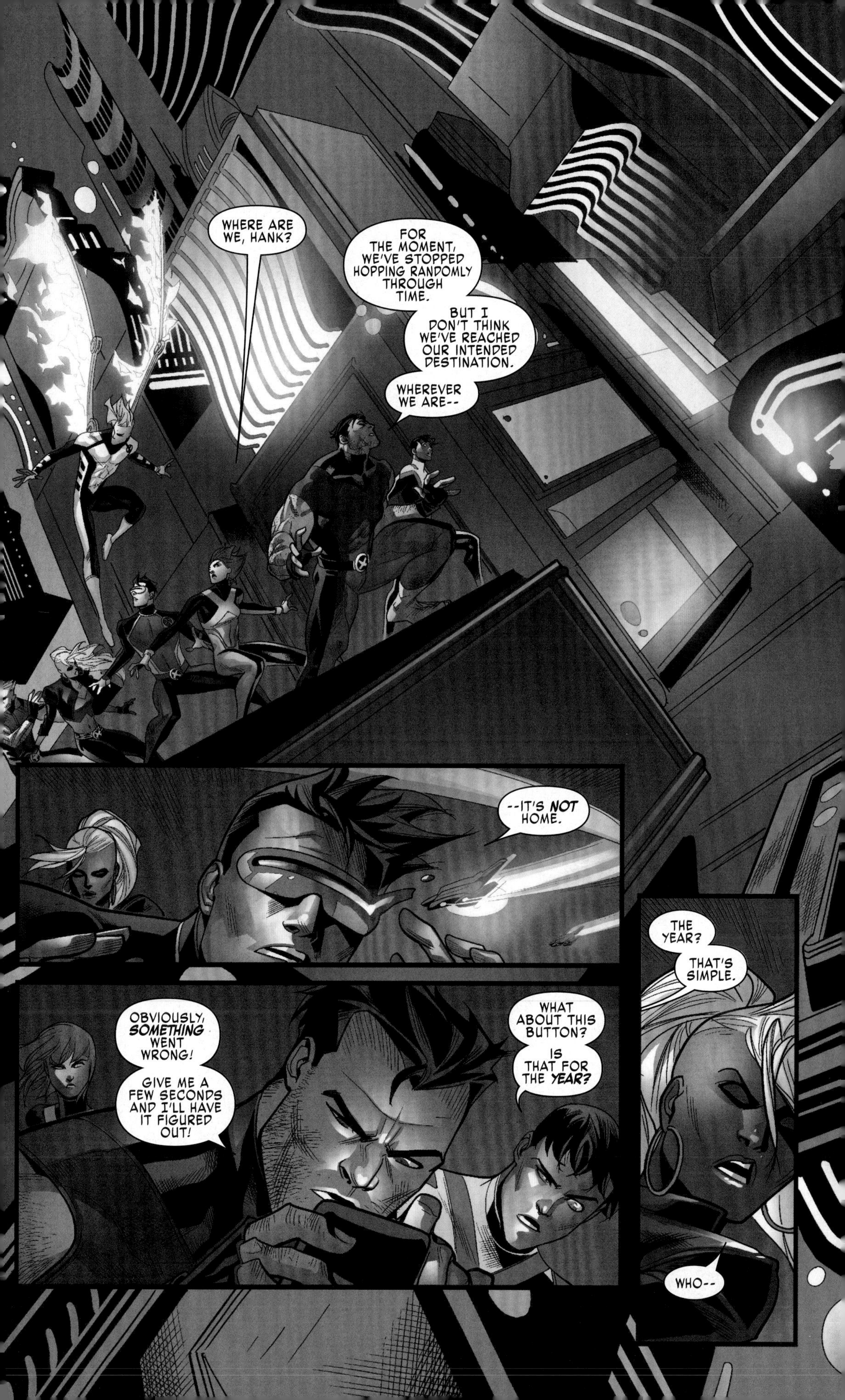
WHERE ARE WE, HANK?
FOR THE MOMENT, WE'VE STOPPED HOPPING RANDOMLY THROUGH TIME.
BUT I DON'T THINK WE'VE REACHED OUR INTENDED DESTINATION.
WHEREVER WE ARE--
--IT'S NOT HOME.
OBVIOUSLY, SOMETHING WENT WRONG!
GIVE ME A FEW SECONDS AND I'LL HAVE IT FIGURED OUT!
WHAT ABOUT THIS BUTTON?
IS THAT FOR THE YEAR?
THE YEAR?
THAT'S SIMPLE.
WHO--

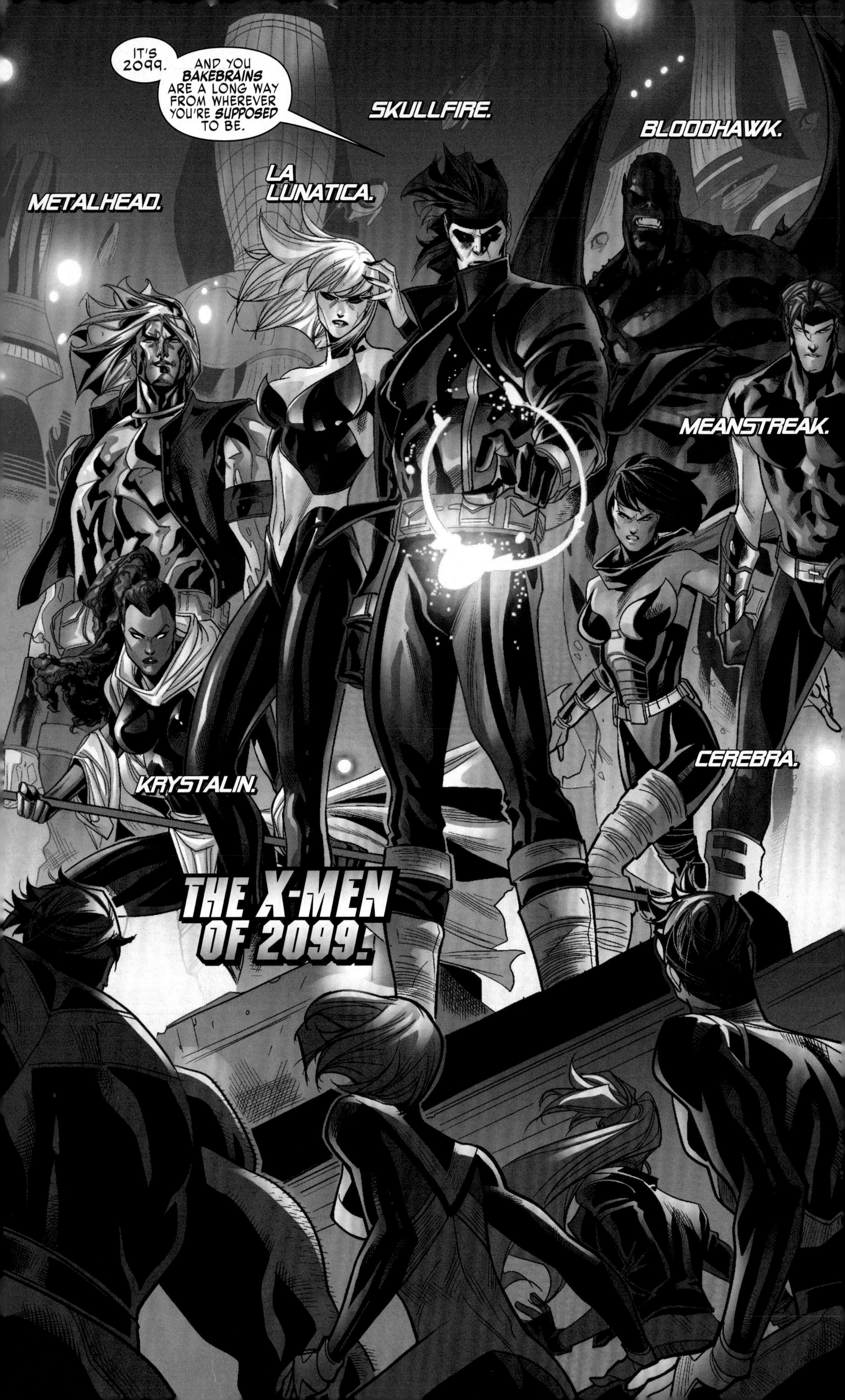
IT'S 2099.
AND YOU BAKEBRAINS ARE A LONG WAY FROM WHEREVER YOU'RE SUPPOSED TO BE.
METALHEAD.
LA LUNATICA.
SKULLFIRE.
BLOODHAWK.
MEANSTREAK.
KRYSTALIN.
CEREBRA.
THE X-MEN OF 2099.

17

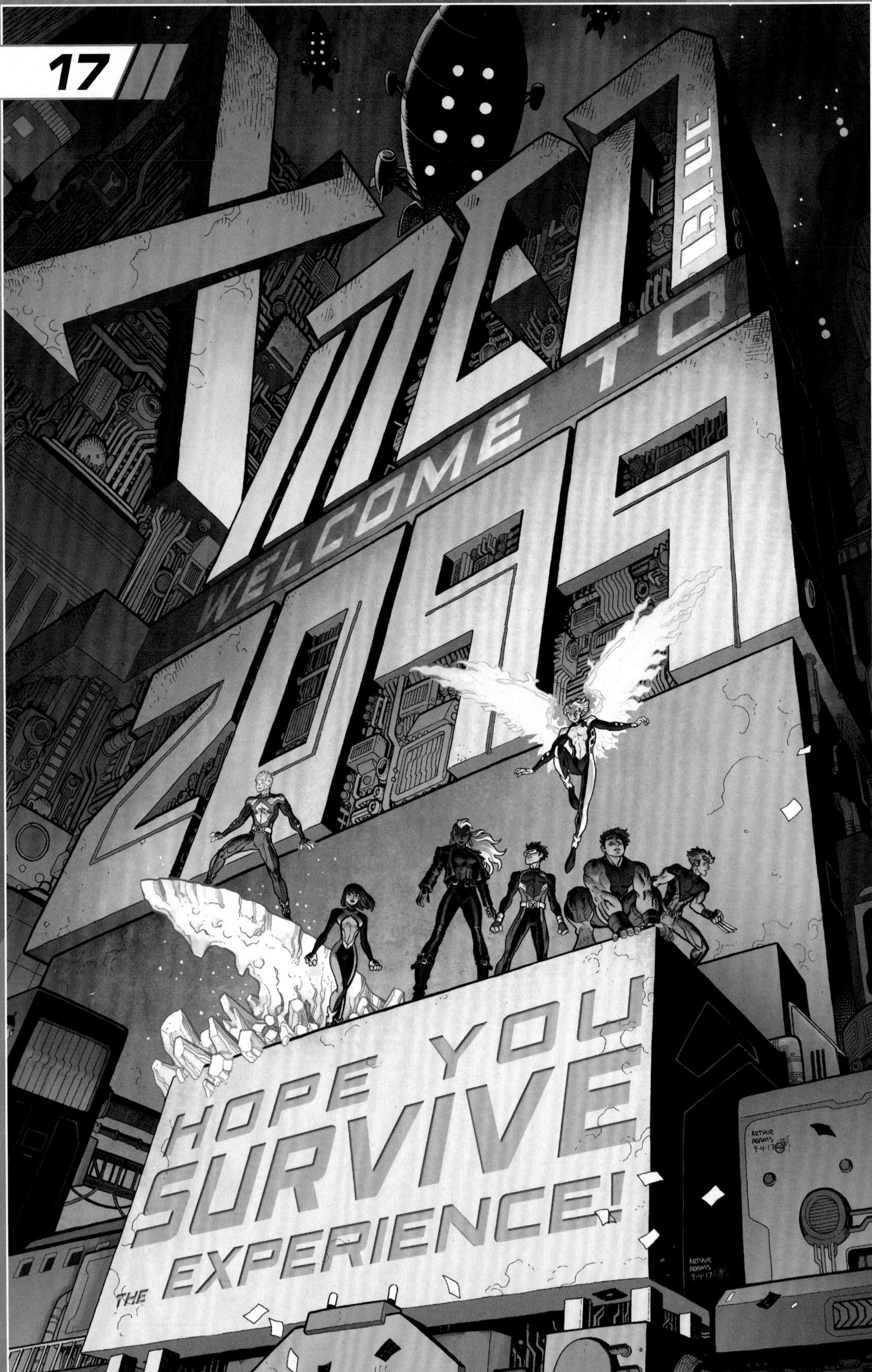
BLUE
WELCOME TO
2099
HOPE YOU SURVIVE THE EXPERIENCE!
ARTHUR ADAMS 9-4-17

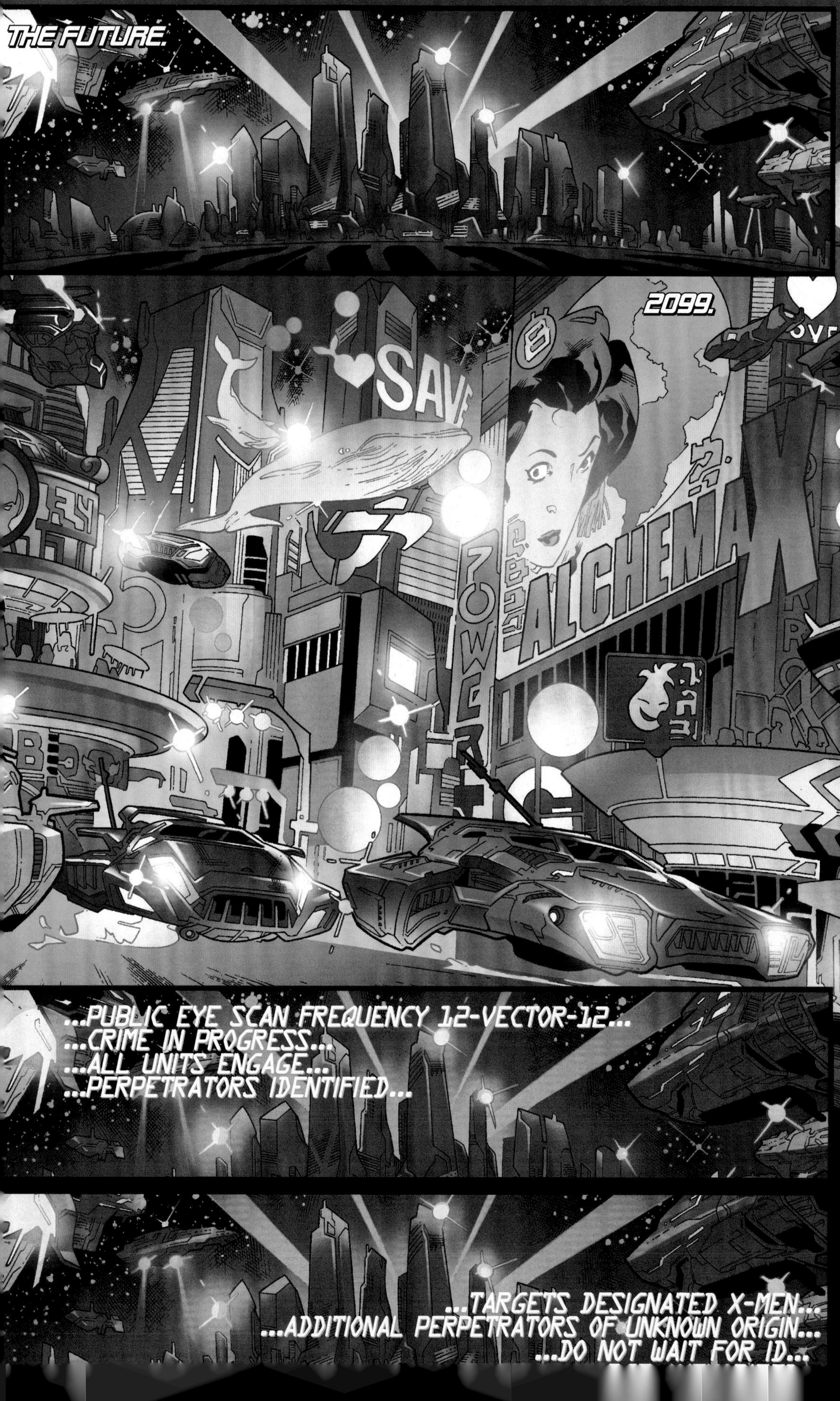
THE FUTURE.
2099.
SAVE
ALCHEMAX
POWER
...PUBLIC EYE SCAN FREQUENCY 12-VECTOR-12...
...CRIME IN PROGRESS...
...ALL UNITS ENGAGE...
...PERPETRATORS IDENTIFIED...
...TARGETS DESIGNATED X-MEN...
...ADDITIONAL PERPETRATORS OF UNKNOWN ORIGIN...
...DO NOT WAIT FOR ID...

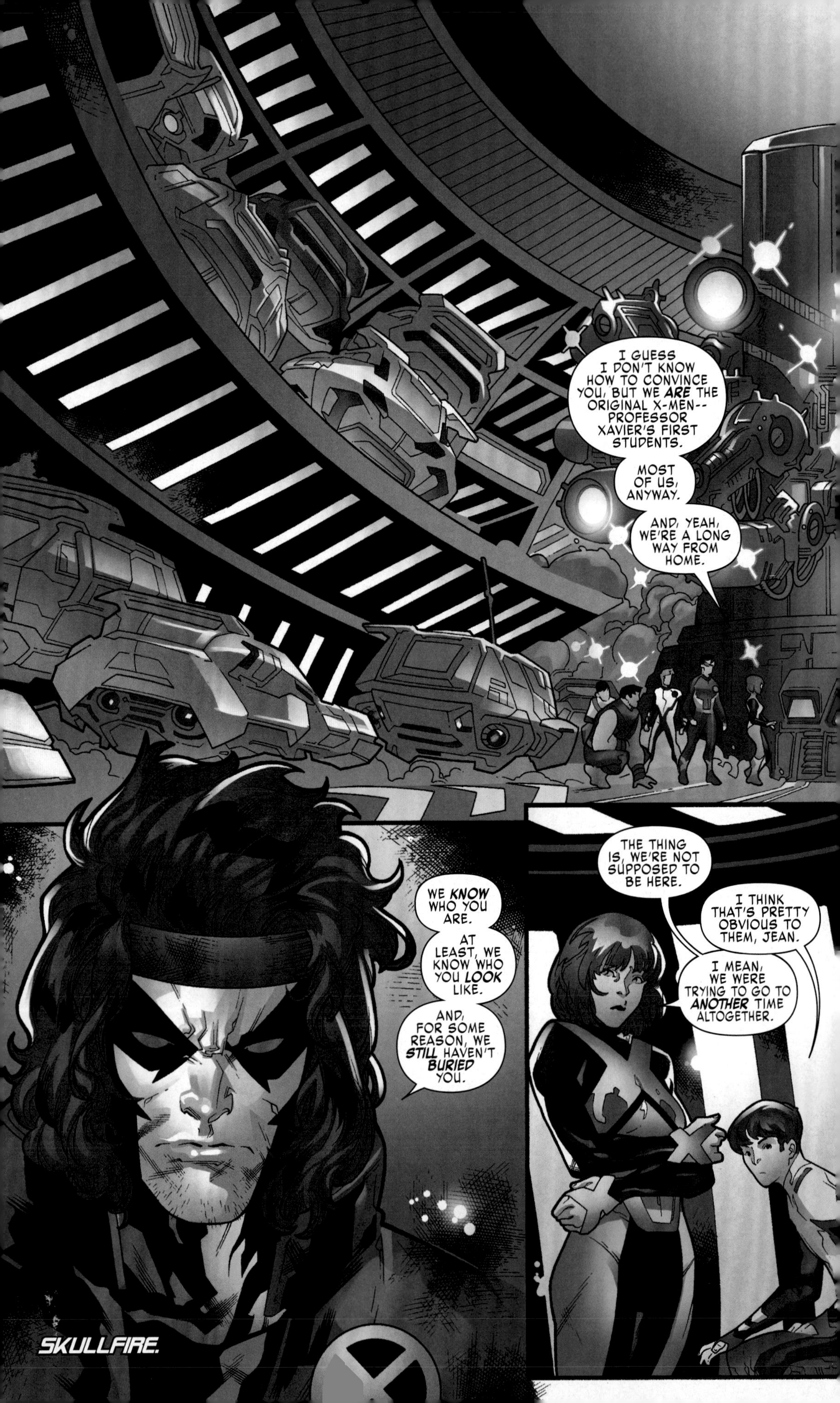
I GUESS I DON'T KNOW HOW TO CONVINCE YOU, BUT WE ARE THE ORIGINAL X-MEN-- PROFESSOR XAVIER'S FIRST STUDENTS.
MOST OF US, ANYWAY.
AND, YEAH, WE'RE A LONG WAY FROM HOME.
WE KNOW WHO YOU ARE.
AT LEAST, WE KNOW WHO YOU LOOK LIKE.
AND, FOR SOME REASON, WE STILL HAVEN'T BURIED YOU.
SKULLFIRE.
THE THING IS, WE'RE NOT SUPPOSED TO BE HERE.
I THINK THAT'S PRETTY OBVIOUS TO THEM, JEAN.
I MEAN, WE WERE TRYING TO GO TO ANOTHER TIME ALTOGETHER.

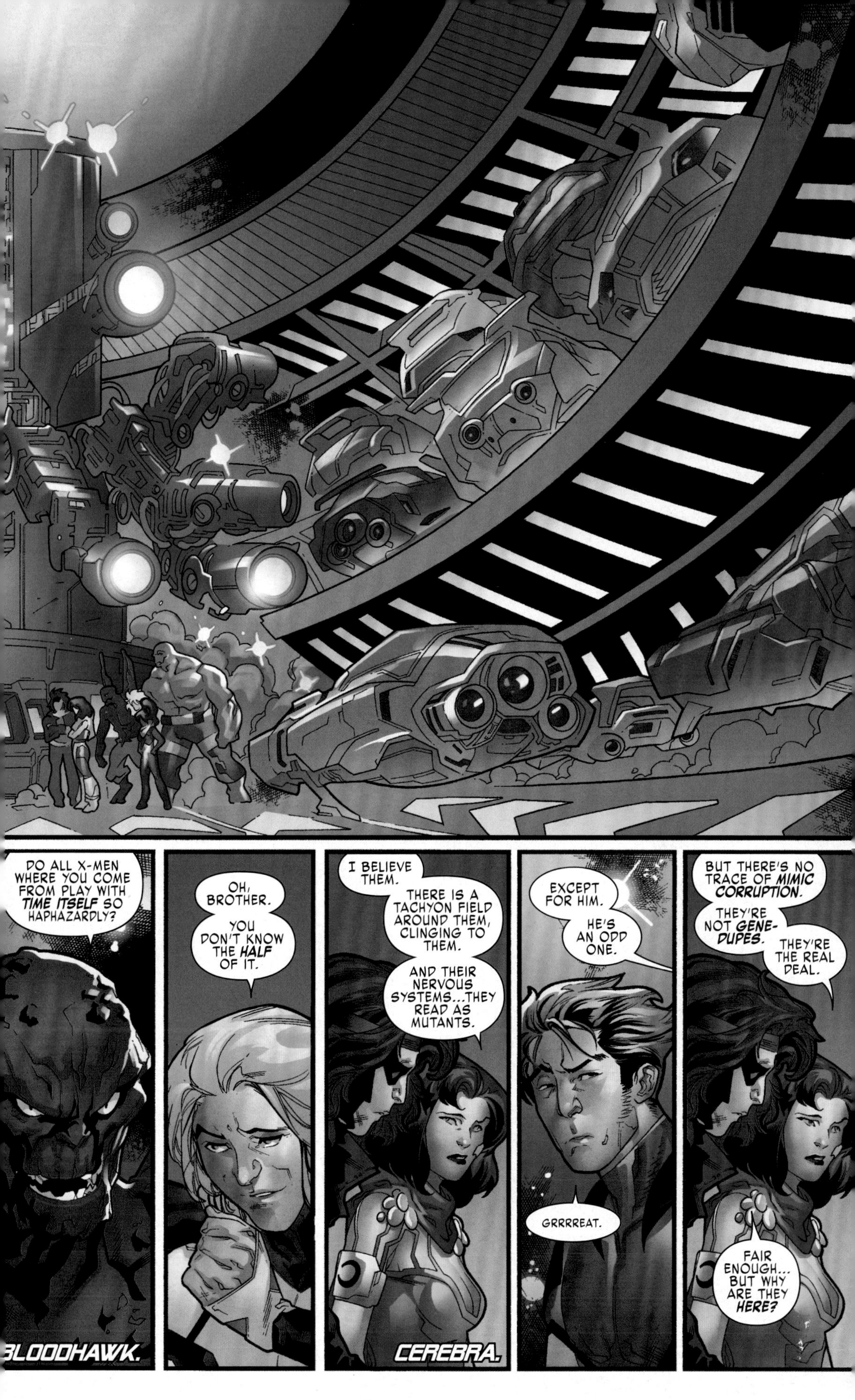
DO ALL X-MEN WHERE YOU COME FROM PLAY WITH TIME ITSELF SO HAPHAZARDLY?
BLOODHAWK.
OH, BROTHER.
YOU DON'T KNOW THE HALF OF IT.
I BELIEVE THEM.
THERE IS A TACHYON FIELD AROUND THEM, CLINGING TO THEM.
AND THEIR NERVOUS SYSTEMS...THEY READ AS MUTANTS.
CEREBRA.
EXCEPT FOR HIM.
HE'S AN ODD ONE.
GRRRREAT.
BUT THERE'S NO TRACE OF MIMIC CORRUPTION.
THEY'RE NOT GENE-DUPES.
THEY'RE THE REAL DEAL.
FAIR ENOUGH... BUT WHY ARE THEY HERE?

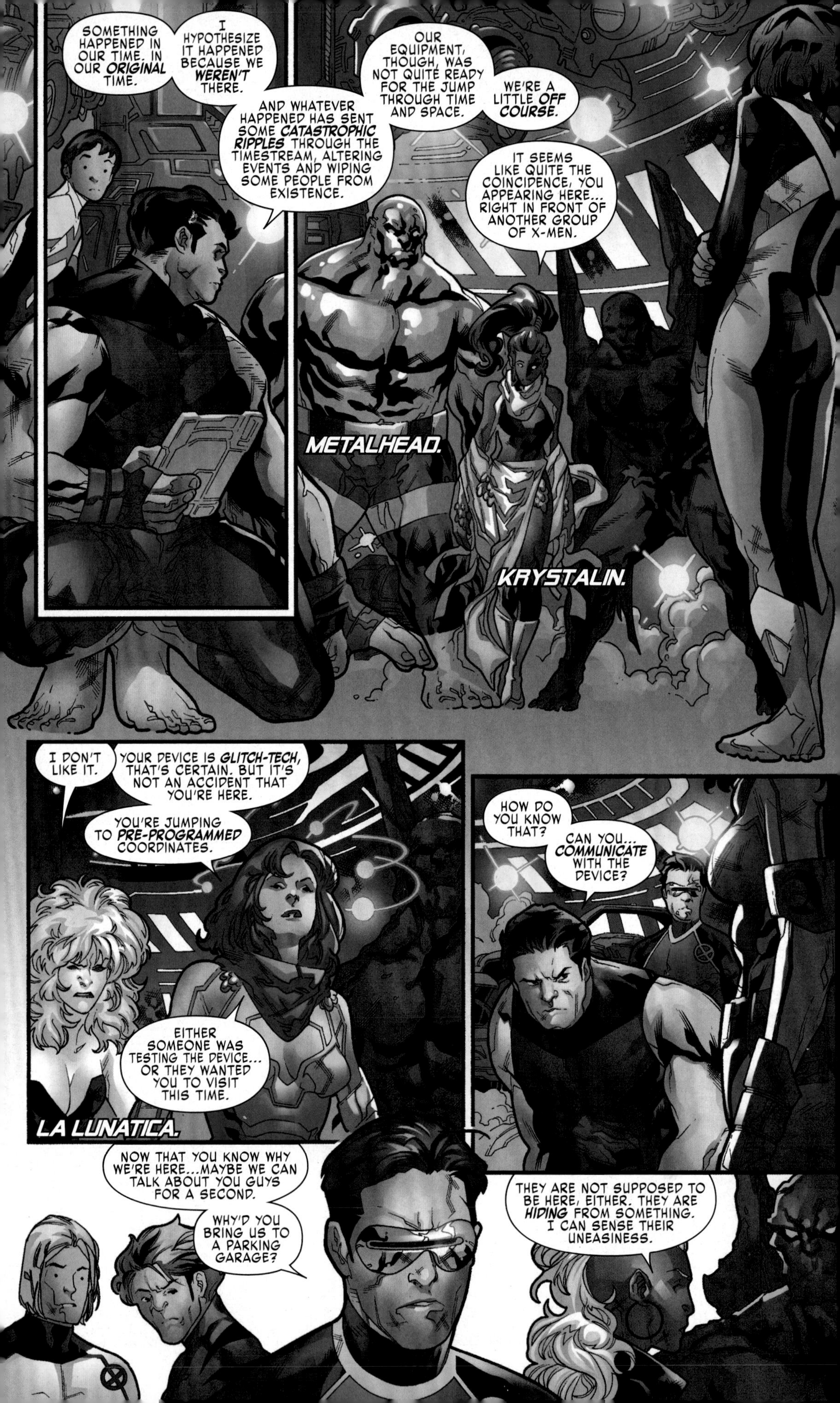

SOMETHING HAPPENED IN OUR TIME. IN OUR ORIGINAL TIME.
I HYPOTHESIZE IT HAPPENED BECAUSE WE WEREN'T THERE.
AND WHATEVER HAPPENED HAS SENT SOME CATASTROPHIC RIPPLES THROUGH THE TIMESTREAM, ALTERING EVENTS AND WIPING SOME PEOPLE FROM EXISTENCE.
OUR EQUIPMENT, THOUGH, WAS NOT QUITE READY FOR THE JUMP THROUGH TIME AND SPACE.
WE'RE A LITTLE OFF COURSE.
IT SEEMS LIKE QUITE THE COINCIDENCE, YOU APPEARING HERE... RIGHT IN FRONT OF ANOTHER GROUP OF X-MEN.
METALHEAD.
KRYSTALIN.
I DON'T LIKE IT.
YOUR DEVICE IS GLITCH-TECH, THAT'S CERTAIN. BUT IT'S NOT AN ACCIDENT THAT YOU'RE HERE.
YOU'RE JUMPING TO PRE-PROGRAMMED COORDINATES.
EITHER SOMEONE WAS TESTING THE DEVICE... OR THEY WANTED YOU TO VISIT THIS TIME.
LA LUNATICA.
HOW DO YOU KNOW THAT?
CAN YOU... COMMUNICATE WITH THE DEVICE?
NOW THAT YOU KNOW WHY WE'RE HERE...MAYBE WE CAN TALK ABOUT YOU GUYS FOR A SECOND.
WHY'D YOU BRING US TO A PARKING GARAGE?
THEY ARE NOT SUPPOSED TO BE HERE, EITHER. THEY ARE HIDING FROM SOMETHING. I CAN SENSE THEIR UNEASINESS.

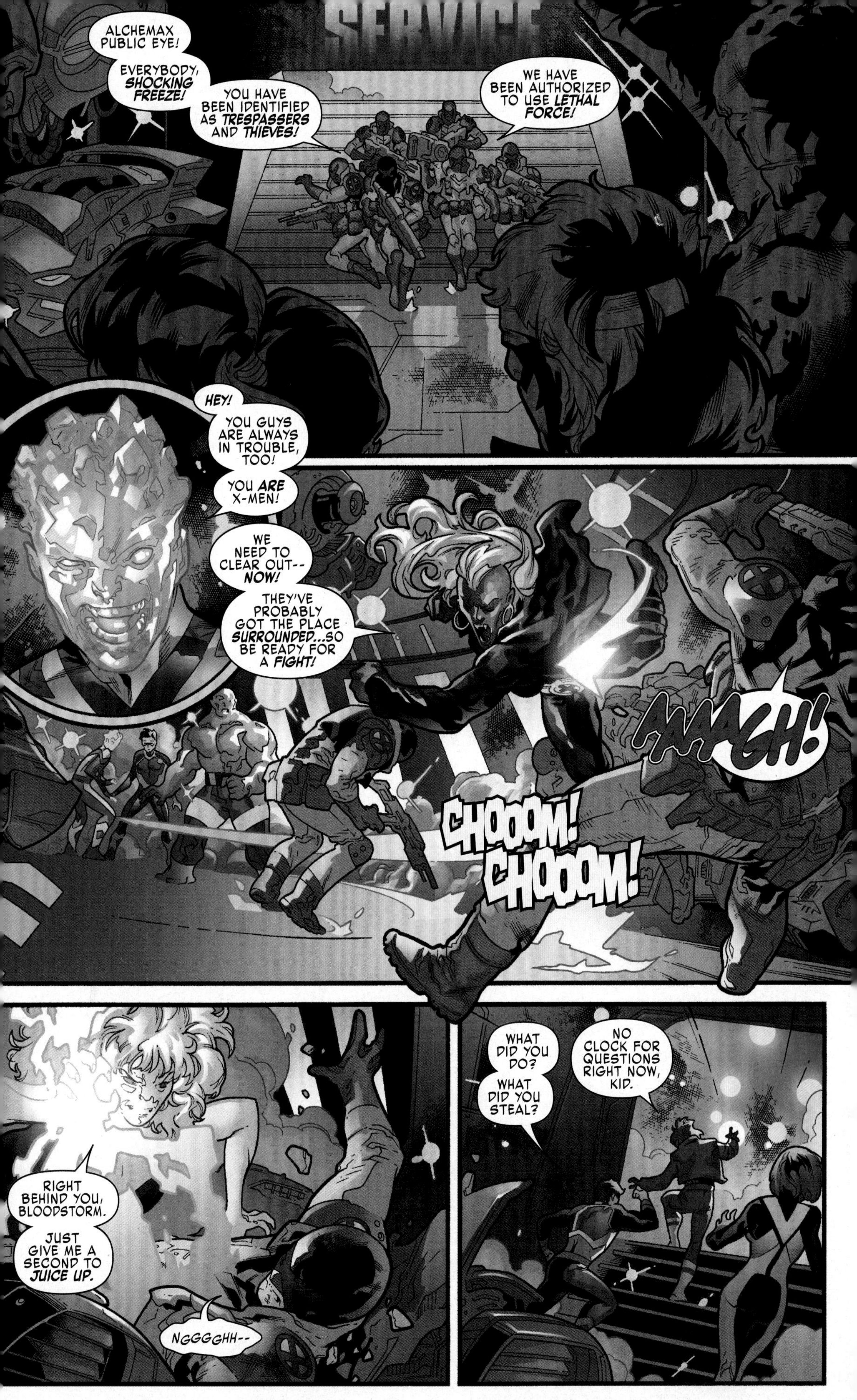
SERVICE
ALCHEMAX PUBLIC EYE!
EVERYBODY, SHOCKING FREEZE!
YOU HAVE BEEN IDENTIFIED AS TRESPASSERS AND THIEVES!
WE HAVE BEEN AUTHORIZED TO USE LETHAL FORCE!
HEY!
YOU GUYS ARE ALWAYS IN TROUBLE, TOO!
YOU ARE X-MEN!
WE NEED TO CLEAR OUT--NOW!
THEY'VE PROBABLY GOT THE PLACE SURROUNDED...SO BE READY FOR A FIGHT!
AAAAGH!
CHOOOM! CHOOOM!
RIGHT BEHIND YOU, BLOODSTORM.
JUST GIVE ME A SECOND TO JUICE UP.
NGGGGHH--
WHAT DID YOU DO?
WHAT DID YOU STEAL?
NO CLOCK FOR QUESTIONS RIGHT NOW, KID.

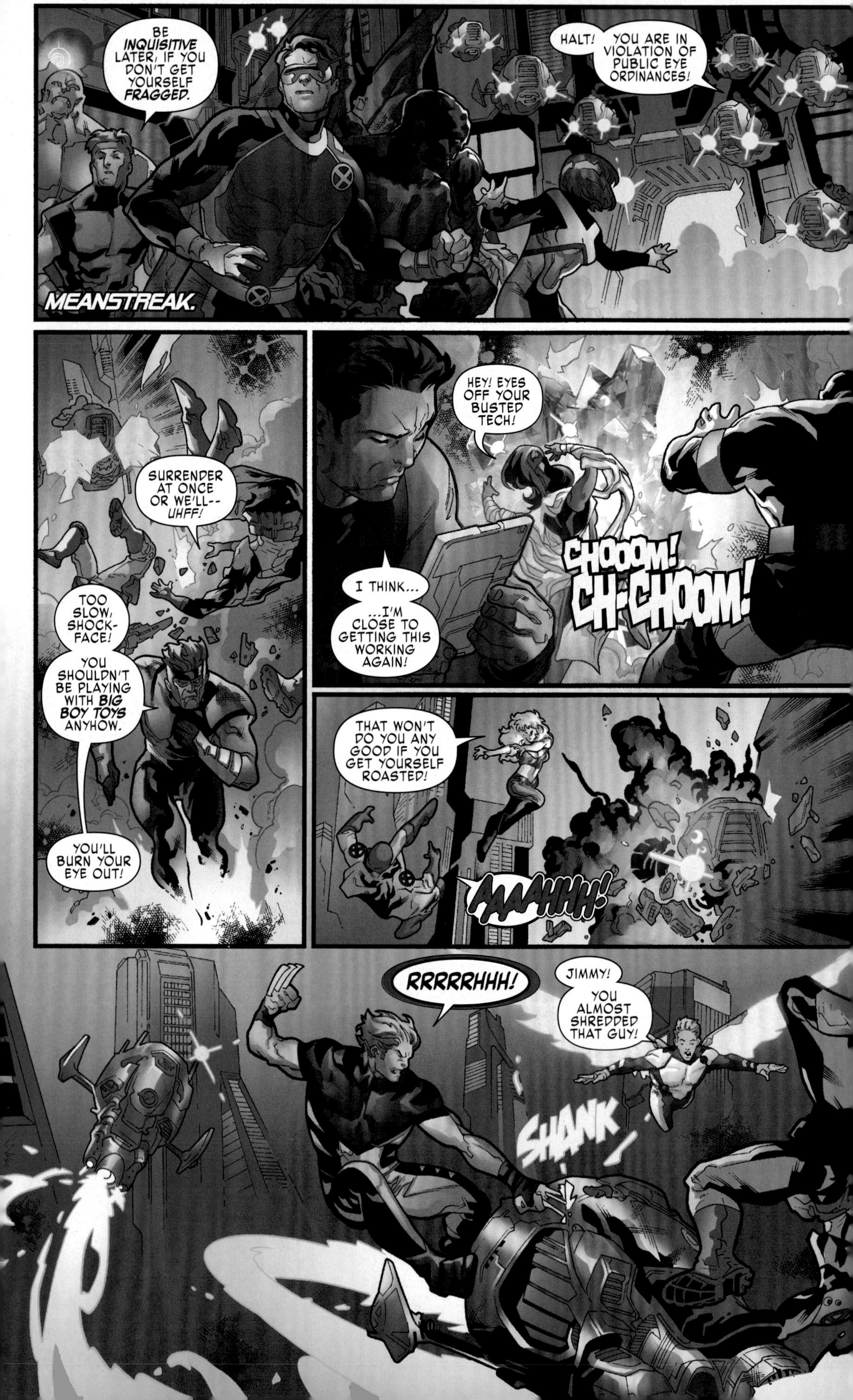

BE INQUISITIVE LATER, IF YOU DON'T GET YOURSELF FRAGGED.
HALT!
YOU ARE IN VIOLATION OF PUBLIC EYE ORDINANCES!
MEANSTREAK.
SURRENDER AT ONCE OR WE'LL-- UHFF!
TOO SLOW, SHOCK-FACE!
YOU SHOULDN'T BE PLAYING WITH BIG BOY TOYS ANYHOW.
YOU'LL BURN YOUR EYE OUT!
HEY! EYES OFF YOUR BUSTED TECH!
I THINK...
...I'M CLOSE TO GETTING THIS WORKING AGAIN!
CHOOOM! CH-CHOOM!
THAT WON'T DO YOU ANY GOOD IF YOU GET YOURSELF ROASTED!
AAAHHH!
RRRRRHHH!
JIMMY!
YOU ALMOST SHREDDED THAT GUY!
SHANK

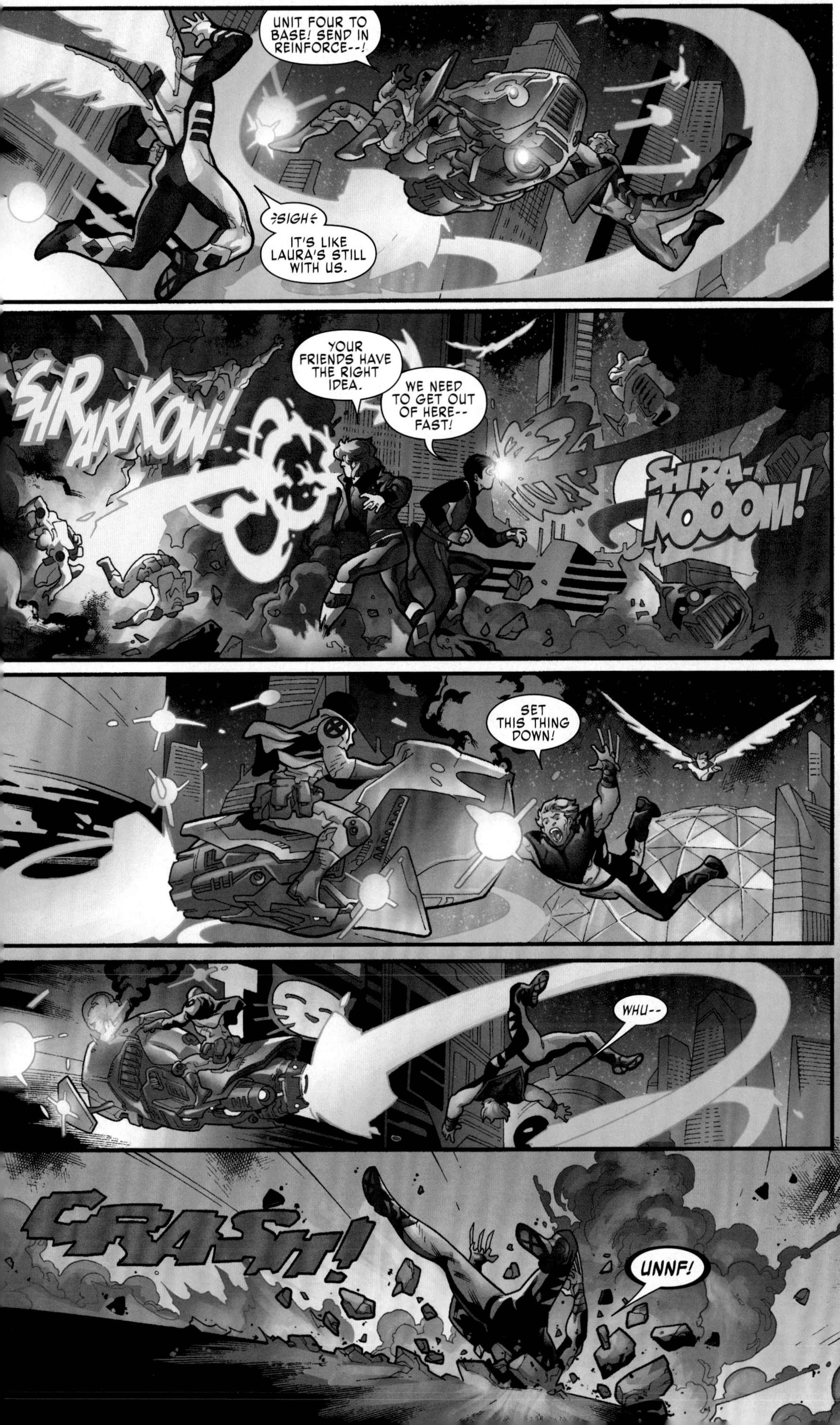
UNIT FOUR TO BASE! SEND IN REINFORCE--!
SIGH
IT'S LIKE LAURA'S STILL WITH US.
SHRAKKOW!
YOUR FRIENDS HAVE THE RIGHT IDEA.
WE NEED TO GET OUT OF HERE-- FAST!
SHRA-KOOOM!
SET THIS THING DOWN!
WHU--
CRASH!
UNNF!

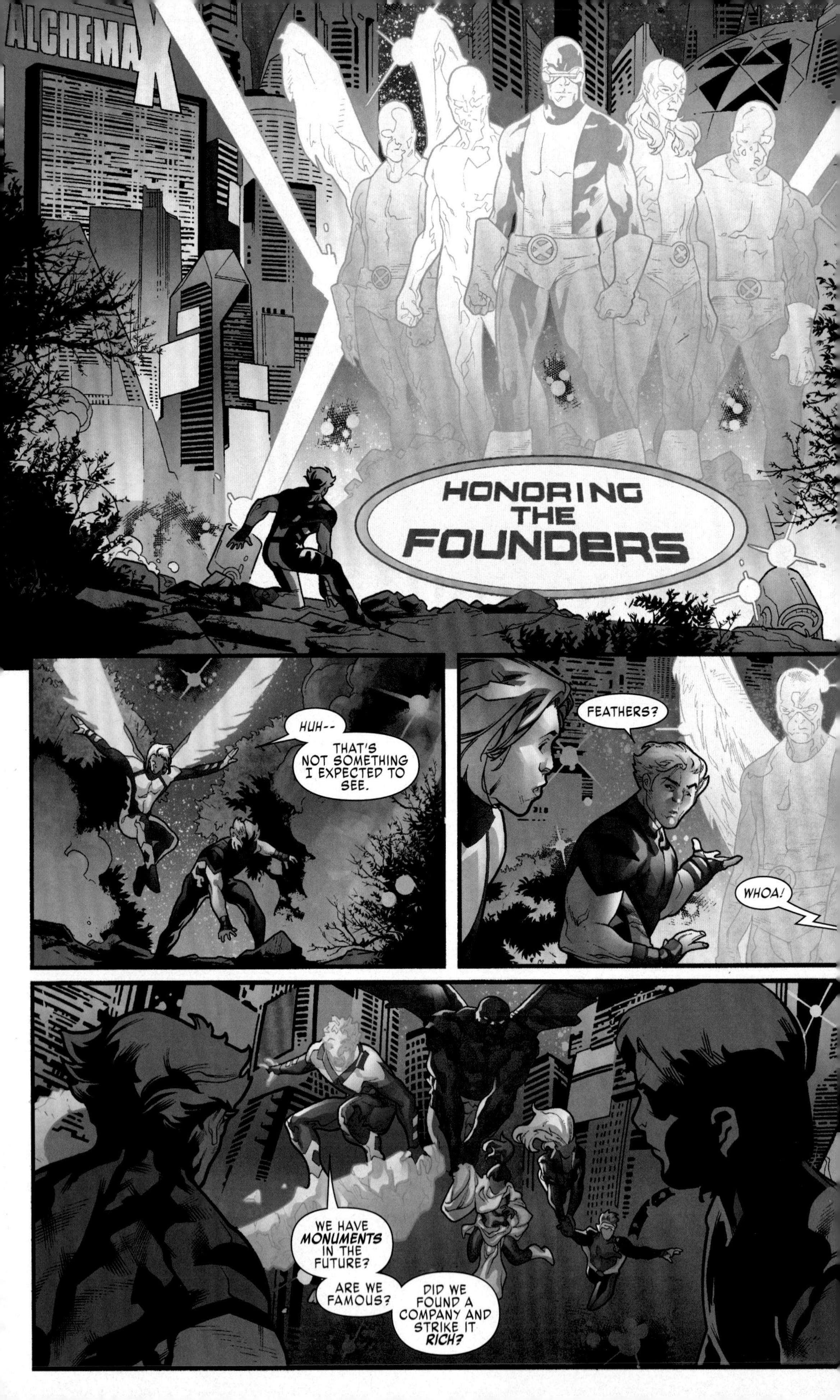

ALCHEMAX
HONORING THE FOUNDERS
HUH-- THAT'S NOT SOMETHING I EXPECTED TO SEE.
FEATHERS?
WHOA!
WE HAVE MONUMENTS IN THE FUTURE?
ARE WE FAMOUS?
DID WE FOUND A COMPANY AND STRIKE IT RICH?

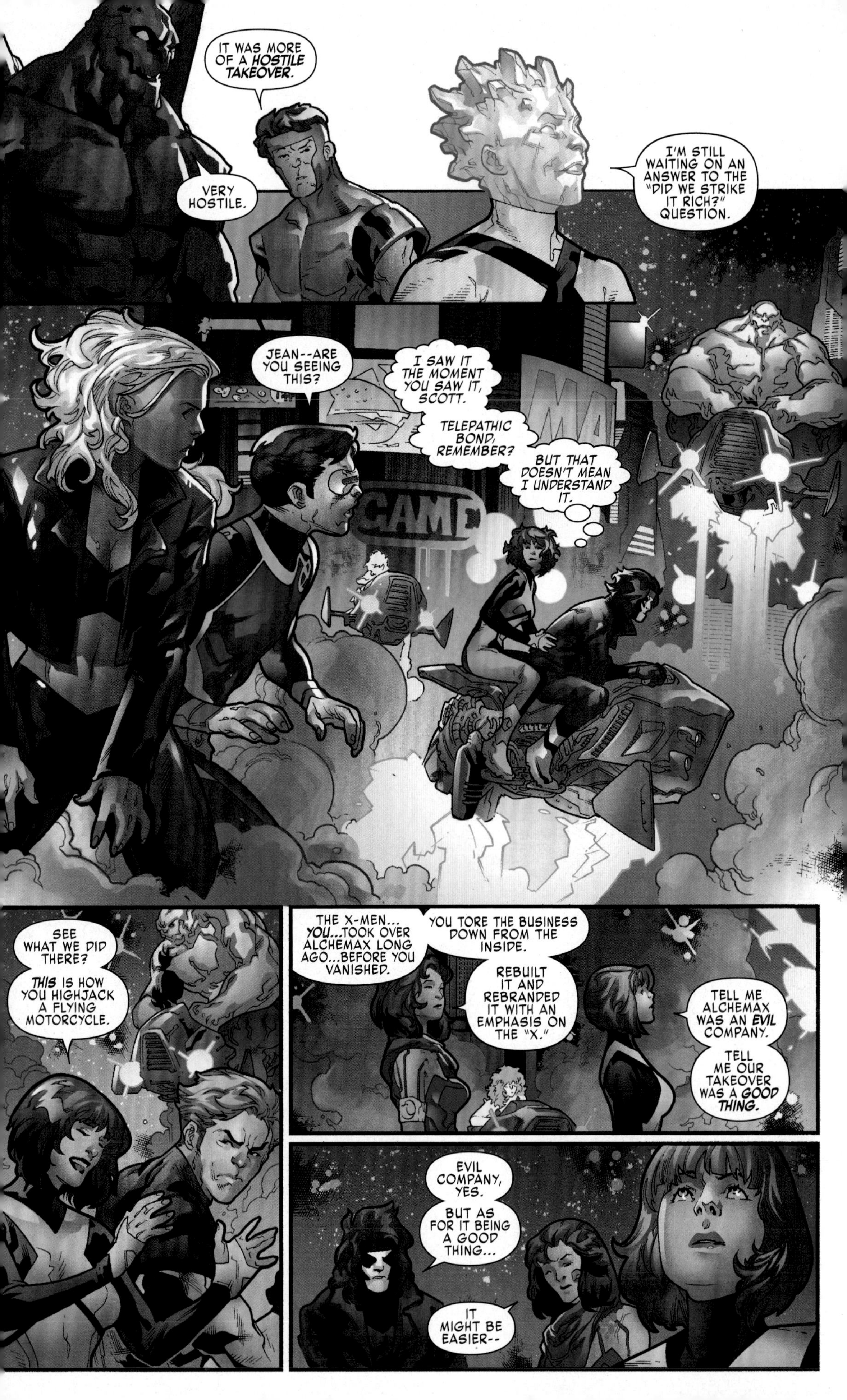
IT WAS MORE OF A HOSTILE TAKEOVER.
VERY HOSTILE.
I'M STILL WAITING ON AN ANSWER TO THE "DID WE STRIKE IT RICH?" QUESTION.
JEAN--ARE YOU SEEING THIS?
I SAW IT THE MOMENT YOU SAW IT, SCOTT.
TELEPATHIC BOND, REMEMBER?
BUT THAT DOESN'T MEAN I UNDERSTAND IT.
GAME
SEE WHAT WE DID THERE?
THIS IS HOW YOU HIGHJACK A FLYING MOTORCYCLE.
THE X-MEN... YOU...TOOK OVER ALCHEMAX LONG AGO...BEFORE YOU VANISHED.
YOU TORE THE BUSINESS DOWN FROM THE INSIDE.
REBUILT IT AND REBRANDED IT WITH AN EMPHASIS ON THE "X."
TELL ME ALCHEMAX WAS AN EVIL COMPANY.
TELL ME OUR TAKEOVER WAS A GOOD THING.
EVIL COMPANY, YES.
BUT AS FOR IT BEING A GOOD THING...
IT MIGHT BE EASIER--

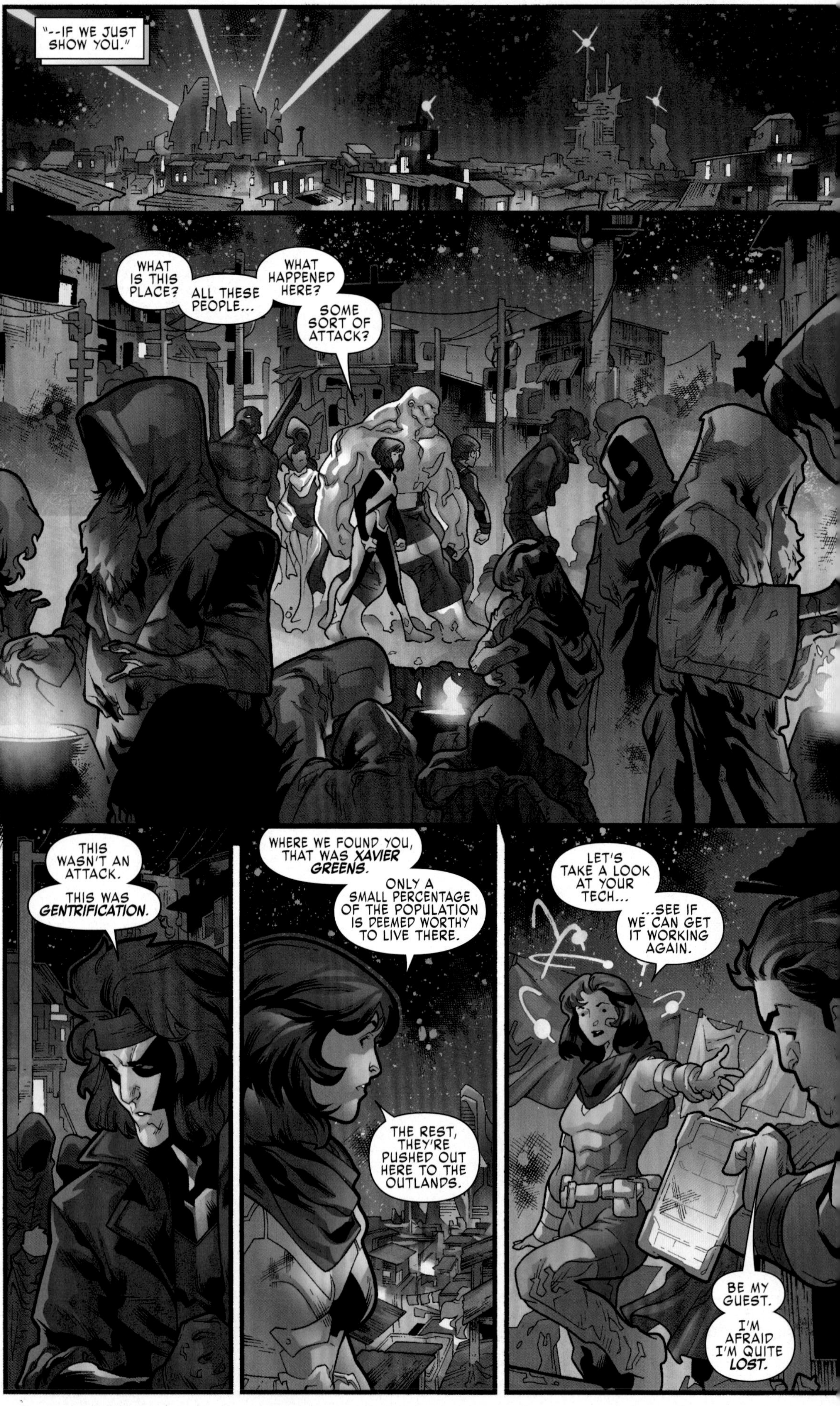
"--IF WE JUST SHOW YOU."
WHAT IS THIS PLACE?
ALL THESE PEOPLE...
WHAT HAPPENED HERE?
SOME SORT OF ATTACK?
THIS WASN'T AN ATTACK.
THIS WAS GENTRIFICATION.
WHERE WE FOUND YOU, THAT WAS XAVIER GREENS.
ONLY A SMALL PERCENTAGE OF THE POPULATION IS DEEMED WORTHY TO LIVE THERE.
THE REST, THEY'RE PUSHED OUT HERE TO THE OUTLANDS.
LET'S TAKE A LOOK AT YOUR TECH...
...SEE IF WE CAN GET IT WORKING AGAIN.
BE MY GUEST.
I'M AFRAID I'M QUITE LOST.

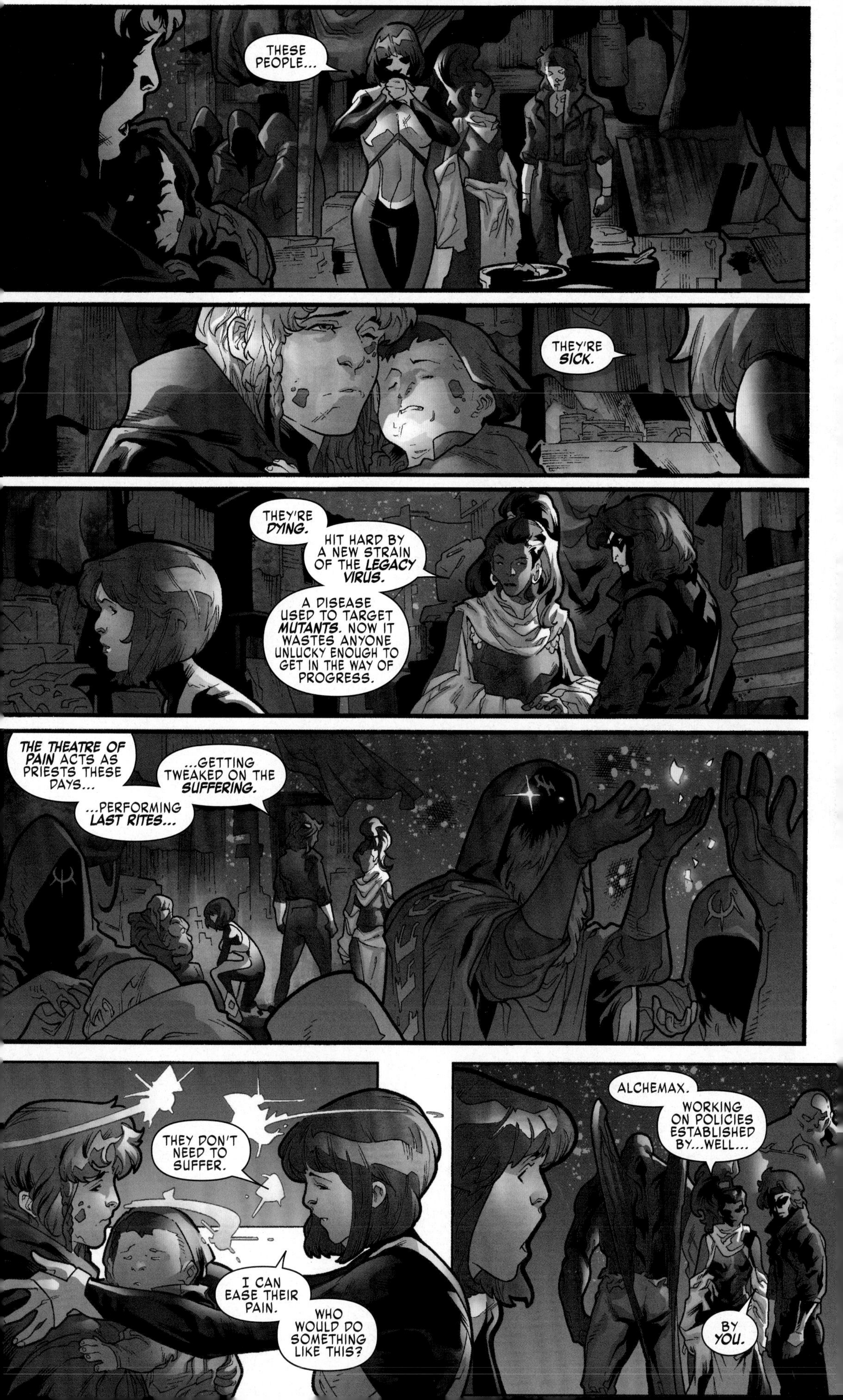
THESE PEOPLE...
THEY'RE SICK.
THEY'RE DYING.
HIT HARD BY A NEW STRAIN OF THE LEGACY VIRUS.
A DISEASE USED TO TARGET MUTANTS. NOW IT WASTES ANYONE UNLUCKY ENOUGH TO GET IN THE WAY OF PROGRESS.
THE THEATRE OF PAIN ACTS AS PRIESTS THESE DAYS...
...PERFORMING LAST RITES...
...GETTING TWEAKED ON THE SUFFERING.
THEY DON'T NEED TO SUFFER.
I CAN EASE THEIR PAIN.
WHO WOULD DO SOMETHING LIKE THIS?
ALCHEMAX.
WORKING ON POLICIES ESTABLISHED BY...WELL...
BY YOU.

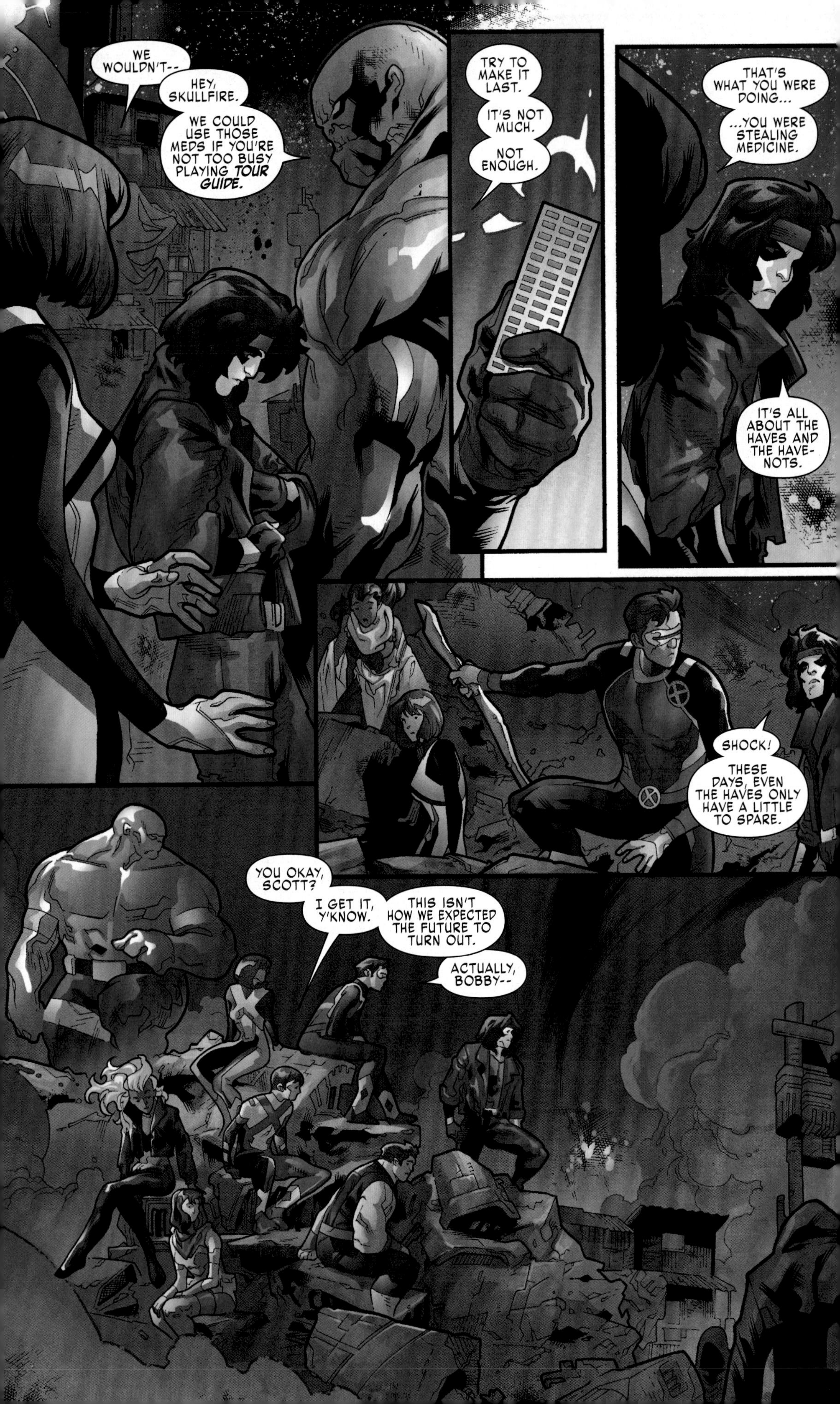
WE WOULDN'T--
HEY, SKULLFIRE.
WE COULD USE THOSE MEDS IF YOU'RE NOT TOO BUSY PLAYING TOUR GUIDE.
TRY TO MAKE IT LAST.
IT'S NOT MUCH.
NOT ENOUGH.
THAT'S WHAT YOU WERE DOING...
...YOU WERE STEALING MEDICINE.
IT'S ALL ABOUT THE HAVES AND THE HAVE-NOTS.
SHOCK!
THESE DAYS, EVEN THE HAVES ONLY HAVE A LITTLE TO SPARE.
YOU OKAY, SCOTT?
I GET IT, Y'KNOW.
THIS ISN'T HOW WE EXPECTED THE FUTURE TO TURN OUT.
ACTUALLY, BOBBY--

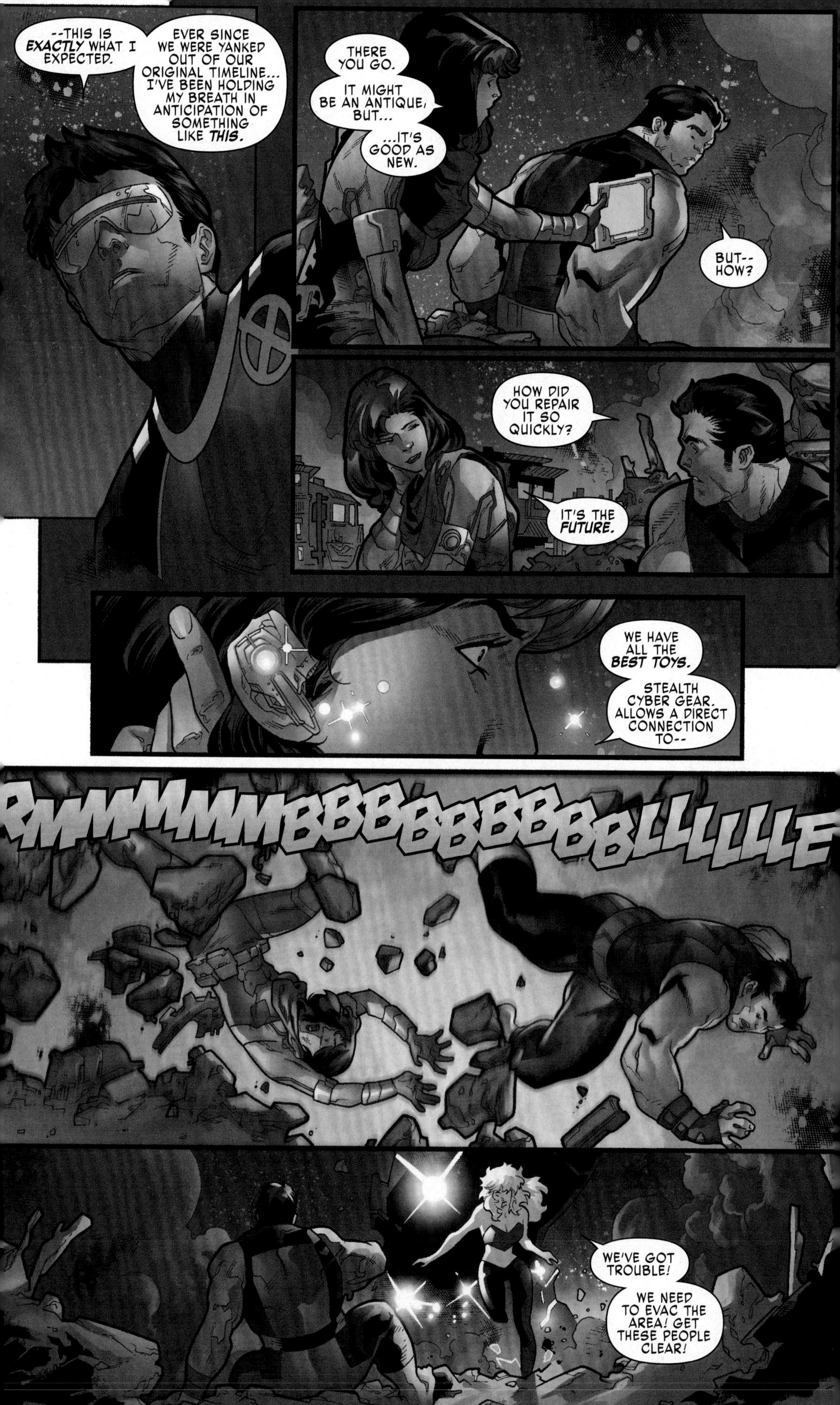
--THIS IS EXACTLY WHAT I EXPECTED.
EVER SINCE WE WERE YANKED OUT OF OUR ORIGINAL TIMELINE... I'VE BEEN HOLDING MY BREATH IN ANTICIPATION OF SOMETHING LIKE THIS.
THERE YOU GO.
IT MIGHT BE AN ANTIQUE, BUT...
...IT'S GOOD AS NEW.
BUT-- HOW?
HOW DID YOU REPAIR IT SO QUICKLY?
IT'S THE FUTURE.
WE HAVE ALL THE BEST TOYS.
STEALTH CYBER GEAR. ALLOWS A DIRECT CONNECTION TO--
RMMMMMMBBBBBBBBBLLLLLLE
WE'VE GOT TROUBLE!
WE NEED TO EVAC THE AREA! GET THESE PEOPLE CLEAR!

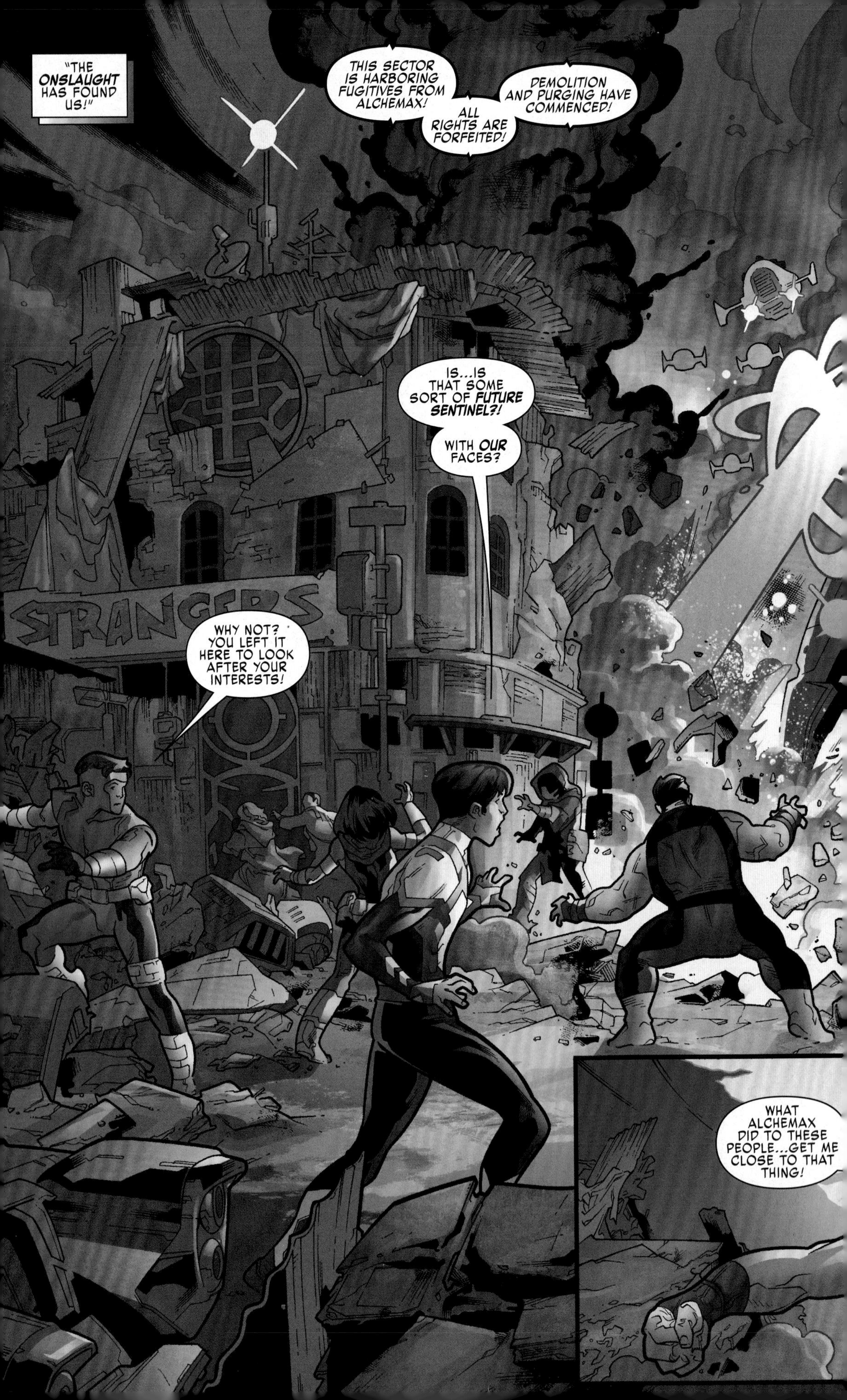
"THE ONSLAUGHT HAS FOUND US!"
THIS SECTOR IS HARBORING FUGITIVES FROM ALCHEMAX!
ALL RIGHTS ARE FORFEITED!
DEMOLITION AND PURGING HAVE COMMENCED!
IS...IS THAT SOME SORT OF FUTURE SENTINEL?!
WITH OUR FACES?
STRANGERS
WHY NOT? YOU LEFT IT HERE TO LOOK AFTER YOUR INTERESTS!
WHAT ALCHEMAX DID TO THESE PEOPLE...GET ME CLOSE TO THAT THING!

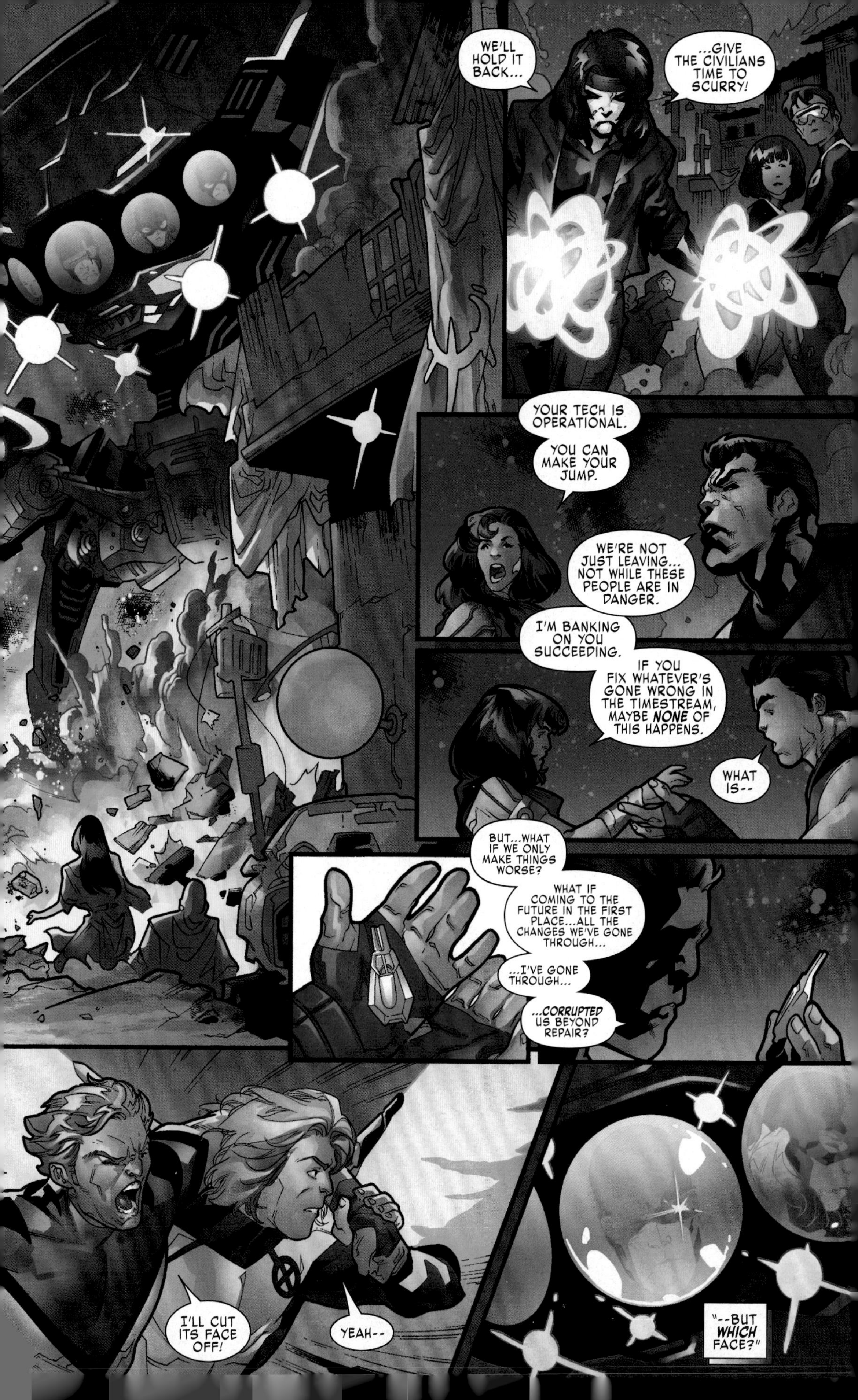

WE'LL HOLD IT BACK...
...GIVE THE CIVILIANS TIME TO SCURRY!
YOUR TECH IS OPERATIONAL.
YOU CAN MAKE YOUR JUMP.
WE'RE NOT JUST LEAVING... NOT WHILE THESE PEOPLE ARE IN DANGER.
I'M BANKING ON YOU SUCCEEDING.
IF YOU FIX WHATEVER'S GONE WRONG IN THE TIMESTREAM, MAYBE NONE OF THIS HAPPENS.
WHAT IS--
BUT...WHAT IF WE ONLY MAKE THINGS WORSE?
WHAT IF COMING TO THE FUTURE IN THE FIRST PLACE...ALL THE CHANGES WE'VE GONE THROUGH...
...I'VE GONE THROUGH...
...CORRUPTED US BEYOND REPAIR?
I'LL CUT ITS FACE OFF!
YEAH--
"--BUT WHICH FACE?"

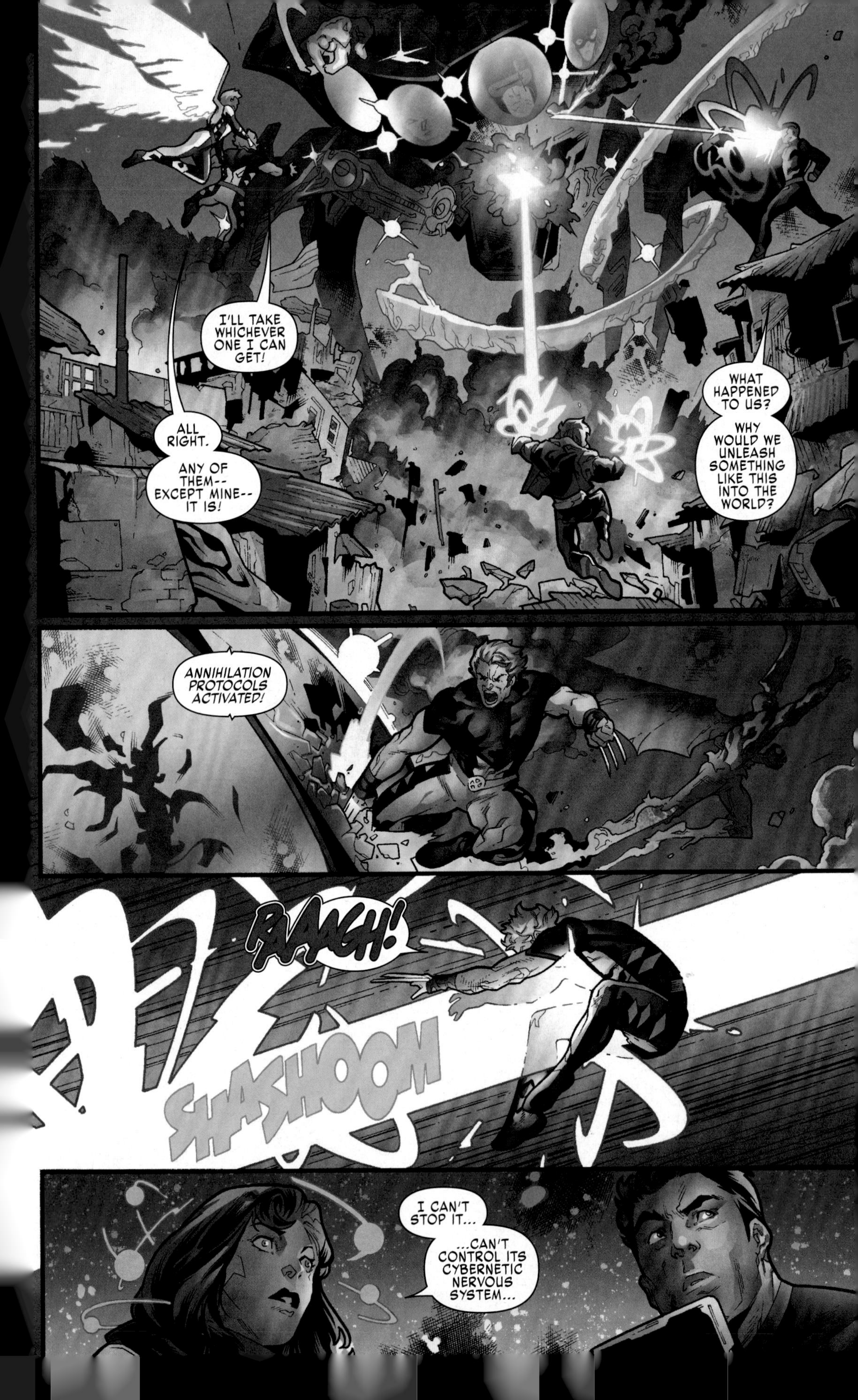
I'LL TAKE WHICHEVER ONE I CAN GET!
ALL RIGHT.
ANY OF THEM--EXCEPT MINE--IT IS!
WHAT HAPPENED TO US?
WHY WOULD WE UNLEASH SOMETHING LIKE THIS INTO THE WORLD?
ANNIHILATION PROTOCOLS ACTIVATED!
RAAAGH!
SHASHOOM
I CAN'T STOP IT...
...CAN'T CONTROL ITS CYBERNETIC NERVOUS SYSTEM...

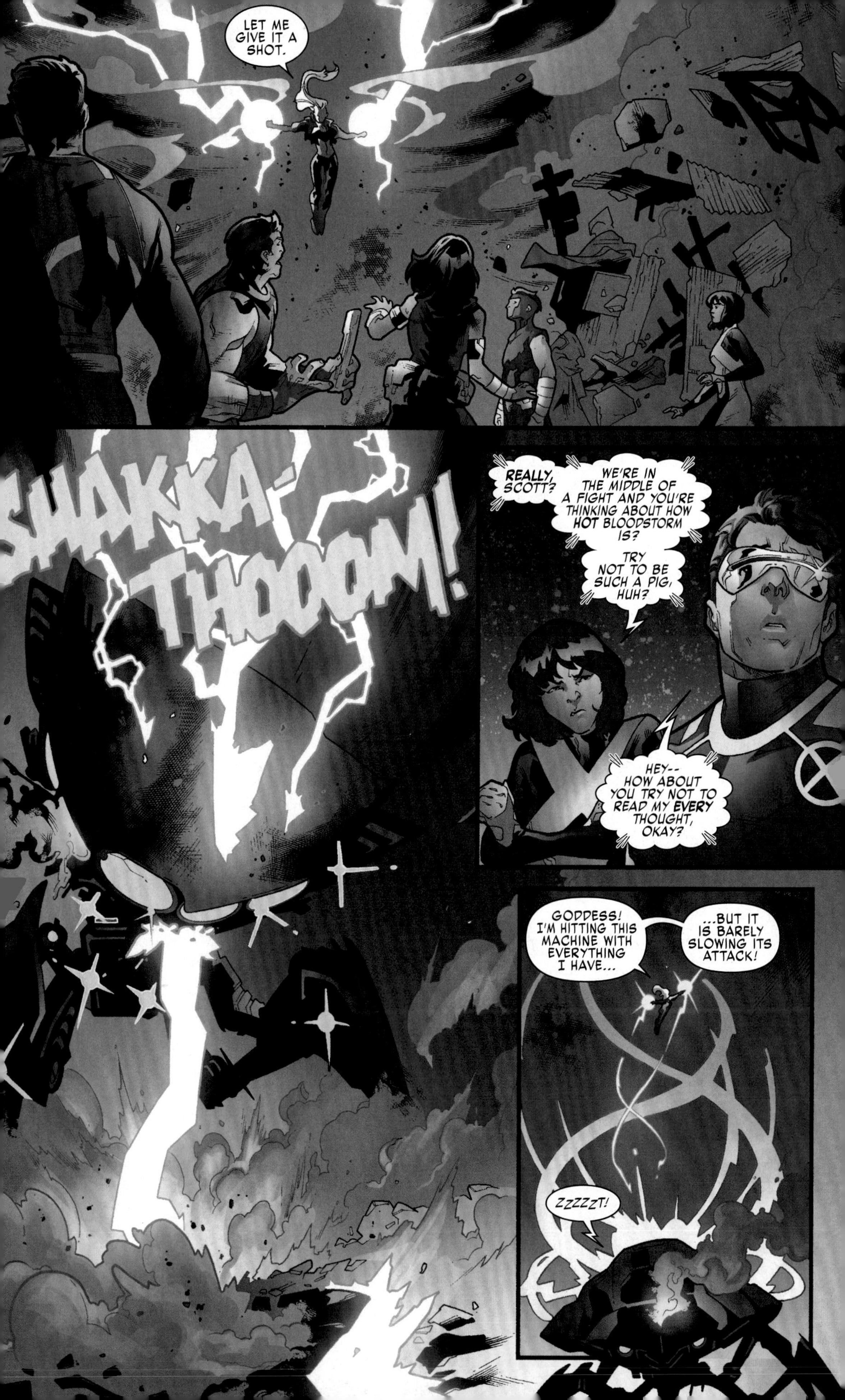
LET ME GIVE IT A SHOT.
SHAKKA-THOOOM!
REALLY, SCOTT?
WE'RE IN THE MIDDLE OF A FIGHT AND YOU'RE THINKING ABOUT HOW HOT BLOODSTORM IS?
TRY NOT TO BE SUCH A PIG, HUH?
HEY-- HOW ABOUT YOU TRY NOT TO READ MY EVERY THOUGHT, OKAY?
GODDESS! I'M HITTING THIS MACHINE WITH EVERYTHING I HAVE...
...BUT IT IS BARELY SLOWING ITS ATTACK!
ZZZZZT!

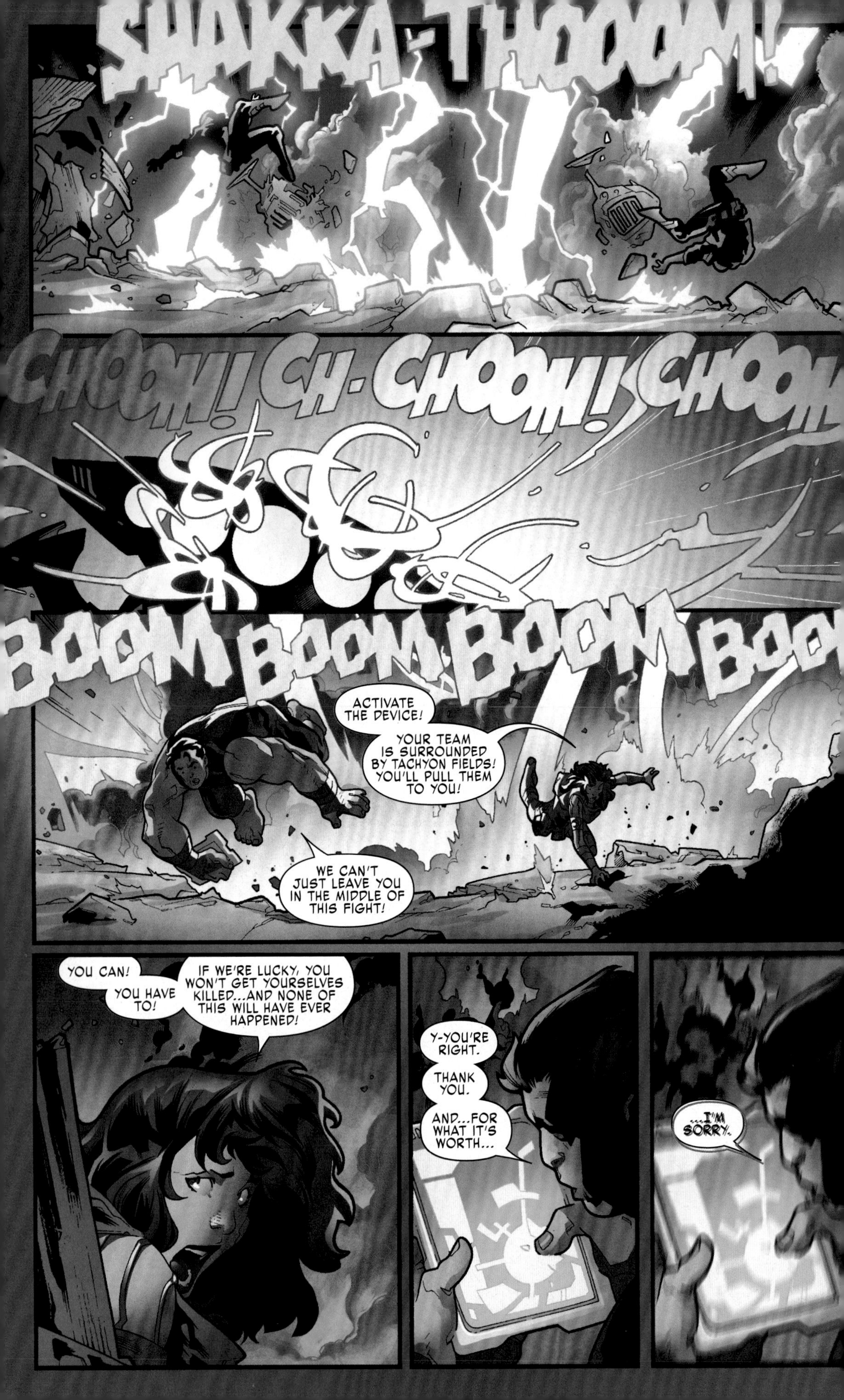
SHAKKA-THOOOM!
CHOOM! CH-CHOOM! CHOOM
BOOM BOOM BOOM BOO
ACTIVATE THE DEVICE!
YOUR TEAM IS SURROUNDED BY TACHYON FIELDS! YOU'LL PULL THEM TO YOU!
WE CAN'T JUST LEAVE YOU IN THE MIDDLE OF THIS FIGHT!
YOU CAN!
YOU HAVE TO!
IF WE'RE LUCKY, YOU WON'T GET YOURSELVES KILLED...AND NONE OF THIS WILL HAVE EVER HAPPENED!
Y-YOU'RE RIGHT.
THANK YOU.
AND...FOR WHAT IT'S WORTH...
...I'M SORRY.

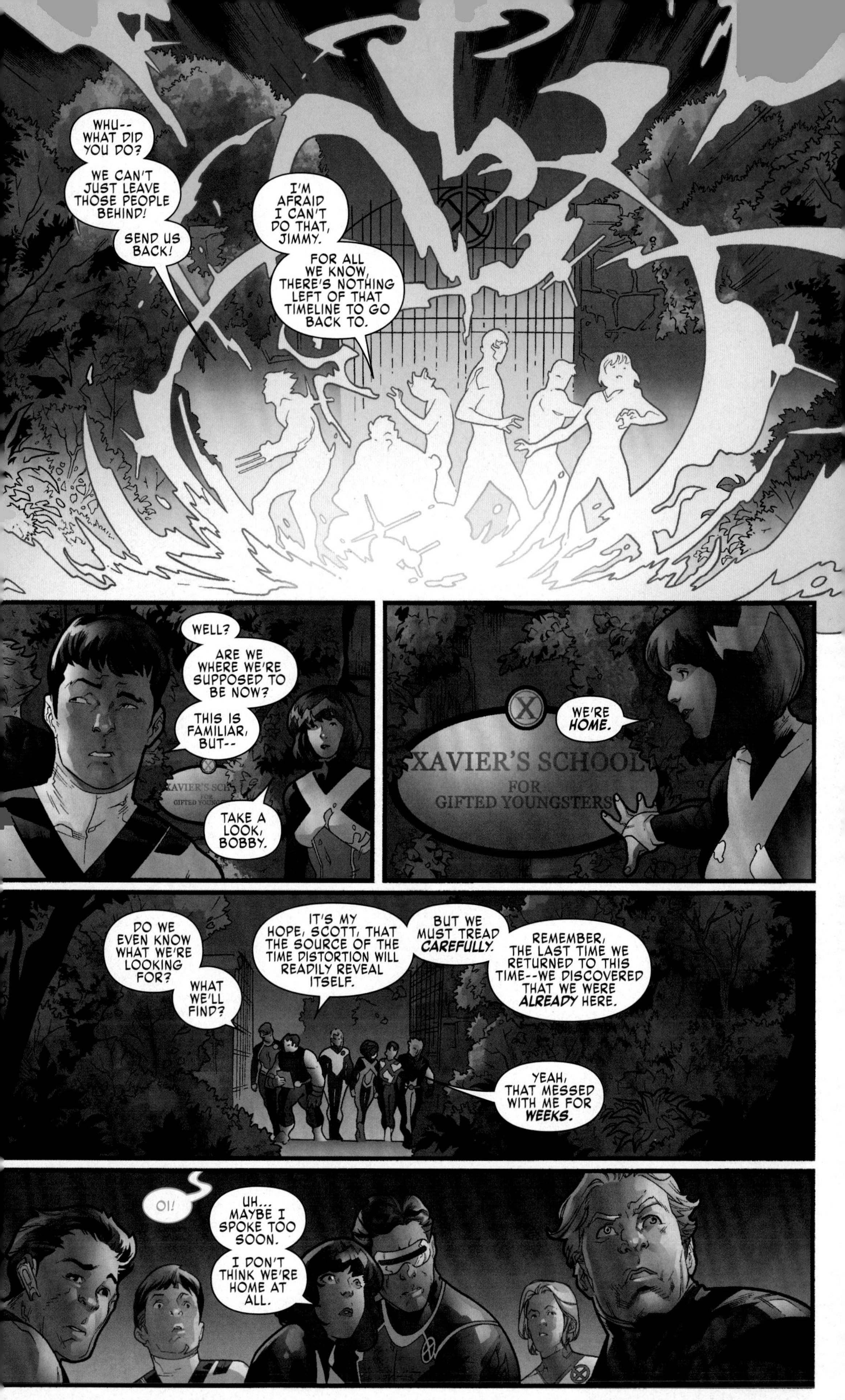
WHU-- WHAT DID YOU DO?
WE CAN'T JUST LEAVE THOSE PEOPLE BEHIND!
SEND US BACK!
I'M AFRAID I CAN'T DO THAT, JIMMY.
FOR ALL WE KNOW, THERE'S NOTHING LEFT OF THAT TIMELINE TO GO BACK TO.
WELL?
ARE WE WHERE WE'RE SUPPOSED TO BE NOW?
THIS IS FAMILIAR, BUT--
TAKE A LOOK, BOBBY.
XAVIER'S SCHOOL FOR GIFTED YOUNGSTERS
WE'RE *HOME.*
DO WE EVEN KNOW WHAT WE'RE LOOKING FOR?
WHAT WE'LL FIND?
IT'S MY HOPE, SCOTT, THAT THE SOURCE OF THE TIME DISTORTION WILL READILY REVEAL ITSELF.
BUT WE MUST TREAD *CAREFULLY.*
REMEMBER, THE LAST TIME WE RETURNED TO THIS TIME--WE DISCOVERED THAT WE WERE *ALREADY* HERE.
YEAH, THAT MESSED WITH ME FOR *WEEKS.*
OI!
UH... MAYBE I SPOKE TOO SOON.
I DON'T THINK WE'RE HOME AT ALL.

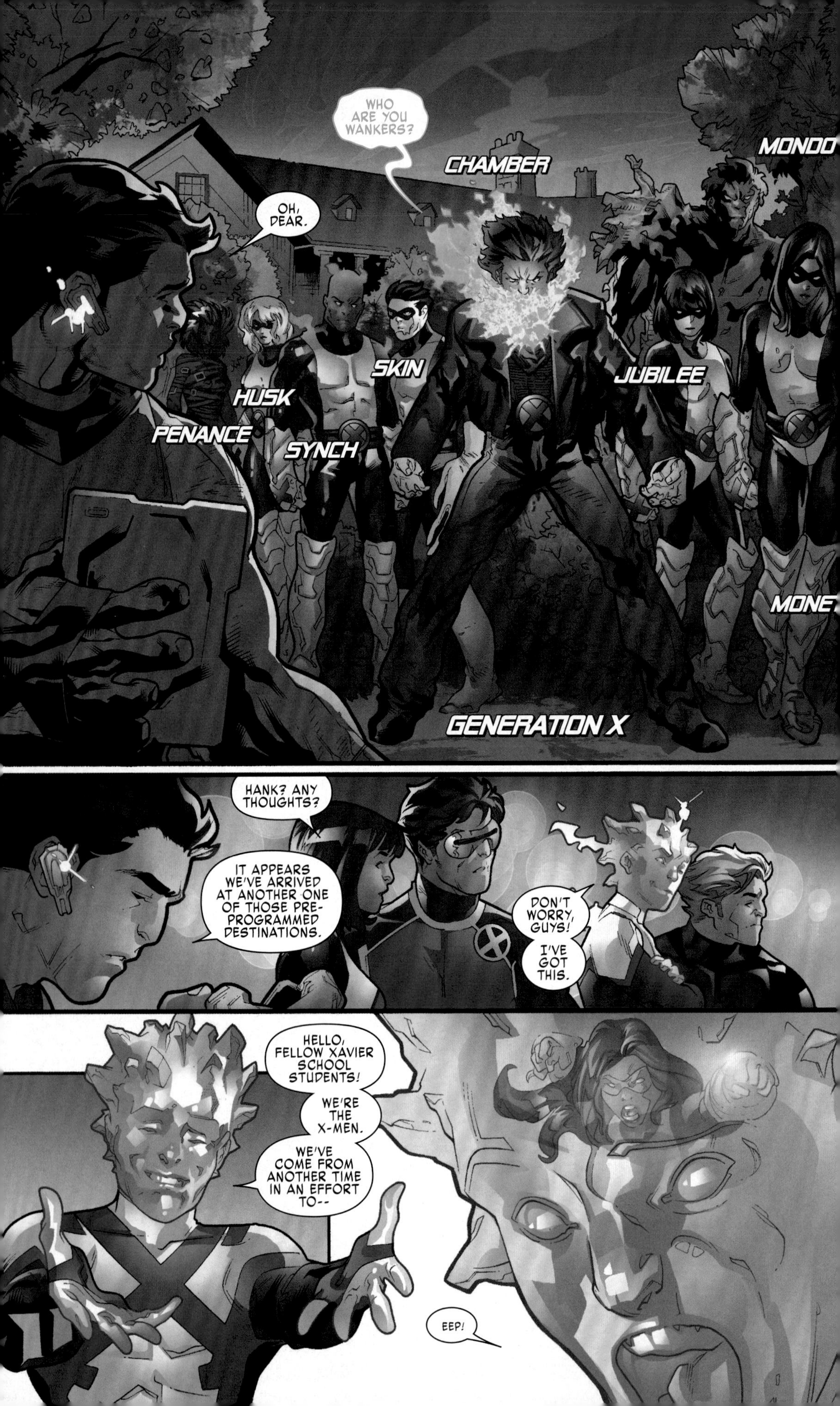
WHO ARE YOU WANKERS?
OH, DEAR.
CHAMBER
MONDO
HUSK
PENANCE
SYNCH
SKIN
JUBILEE
MONE
GENERATION X
HANK? ANY THOUGHTS?
IT APPEARS WE'VE ARRIVED AT ANOTHER ONE OF THOSE PRE-PROGRAMMED DESTINATIONS.
DON'T WORRY, GUYS!
I'VE GOT THIS.
HELLO, FELLOW XAVIER SCHOOL STUDENTS!
WE'RE THE X-MEN.
WE'VE COME FROM ANOTHER TIME IN AN EFFORT TO--
EEP!

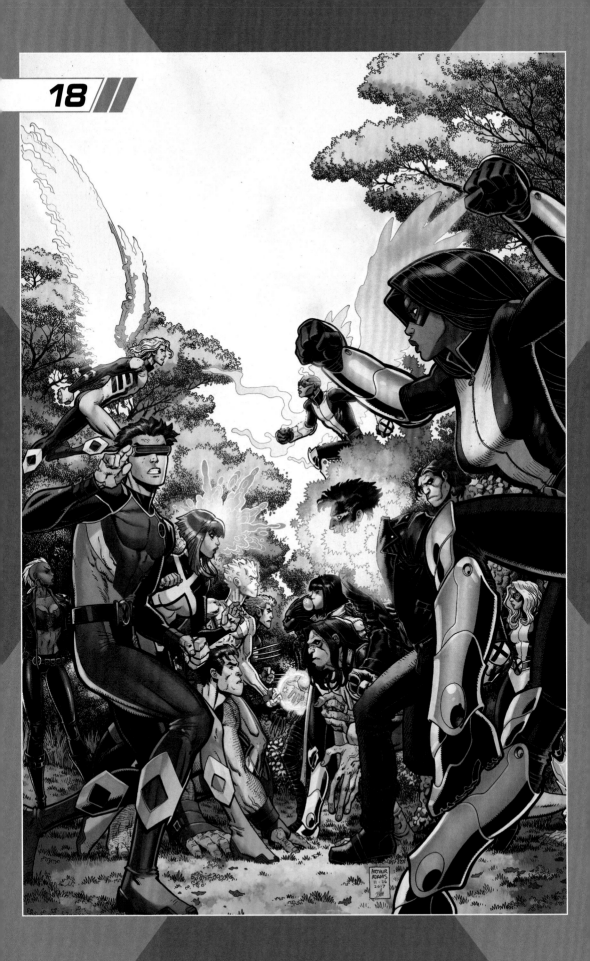

ARTHUR ADAMS
11.26.2017

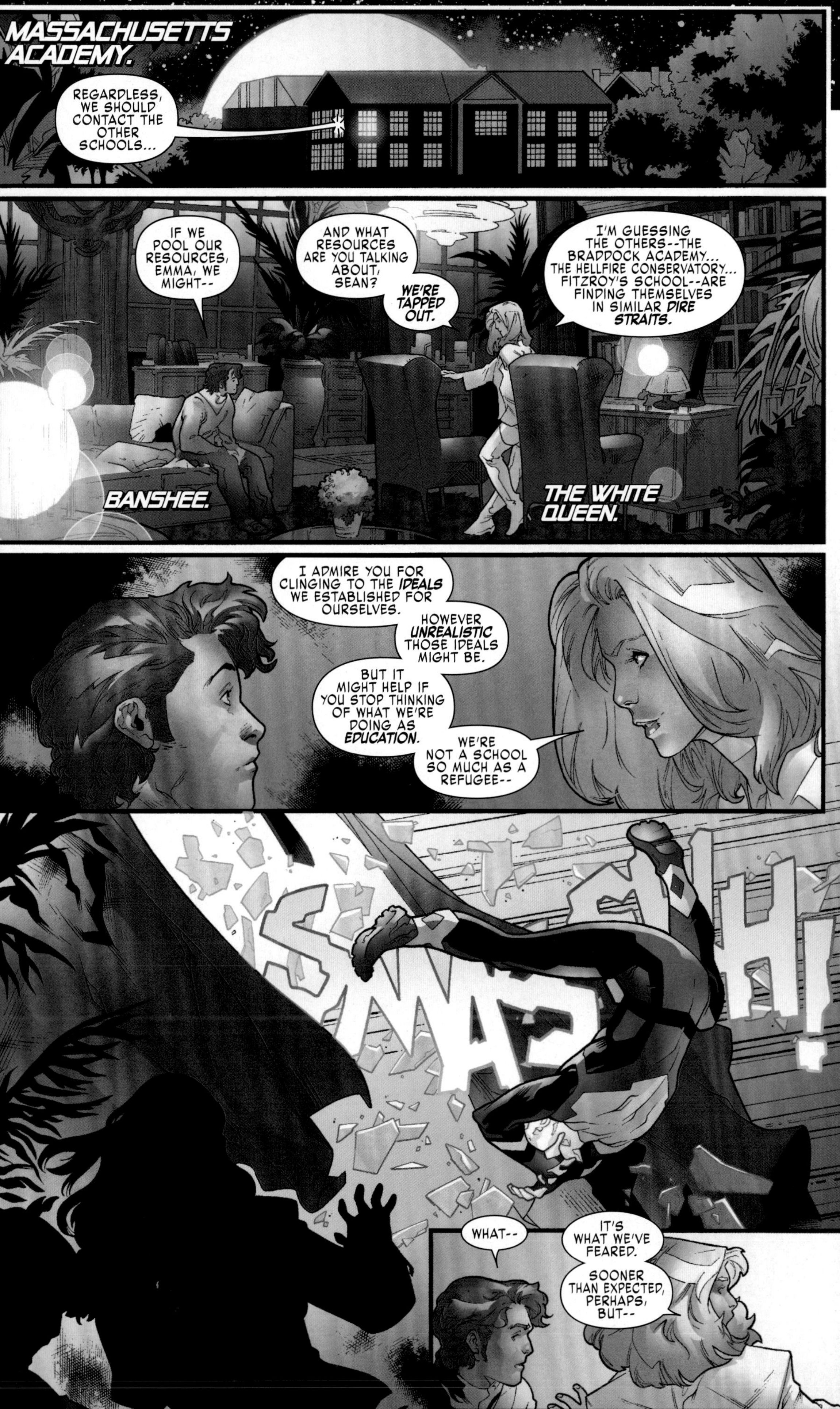

MASSACHUSETTS ACADEMY.
REGARDLESS, WE SHOULD CONTACT THE OTHER SCHOOLS...
IF WE POOL OUR RESOURCES, EMMA, WE MIGHT--
AND WHAT RESOURCES ARE YOU TALKING ABOUT, SEAN?
WE'RE TAPPED OUT.
I'M GUESSING THE OTHERS--THE BRADDOCK ACADEMY... THE HELLFIRE CONSERVATORY... FITZROY'S SCHOOL--ARE FINDING THEMSELVES IN SIMILAR DIRE STRAITS.
BANSHEE.
THE WHITE QUEEN.
I ADMIRE YOU FOR CLINGING TO THE IDEALS WE ESTABLISHED FOR OURSELVES.
HOWEVER UNREALISTIC THOSE IDEALS MIGHT BE.
BUT IT MIGHT HELP IF YOU STOP THINKING OF WHAT WE'RE DOING AS EDUCATION.
WE'RE NOT A SCHOOL SO MUCH AS A REFUGEE--
SMASH!
WHAT--
IT'S WHAT WE'VE FEARED.
SOONER THAN EXPECTED, PERHAPS, BUT--

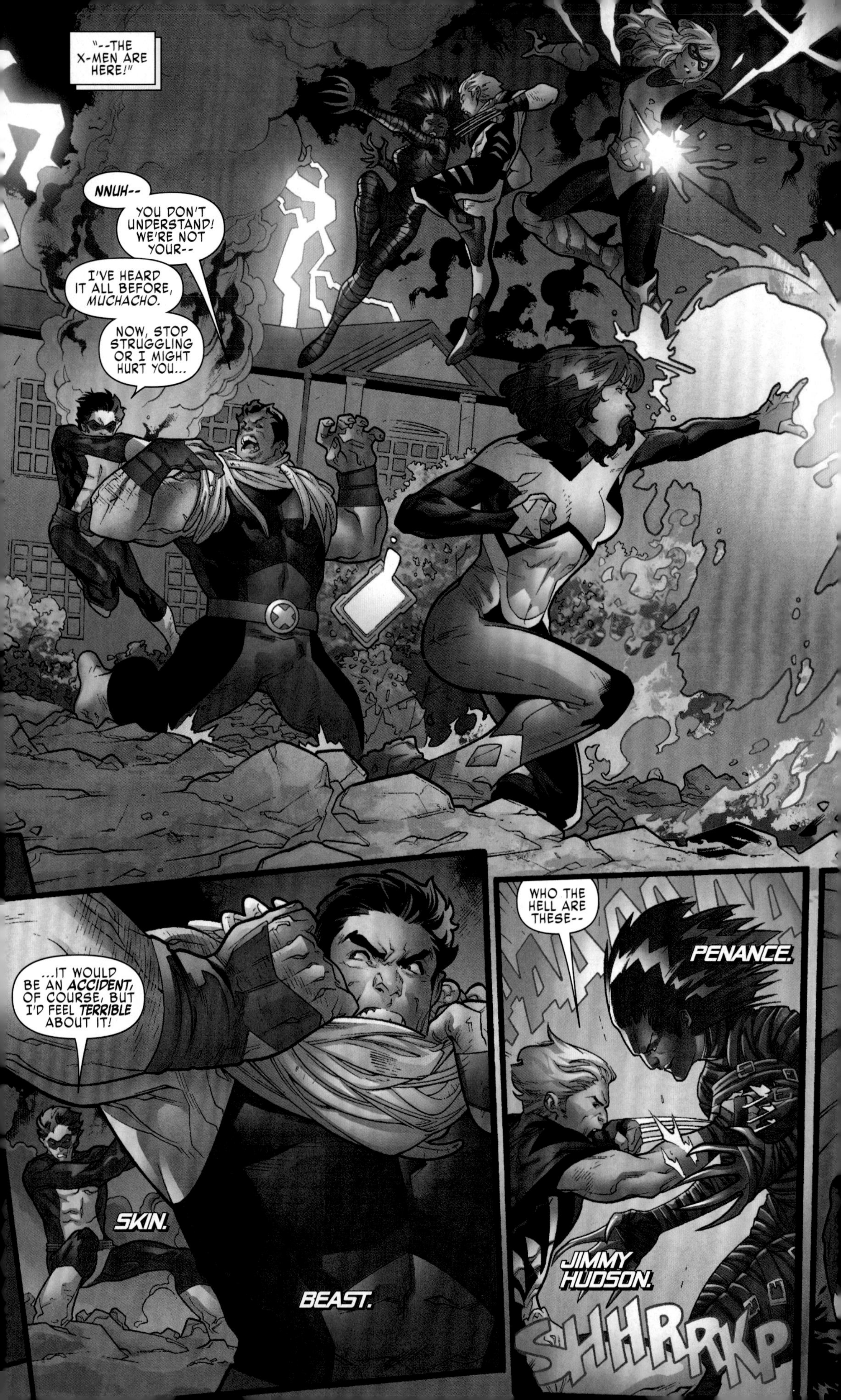
"--THE X-MEN ARE HERE!"
NNUH--
YOU DON'T UNDERSTAND! WE'RE NOT YOUR--
I'VE HEARD IT ALL BEFORE, MUCHACHO.
NOW, STOP STRUGGLING OR I MIGHT HURT YOU...
...IT WOULD BE AN ACCIDENT, OF COURSE, BUT I'D FEEL TERRIBLE ABOUT IT!
SKIN.
BEAST.
WHO THE HELL ARE THESE--
PENANCE.
JIMMY HUDSON.
SHHRRKP

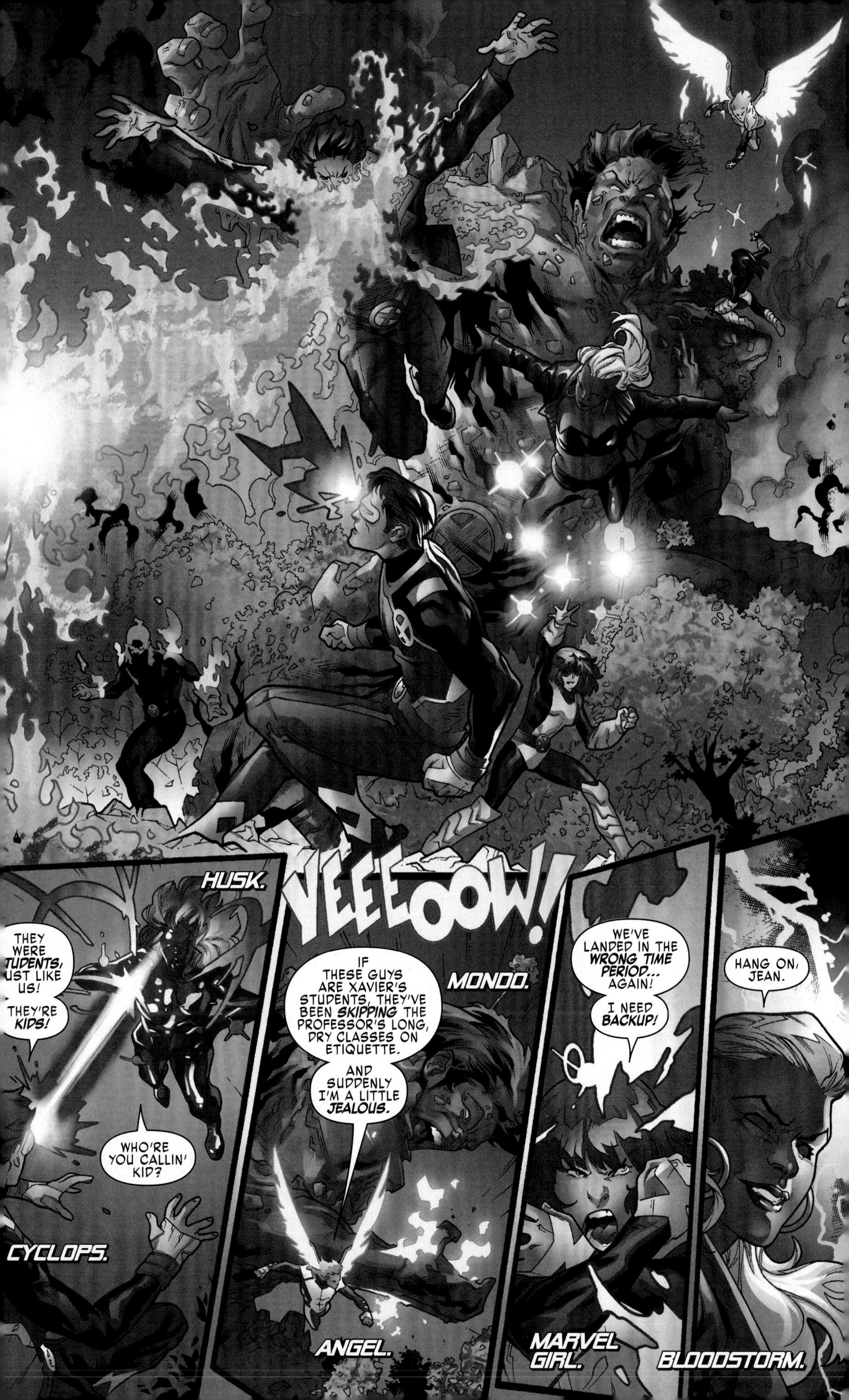
HUSK.
THEY WERE STUDENTS, JUST LIKE US!
THEY'RE KIDS!
WHO'RE YOU CALLIN' KID?
CYCLOPS.
VEEEOOW!
IF THESE GUYS ARE XAVIER'S STUDENTS, THEY'VE BEEN SKIPPING THE PROFESSOR'S LONG, DRY CLASSES ON ETIQUETTE.
AND SUDDENLY I'M A LITTLE JEALOUS.
MONDO.
ANGEL.
WE'VE LANDED IN THE WRONG TIME PERIOD... AGAIN!
I NEED BACKUP!
MARVEL GIRL.
HANG ON, JEAN.
BLOODSTORM.

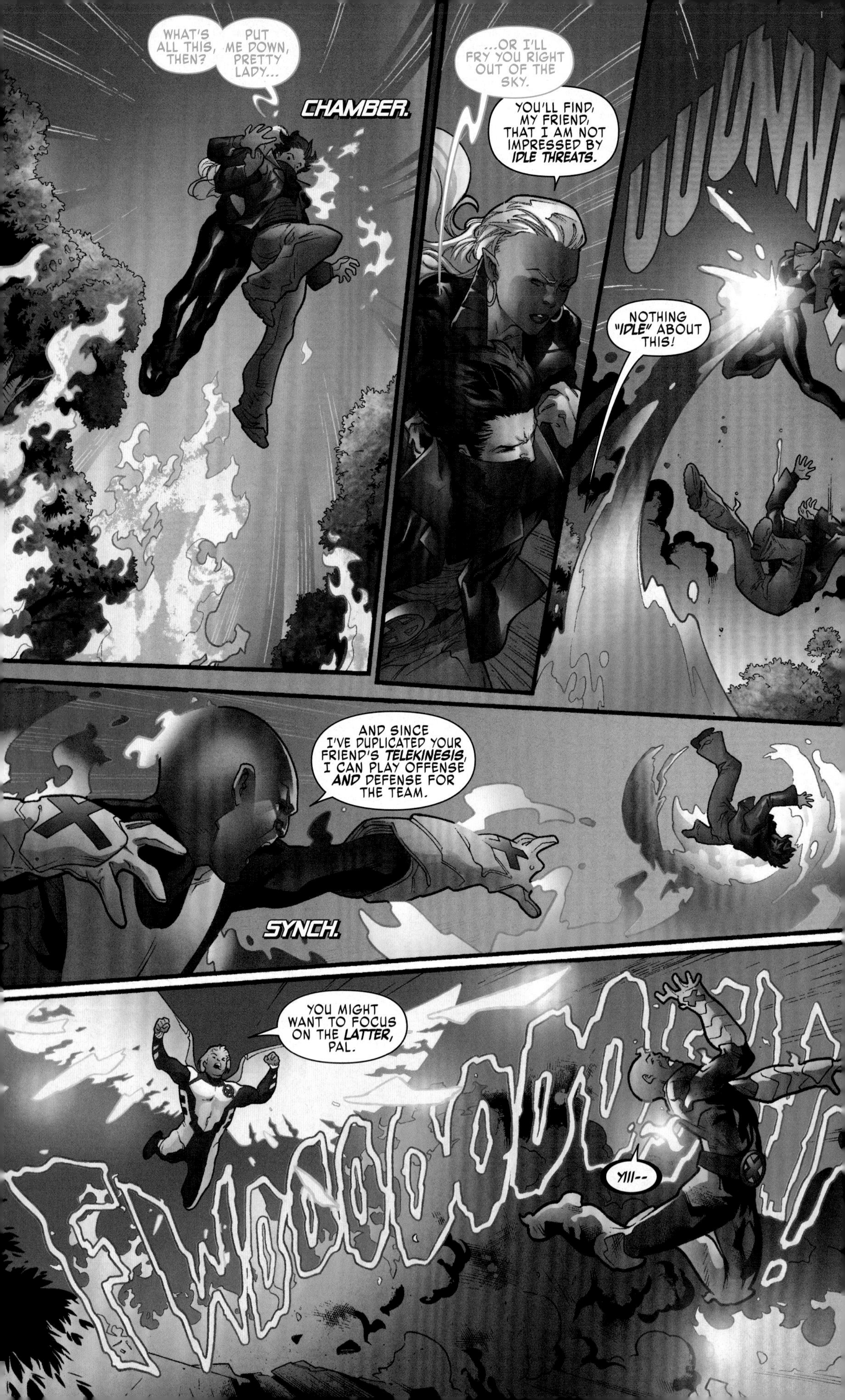
WHAT'S ALL THIS, THEN?
PUT ME DOWN, PRETTY LADY...
CHAMBER.
...OR I'LL FRY YOU RIGHT OUT OF THE SKY.
YOU'LL FIND, MY FRIEND, THAT I AM NOT IMPRESSED BY IDLE THREATS.
NOTHING "IDLE" ABOUT THIS!
AND SINCE I'VE DUPLICATED YOUR FRIEND'S TELEKINESIS, I CAN PLAY OFFENSE AND DEFENSE FOR THE TEAM.
SYNCH.
YOU MIGHT WANT TO FOCUS ON THE LATTER, PAL.
YIII--

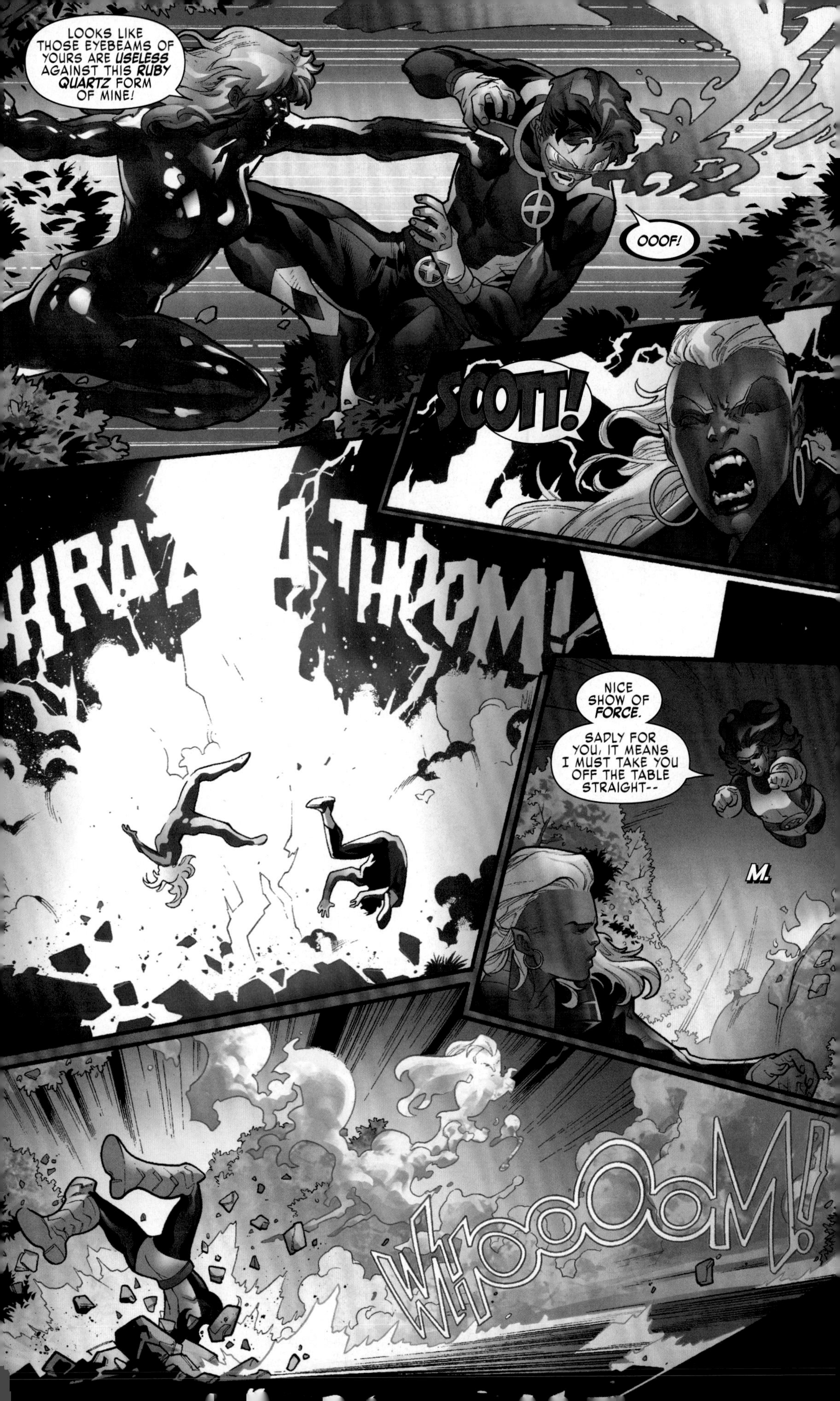
LOOKS LIKE THOSE EYEBEAMS OF YOURS ARE USELESS AGAINST THIS RUBY QUARTZ FORM OF MINE!
OOOF!
SCOTT!
NICE SHOW OF FORCE.
SADLY FOR YOU, IT MEANS I MUST TAKE YOU OFF THE TABLE STRAIGHT--
M.
WHOOOOOM!

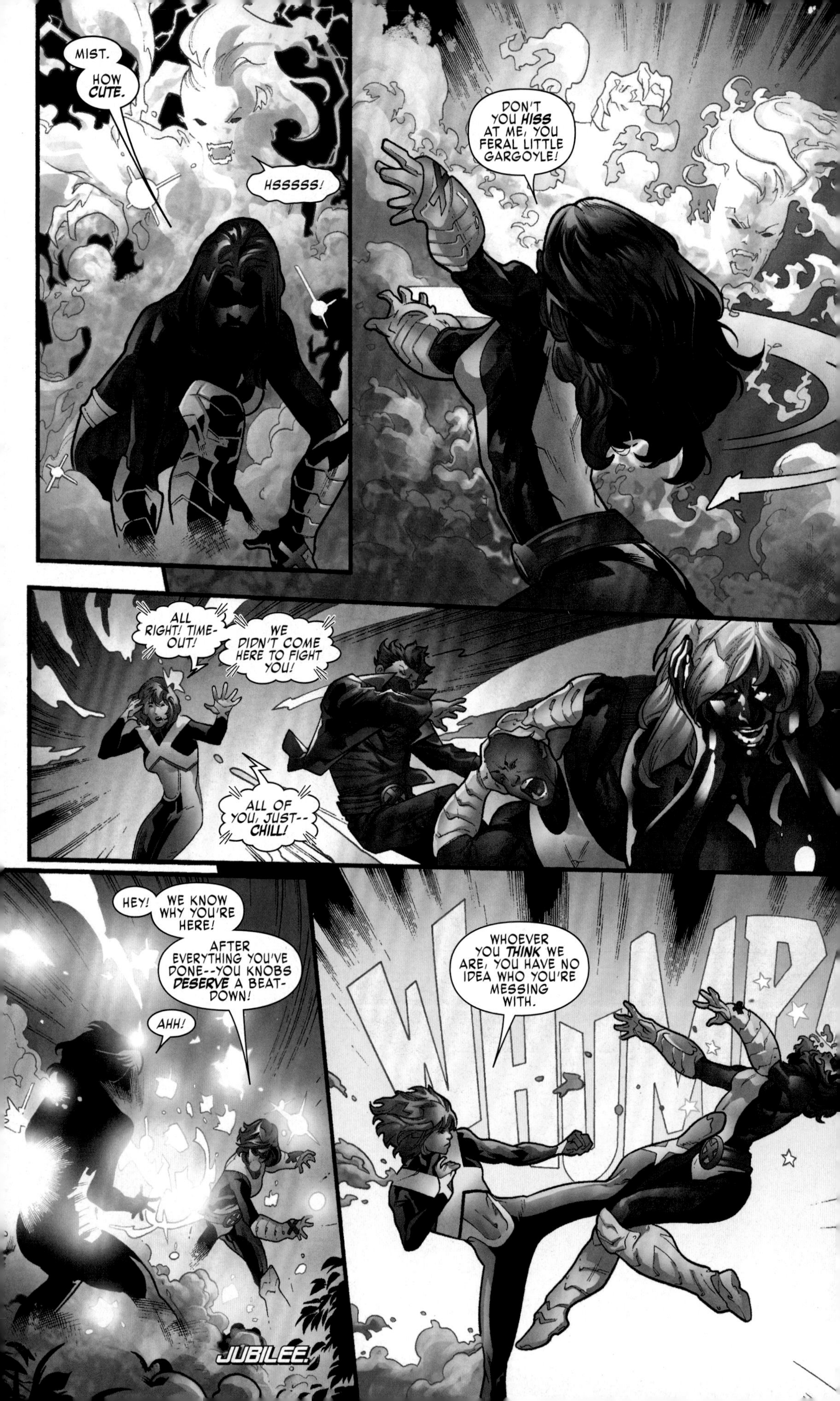
MIST.
HOW CUTE.
HSSSSS!
DON'T YOU HISS AT ME, YOU FERAL LITTLE GARGOYLE!
ALL RIGHT! TIME-OUT!
WE DIDN'T COME HERE TO FIGHT YOU!
ALL OF YOU, JUST-- CHILL!
HEY!
WE KNOW WHY YOU'RE HERE!
AFTER EVERYTHING YOU'VE DONE--YOU KNOBS DESERVE A BEAT-DOWN!
AHH!
JUBILEE.
WHOEVER YOU THINK WE ARE, YOU HAVE NO IDEA WHO YOU'RE MESSING WITH.

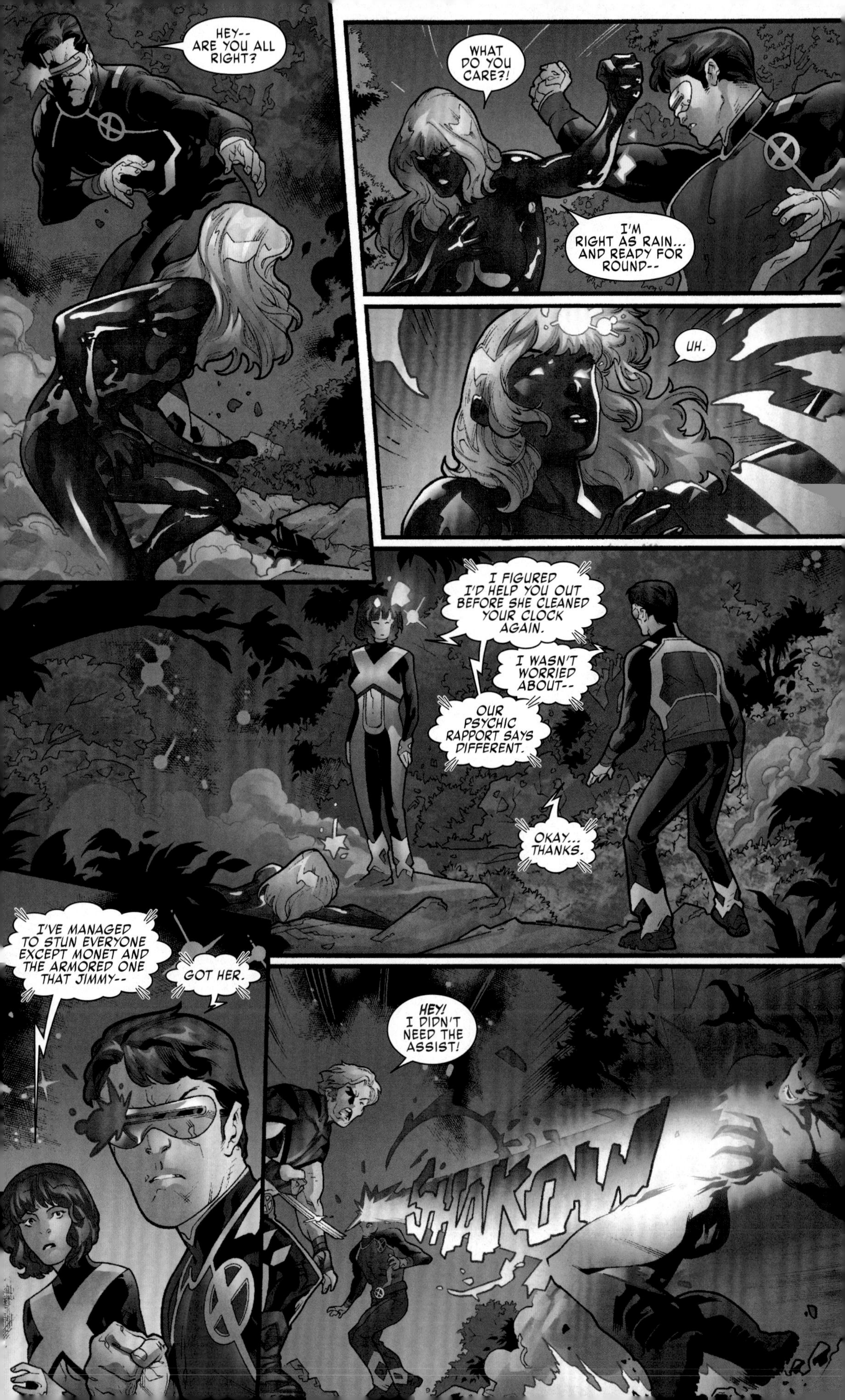
HEY-- ARE YOU ALL RIGHT?
WHAT DO YOU CARE?!
I'M RIGHT AS RAIN... AND READY FOR ROUND--
UH.
I FIGURED I'D HELP YOU OUT BEFORE SHE CLEANED YOUR CLOCK AGAIN.
I WASN'T WORRIED ABOUT--
OUR PSYCHIC RAPPORT SAYS DIFFERENT.
OKAY... THANKS.
I'VE MANAGED TO STUN EVERYONE EXCEPT MONET AND THE ARMORED ONE THAT JIMMY--
GOT HER.
HEY! I DIDN'T NEED THE ASSIST!
SHAKOW

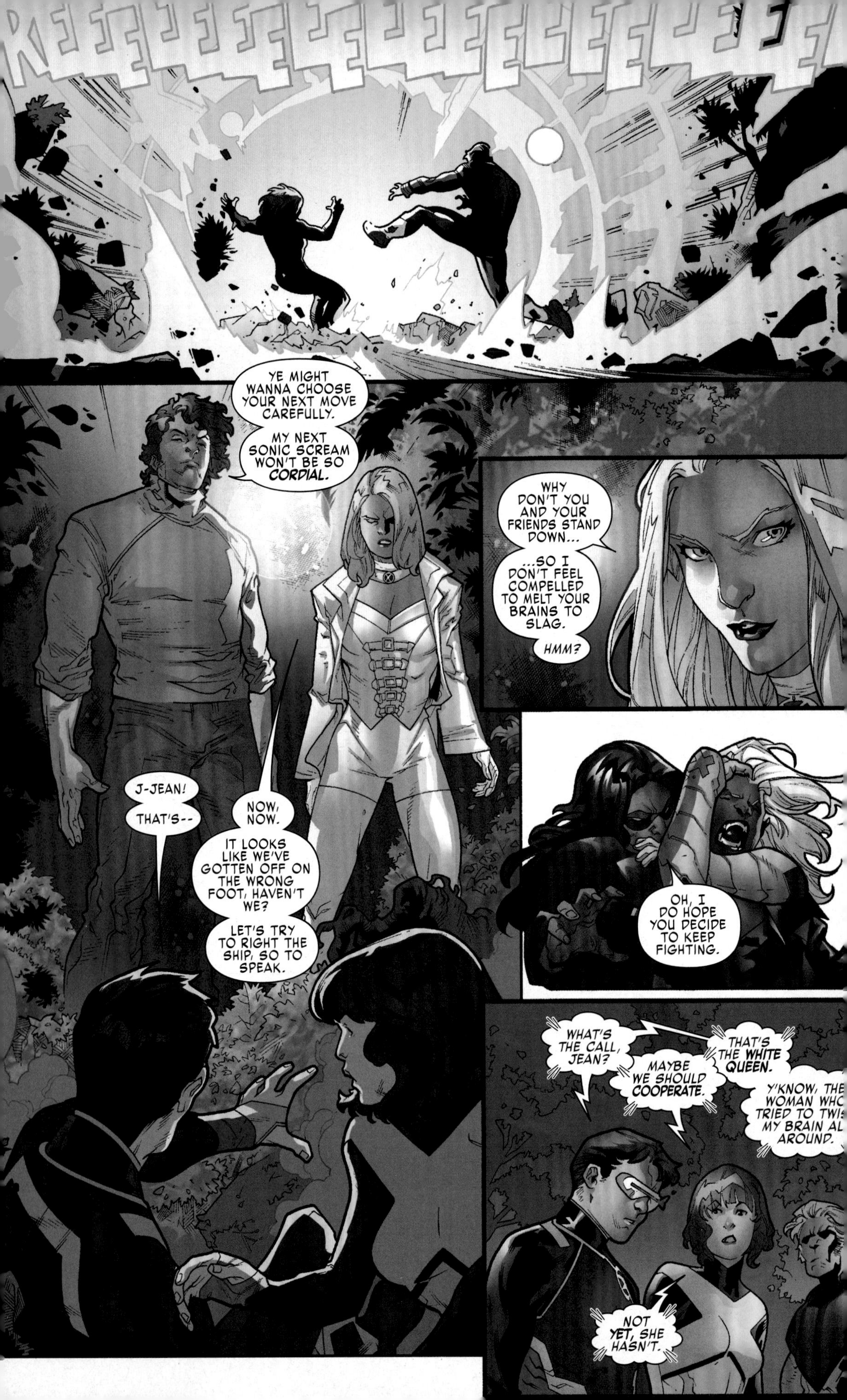
REEEEEEEEEEEEEEEEE
YE MIGHT WANNA CHOOSE YOUR NEXT MOVE CAREFULLY.
MY NEXT SONIC SCREAM WON'T BE SO CORDIAL.
WHY DON'T YOU AND YOUR FRIENDS STAND DOWN...
...SO I DON'T FEEL COMPELLED TO MELT YOUR BRAINS TO SLAG.
HMM?
J-JEAN!
THAT'S--
NOW, NOW.
IT LOOKS LIKE WE'VE GOTTEN OFF ON THE WRONG FOOT, HAVEN'T WE?
LET'S TRY TO RIGHT THE SHIP, SO TO SPEAK.
OH, I DO HOPE YOU DECIDE TO KEEP FIGHTING.
WHAT'S THE CALL, JEAN?
MAYBE WE SHOULD COOPERATE.
THAT'S THE WHITE QUEEN.
NOT YET, SHE HASN'T.

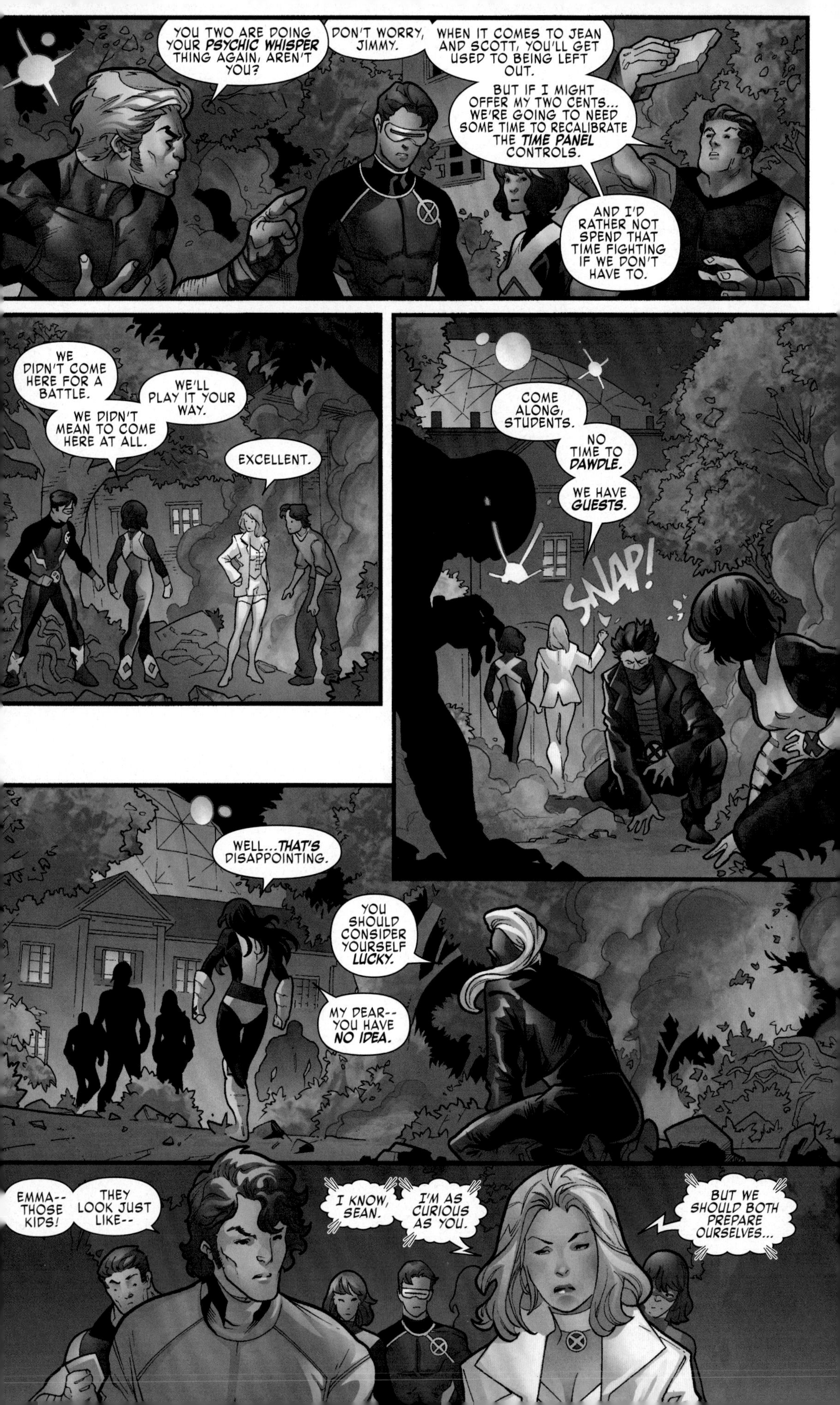

YOU TWO ARE DOING YOUR **PSYCHIC WHISPER** THING AGAIN, AREN'T YOU?
DON'T WORRY, JIMMY.
WHEN IT COMES TO JEAN AND SCOTT, YOU'LL GET USED TO BEING LEFT OUT.
BUT IF I MIGHT OFFER MY TWO CENTS... WE'RE GOING TO NEED SOME TIME TO RECALIBRATE THE **TIME PANEL** CONTROLS.
AND I'D RATHER NOT SPEND THAT TIME FIGHTING IF WE DON'T HAVE TO.
WE DIDN'T COME HERE FOR A BATTLE.
WE DIDN'T MEAN TO COME HERE AT ALL.
WE'LL PLAY IT YOUR WAY.
EXCELLENT.
COME ALONG, STUDENTS.
NO TIME TO **DAWDLE.**
WE HAVE **GUESTS.**
SNAP!
WELL...**THAT'S** DISAPPOINTING.
YOU SHOULD CONSIDER YOURSELF **LUCKY.**
MY DEAR--YOU HAVE **NO IDEA.**
EMMA--THOSE KIDS!
THEY LOOK JUST LIKE--
I KNOW, SEAN.
I'M AS CURIOUS AS YOU.
BUT WE SHOULD BOTH PREPARE OURSELVES...

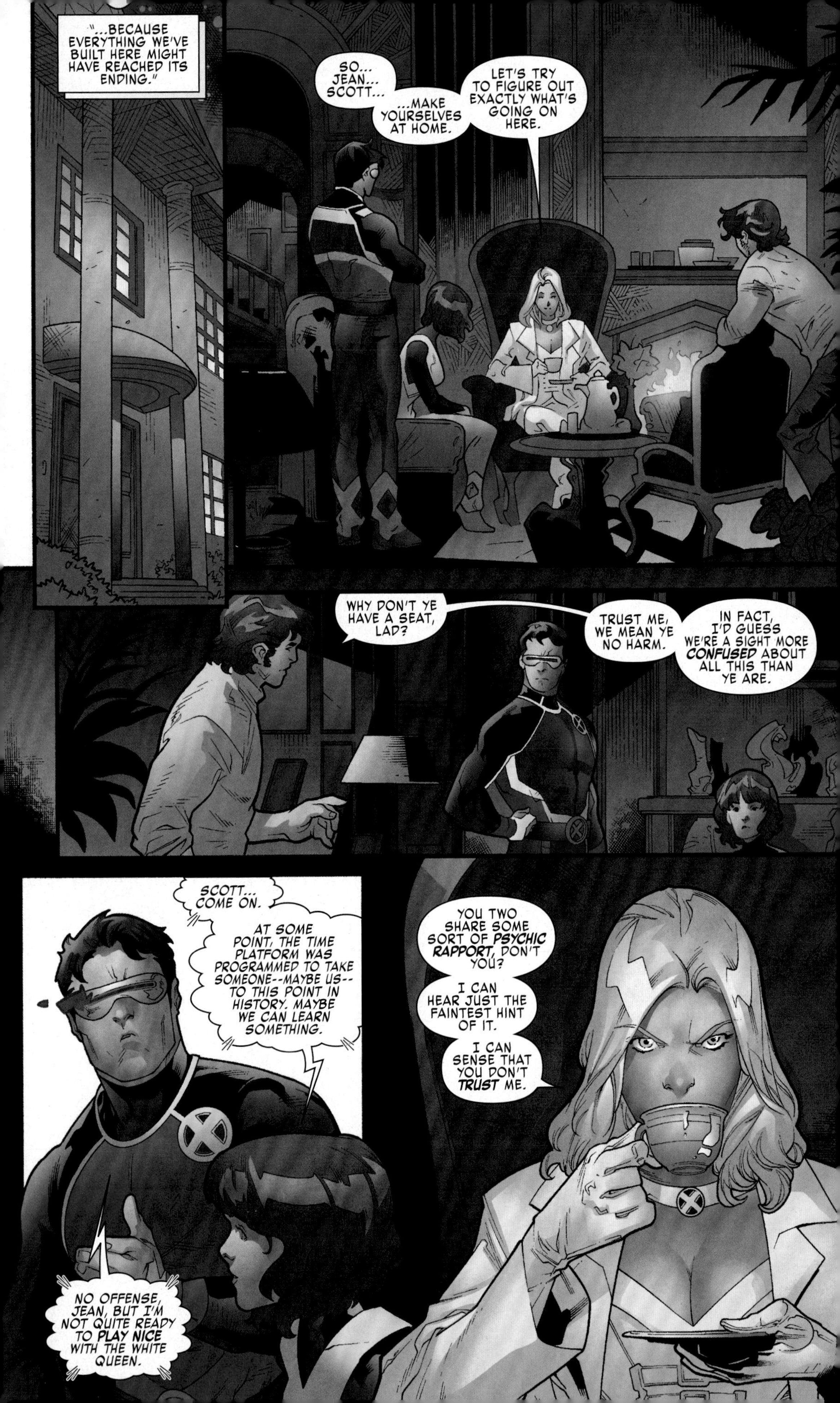
"...BECAUSE EVERYTHING WE'VE BUILT HERE MIGHT HAVE REACHED ITS ENDING."
SO... JEAN... SCOTT...
...MAKE YOURSELVES AT HOME.
LET'S TRY TO FIGURE OUT EXACTLY WHAT'S GOING ON HERE.
WHY DON'T YE HAVE A SEAT, LAD?
TRUST ME, WE MEAN YE NO HARM.
IN FACT, I'D GUESS WE'RE A SIGHT MORE CONFUSED ABOUT ALL THIS THAN YE ARE.
SCOTT... COME ON.
AT SOME POINT, THE TIME PLATFORM WAS PROGRAMMED TO TAKE SOMEONE--MAYBE US--TO THIS POINT IN HISTORY. MAYBE WE CAN LEARN SOMETHING.
NO OFFENSE, JEAN, BUT I'M NOT QUITE READY TO PLAY NICE WITH THE WHITE QUEEN.
YOU TWO SHARE SOME SORT OF PSYCHIC RAPPORT, DON'T YOU?
I CAN HEAR JUST THE FAINTEST HINT OF IT.
I CAN SENSE THAT YOU DON'T TRUST ME.

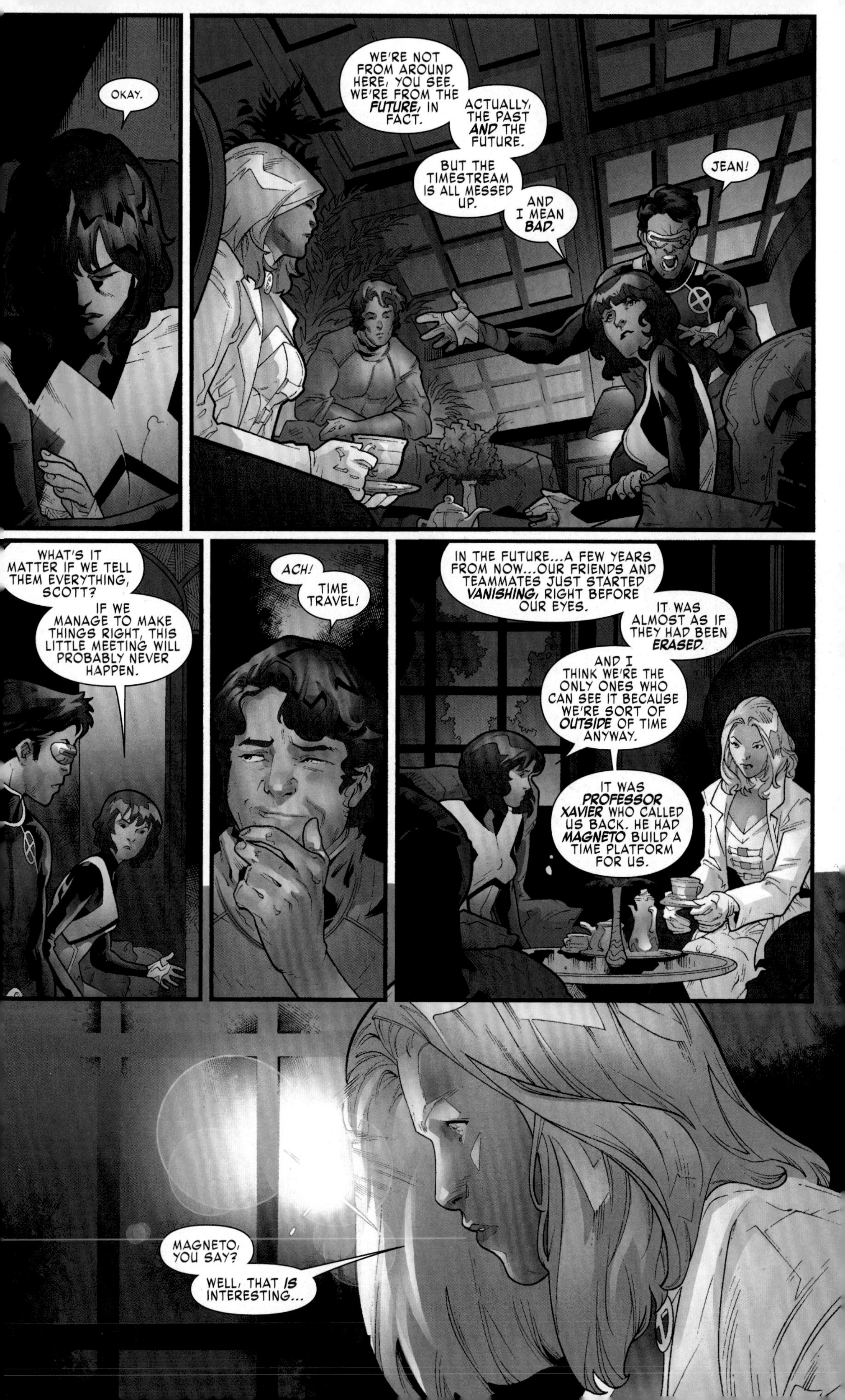
OKAY.
WE'RE NOT FROM AROUND HERE, YOU SEE. WE'RE FROM THE FUTURE, IN FACT.
ACTUALLY, THE PAST AND THE FUTURE.
BUT THE TIMESTREAM IS ALL MESSED UP.
AND I MEAN BAD.
JEAN!
WHAT'S IT MATTER IF WE TELL THEM EVERYTHING, SCOTT?
IF WE MANAGE TO MAKE THINGS RIGHT, THIS LITTLE MEETING WILL PROBABLY NEVER HAPPEN.
ACH!
TIME TRAVEL!
IN THE FUTURE...A FEW YEARS FROM NOW...OUR FRIENDS AND TEAMMATES JUST STARTED VANISHING, RIGHT BEFORE OUR EYES.
IT WAS ALMOST AS IF THEY HAD BEEN ERASED.
AND I THINK WE'RE THE ONLY ONES WHO CAN SEE IT BECAUSE WE'RE SORT OF OUTSIDE OF TIME ANYWAY.
IT WAS PROFESSOR XAVIER WHO CALLED US BACK. HE HAD MAGNETO BUILD A TIME PLATFORM FOR US.
MAGNETO, YOU SAY?
WELL, THAT IS INTERESTING...

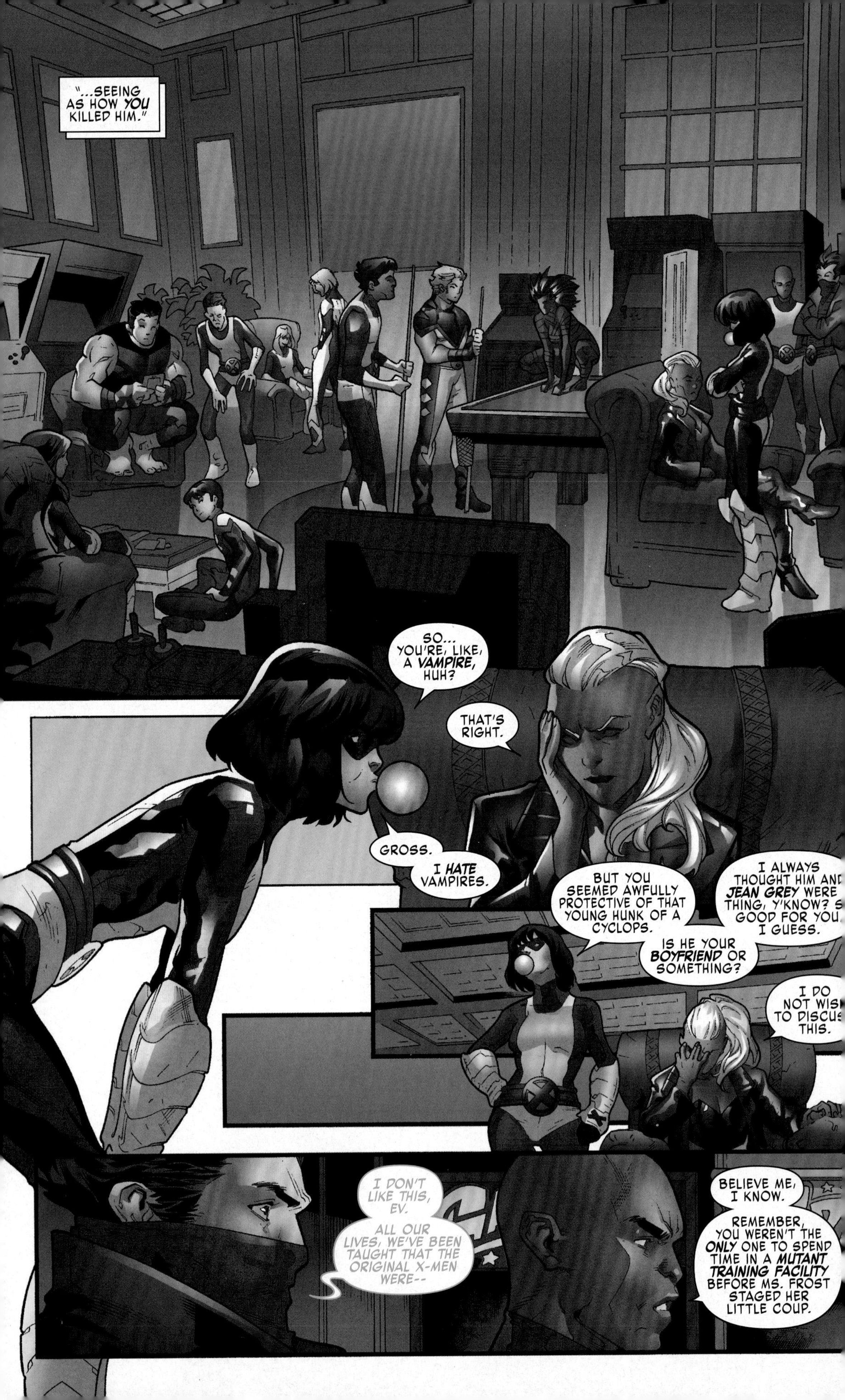
"...SEEING AS HOW YOU KILLED HIM."
SO... YOU'RE, LIKE, A VAMPIRE, HUH?
THAT'S RIGHT.
GROSS.
I HATE VAMPIRES.
BUT YOU SEEMED AWFULLY PROTECTIVE OF THAT YOUNG HUNK OF A CYCLOPS.
IS HE YOUR BOYFRIEND OR SOMETHING?
I ALWAYS THOUGHT HIM AND JEAN GREY WERE THING, Y'KNOW? GOOD FOR YOU. I GUESS.
I DO NOT WISH TO DISCUS THIS.
I DON'T LIKE THIS, EV.
ALL OUR LIVES, WE'VE BEEN TAUGHT THAT THE ORIGINAL X-MEN WERE--
BELIEVE ME, I KNOW.
REMEMBER, YOU WEREN'T THE ONLY ONE TO SPEND TIME IN A MUTANT TRAINING FACILITY BEFORE MS. FROST STAGED HER LITTLE COUP.

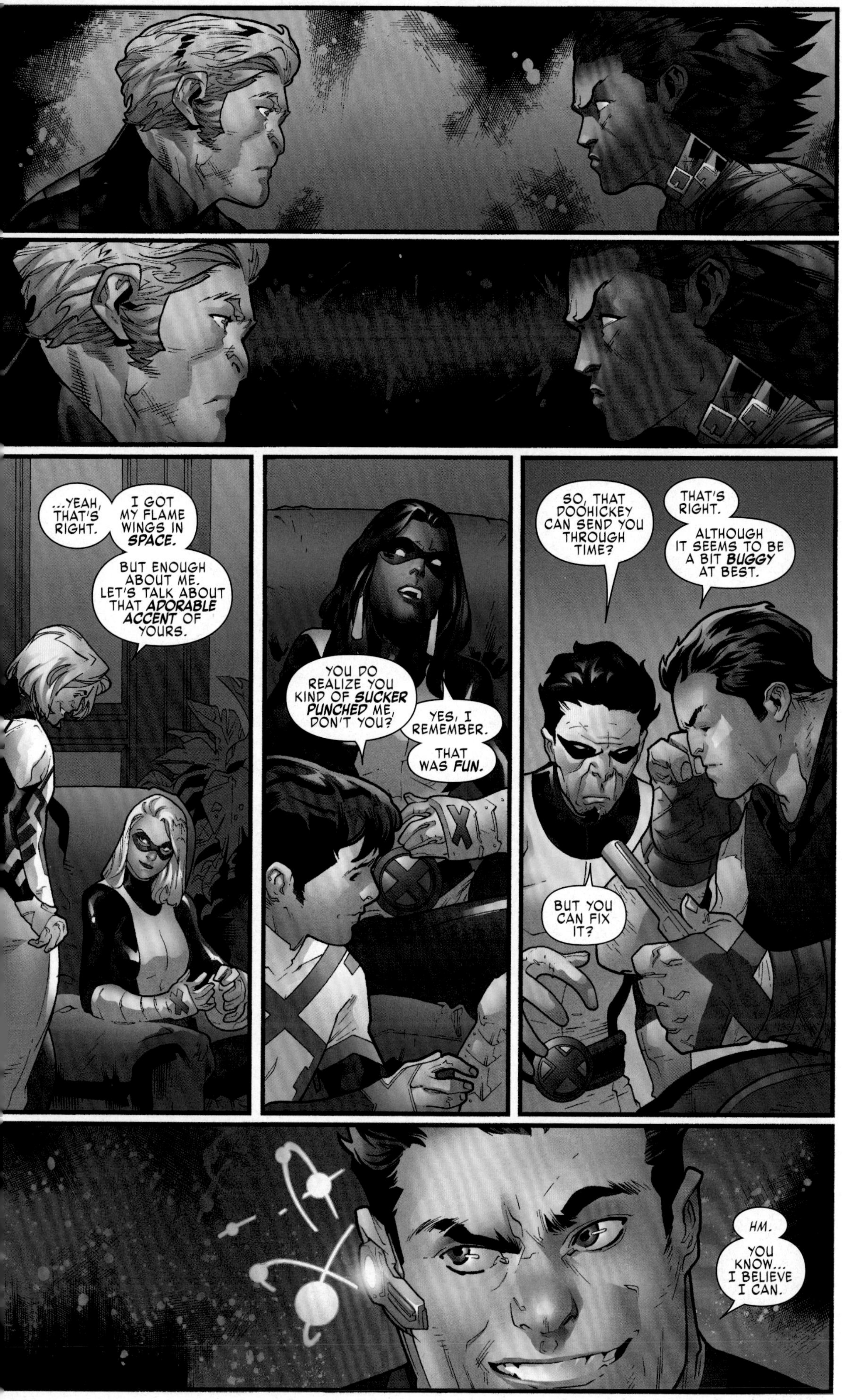
...YEAH, THAT'S RIGHT.
I GOT MY FLAME WINGS IN SPACE.
BUT ENOUGH ABOUT ME. LET'S TALK ABOUT THAT ADORABLE ACCENT OF YOURS.
YOU DO REALIZE YOU KIND OF SUCKER PUNCHED ME, DON'T YOU?
YES, I REMEMBER.
THAT WAS FUN.
SO, THAT DOOHICKEY CAN SEND YOU THROUGH TIME?
THAT'S RIGHT.
ALTHOUGH IT SEEMS TO BE A BIT BUGGY AT BEST.
BUT YOU CAN FIX IT?
HM.
YOU KNOW... I BELIEVE I CAN.

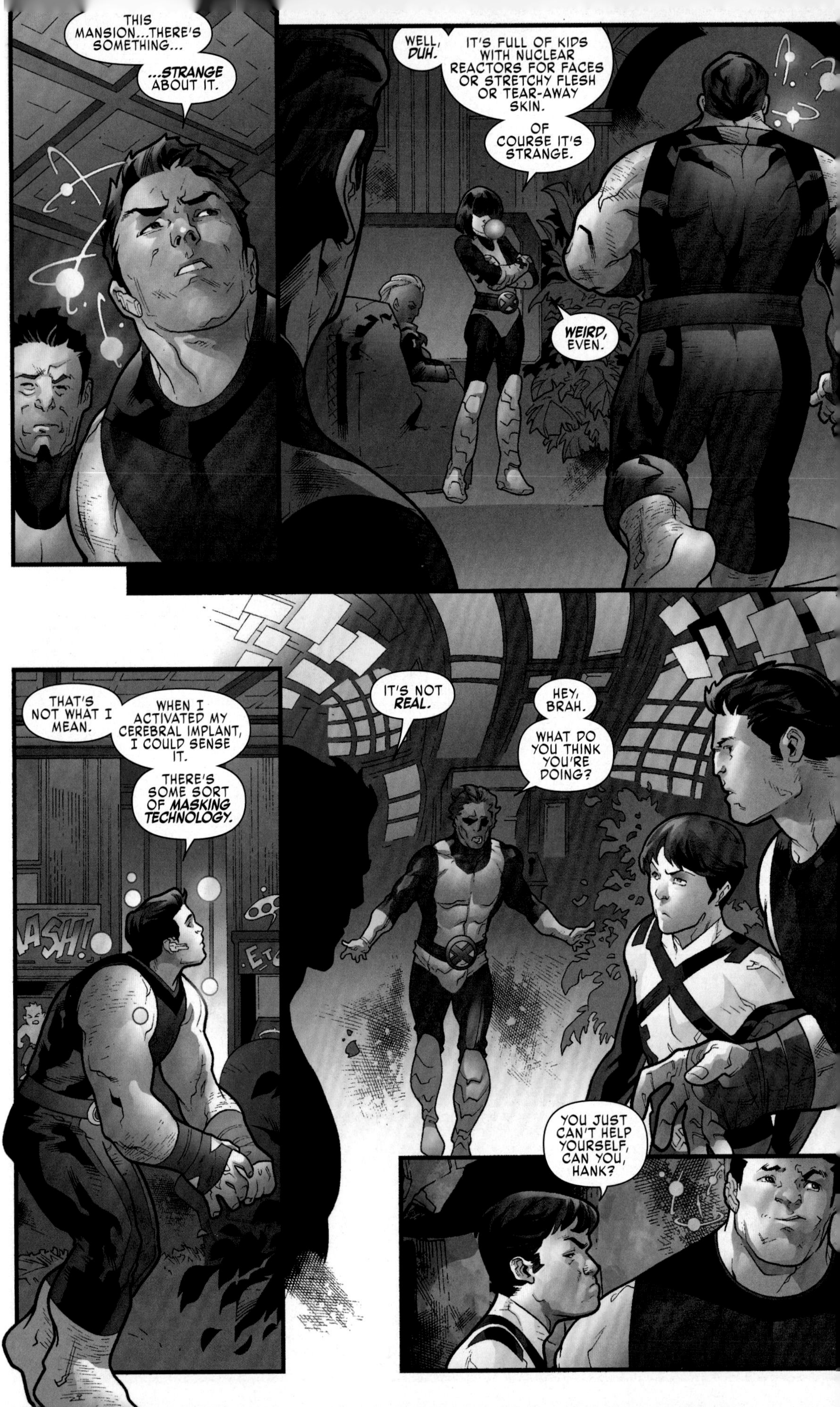

THIS MANSION...THERE'S SOMETHING...
...STRANGE ABOUT IT.
WELL, DUH.
IT'S FULL OF KIDS WITH NUCLEAR REACTORS FOR FACES OR STRETCHY FLESH OR TEAR-AWAY SKIN.
OF COURSE IT'S STRANGE.
WEIRD, EVEN.
THAT'S NOT WHAT I MEAN.
WHEN I ACTIVATED MY CEREBRAL IMPLANT, I COULD SENSE IT.
THERE'S SOME SORT OF MASKING TECHNOLOGY.
IT'S NOT REAL.
HEY, BRAH.
WHAT DO YOU THINK YOU'RE DOING?
YOU JUST CAN'T HELP YOURSELF, CAN YOU, HANK?

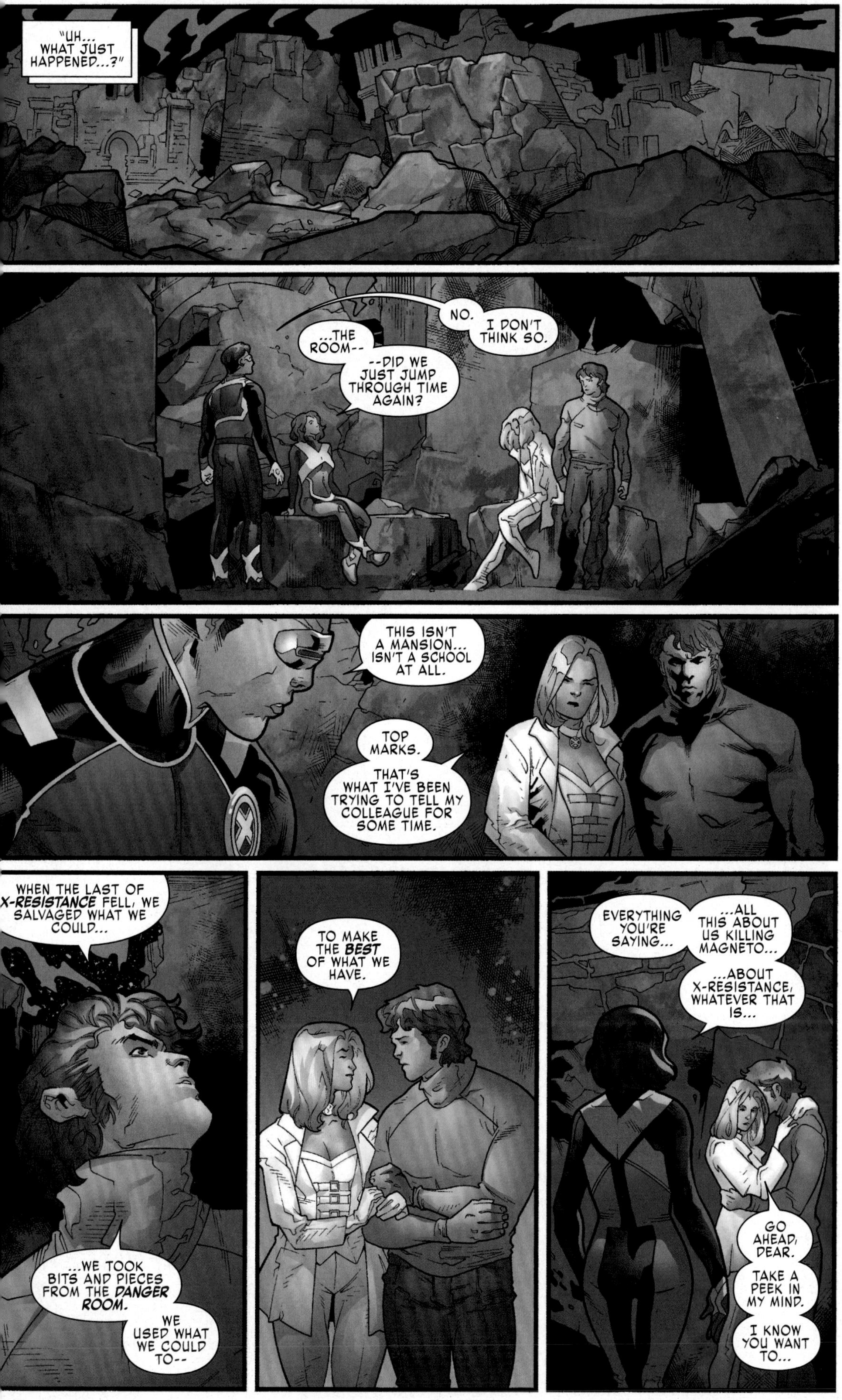
"UH... WHAT JUST HAPPENED...?"
...THE ROOM--
--DID WE JUST JUMP THROUGH TIME AGAIN?
NO. I DON'T THINK SO.
THIS ISN'T A MANSION... ISN'T A SCHOOL AT ALL.
TOP MARKS.
THAT'S WHAT I'VE BEEN TRYING TO TELL MY COLLEAGUE FOR SOME TIME.
WHEN THE LAST OF X-RESISTANCE FELL, WE SALVAGED WHAT WE COULD...
...WE TOOK BITS AND PIECES FROM THE DANGER ROOM.
WE USED WHAT WE COULD TO--
TO MAKE THE BEST OF WHAT WE HAVE.
EVERYTHING YOU'RE SAYING...
...ALL THIS ABOUT US KILLING MAGNETO...
...ABOUT X-RESISTANCE, WHATEVER THAT IS...
GO AHEAD, DEAR.
TAKE A PEEK IN MY MIND.
I KNOW YOU WANT TO...

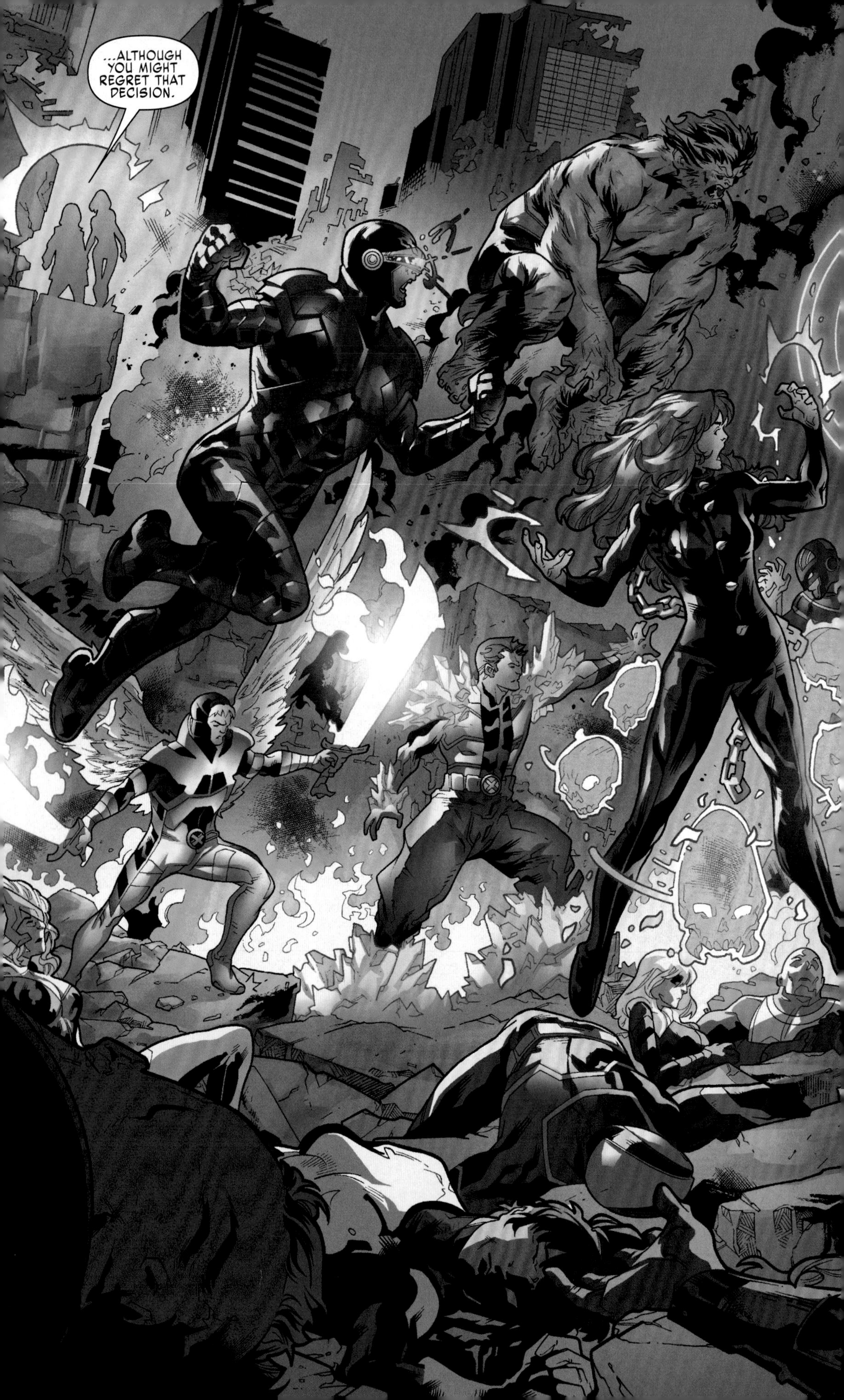
...ALTHOUGH YOU MIGHT REGRET THAT DECISION.

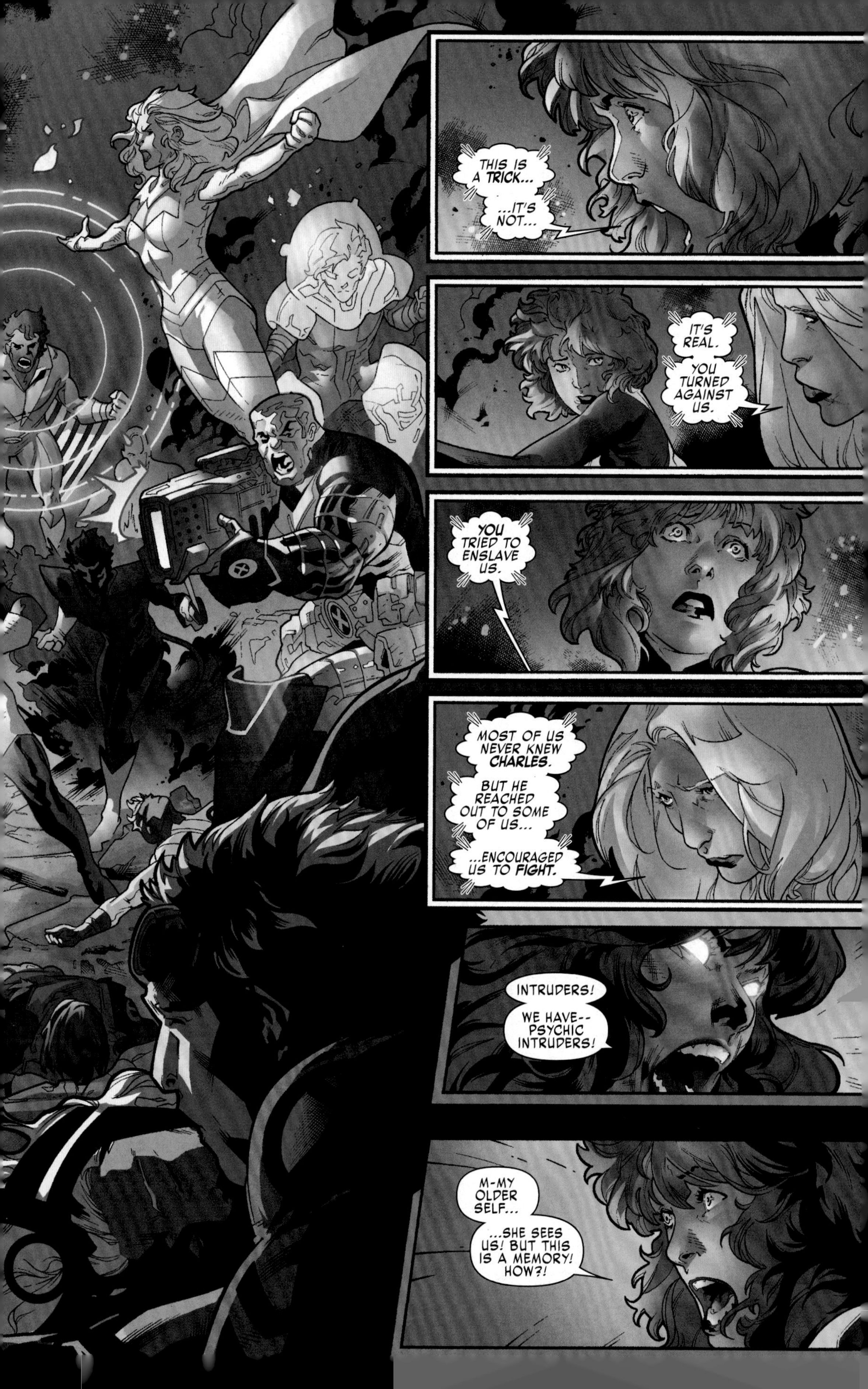
THIS IS A TRICK...
...IT'S NOT...
IT'S REAL.
YOU TURNED AGAINST US.
YOU TRIED TO ENSLAVE US.
MOST OF US NEVER KNEW CHARLES.
BUT HE REACHED OUT TO SOME OF US...
...ENCOURAGED US TO FIGHT.
INTRUDERS!
WE HAVE--PSYCHIC INTRUDERS!
M-MY OLDER SELF...
...SHE SEES US! BUT THIS IS A MEMORY! HOW?!

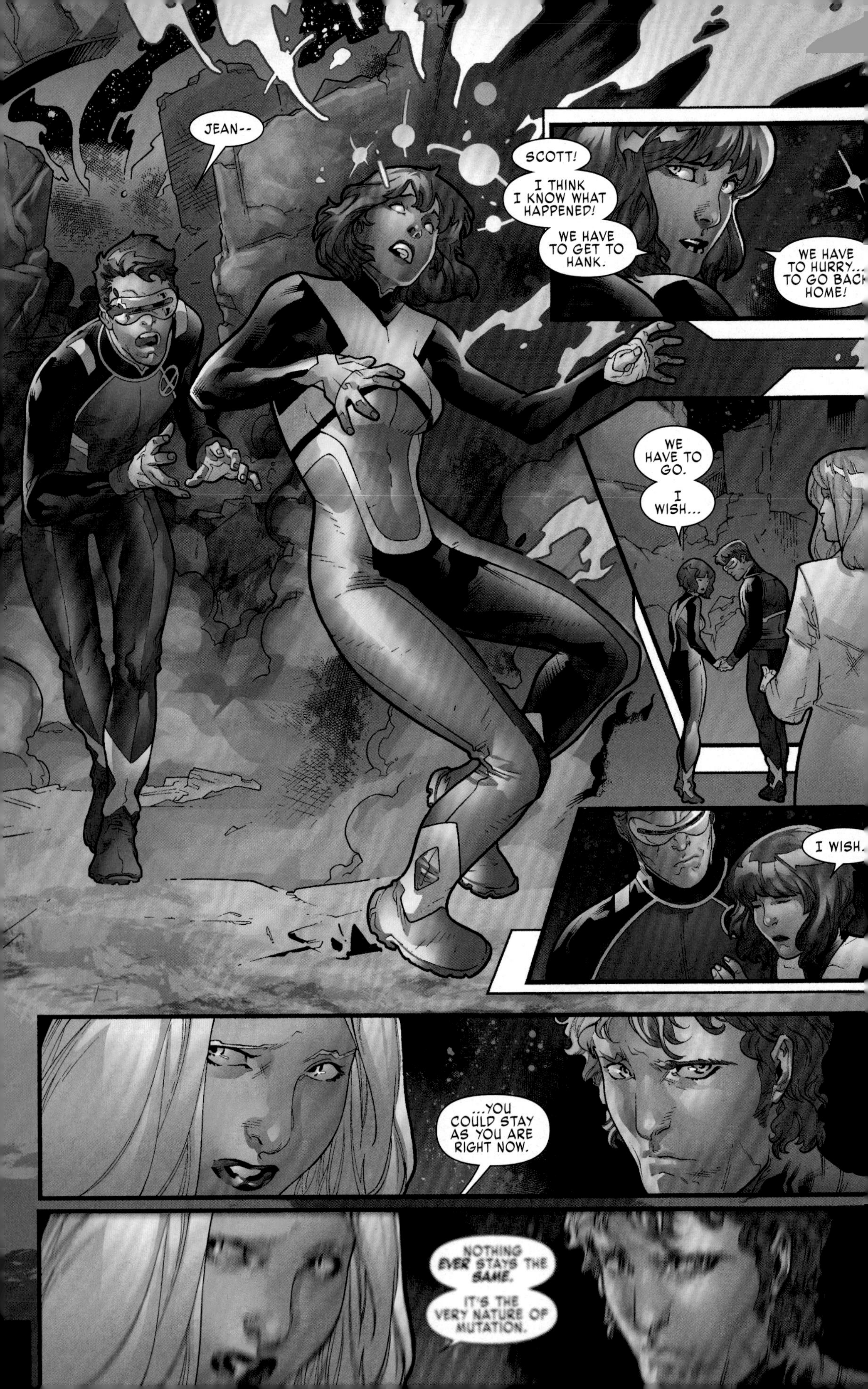
JEAN--
SCOTT!
I THINK I KNOW WHAT HAPPENED!
WE HAVE TO GET TO HANK.
WE HAVE TO HURRY... TO GO BAC
HOME!
WE HAVE TO GO.
I WISH...
I WISH.
...YOU COULD STAY AS YOU ARE RIGHT NOW.
NOTHING EVER STAYS THE SAME.
IT'S THE VERY NATURE OF MUTATION.

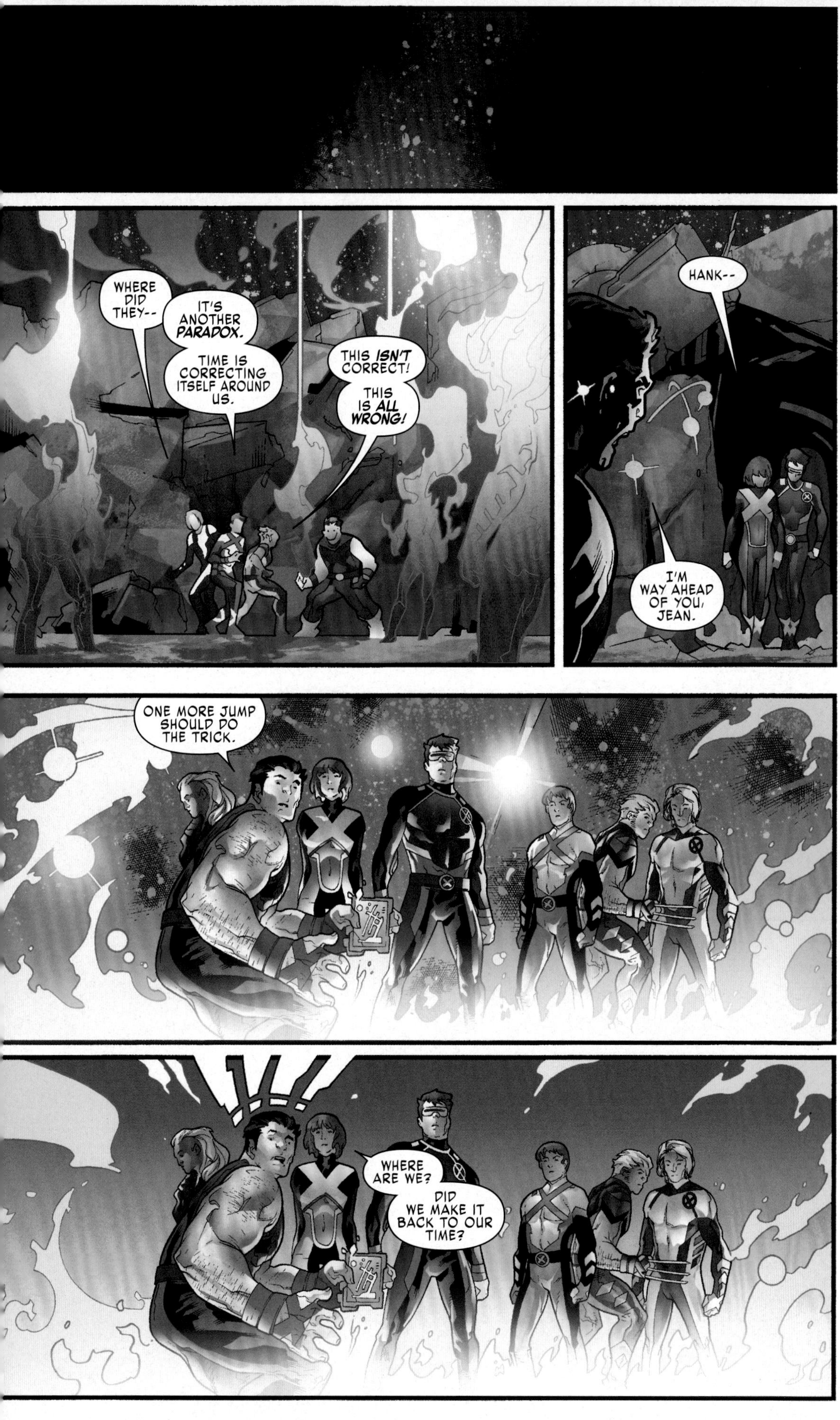
WHERE DID THEY--
IT'S ANOTHER PARADOX.
TIME IS CORRECTING ITSELF AROUND US.
THIS ISN'T CORRECT!
THIS IS ALL WRONG!
HANK--
I'M WAY AHEAD OF YOU, JEAN.
ONE MORE JUMP SHOULD DO THE TRICK.
WHERE ARE WE?
DID WE MAKE IT BACK TO OUR TIME?

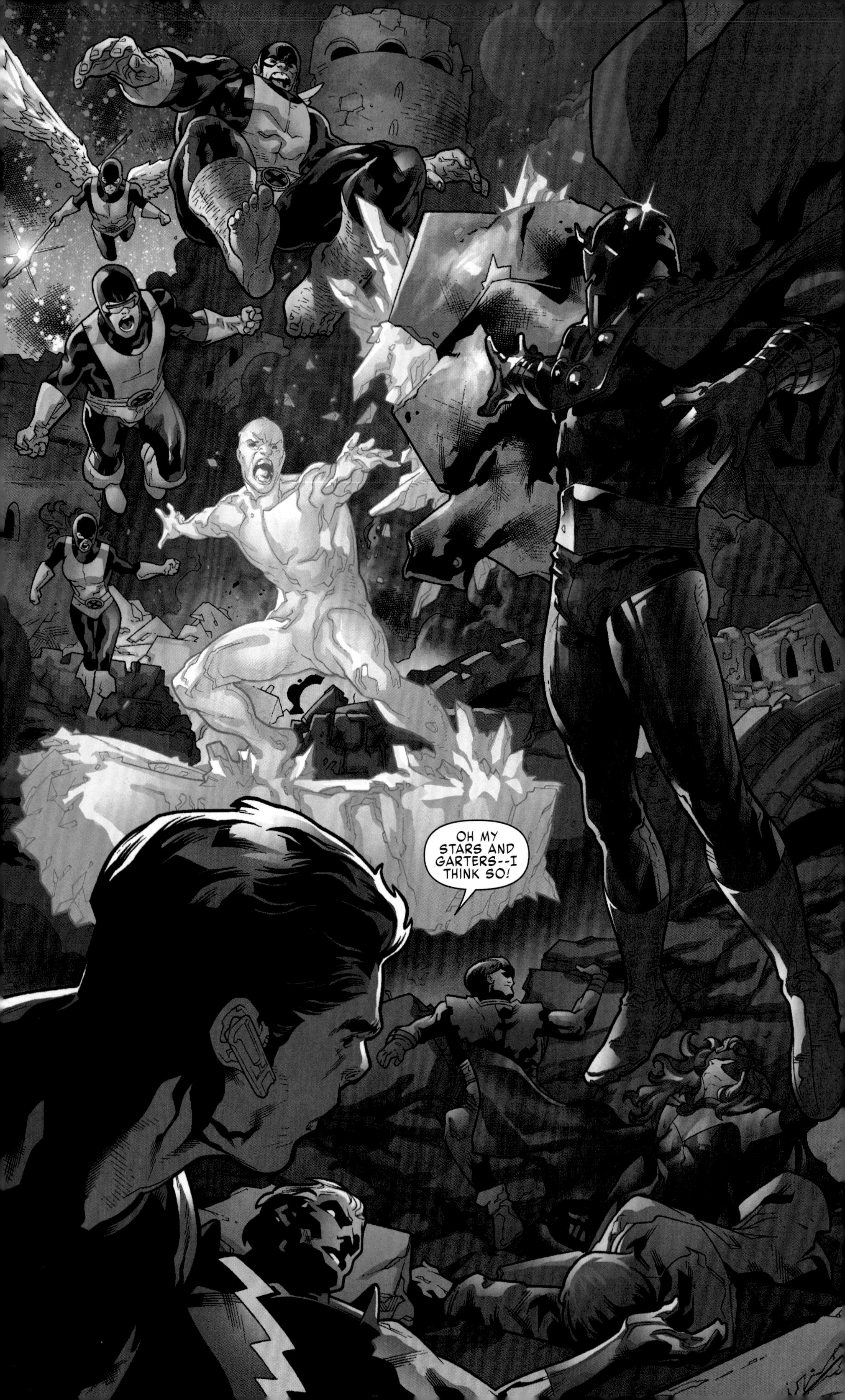
OH MY STARS AND GARTERS--I THINK SO!

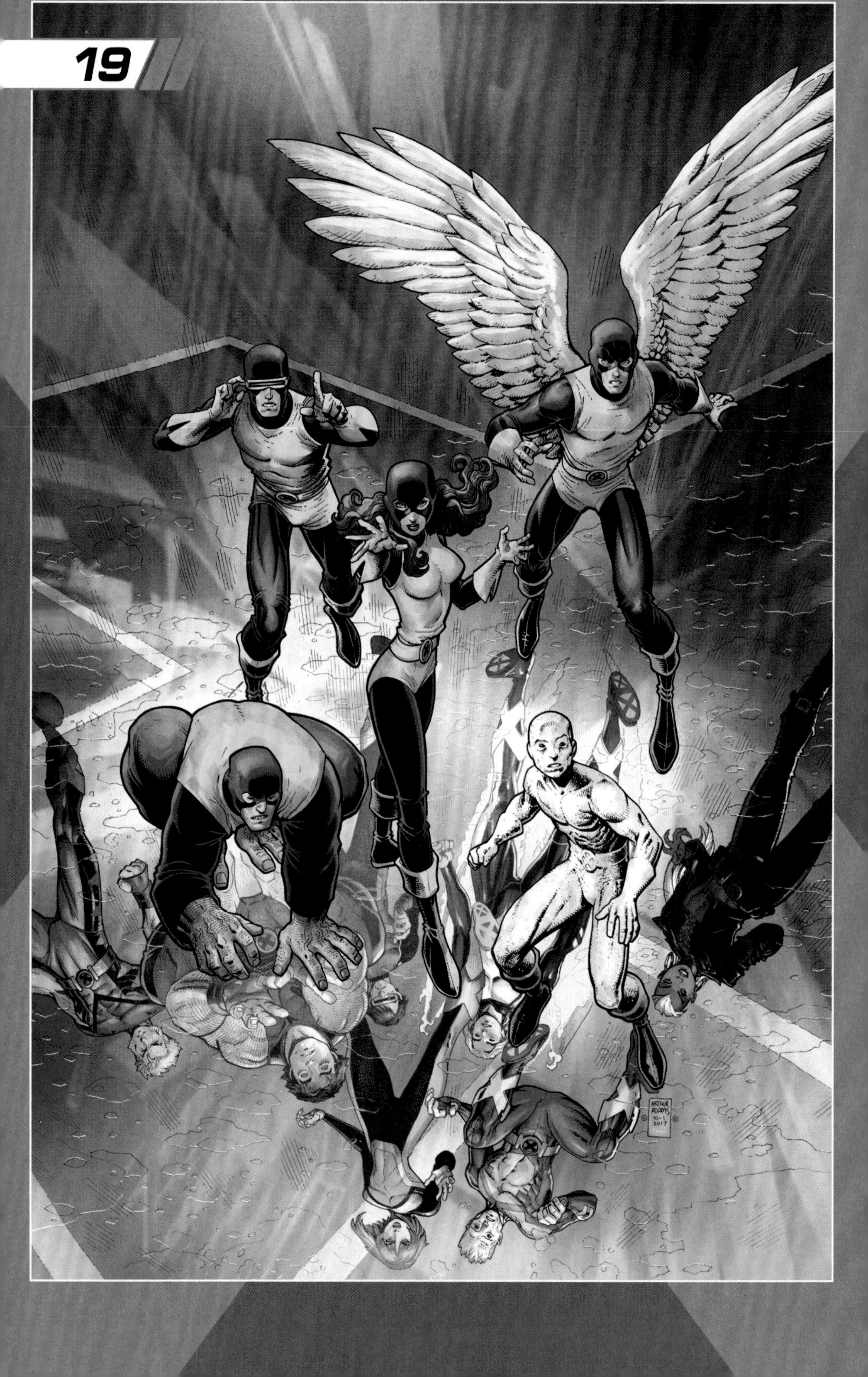
19
ARTHUR ADAMS
10-1
2017

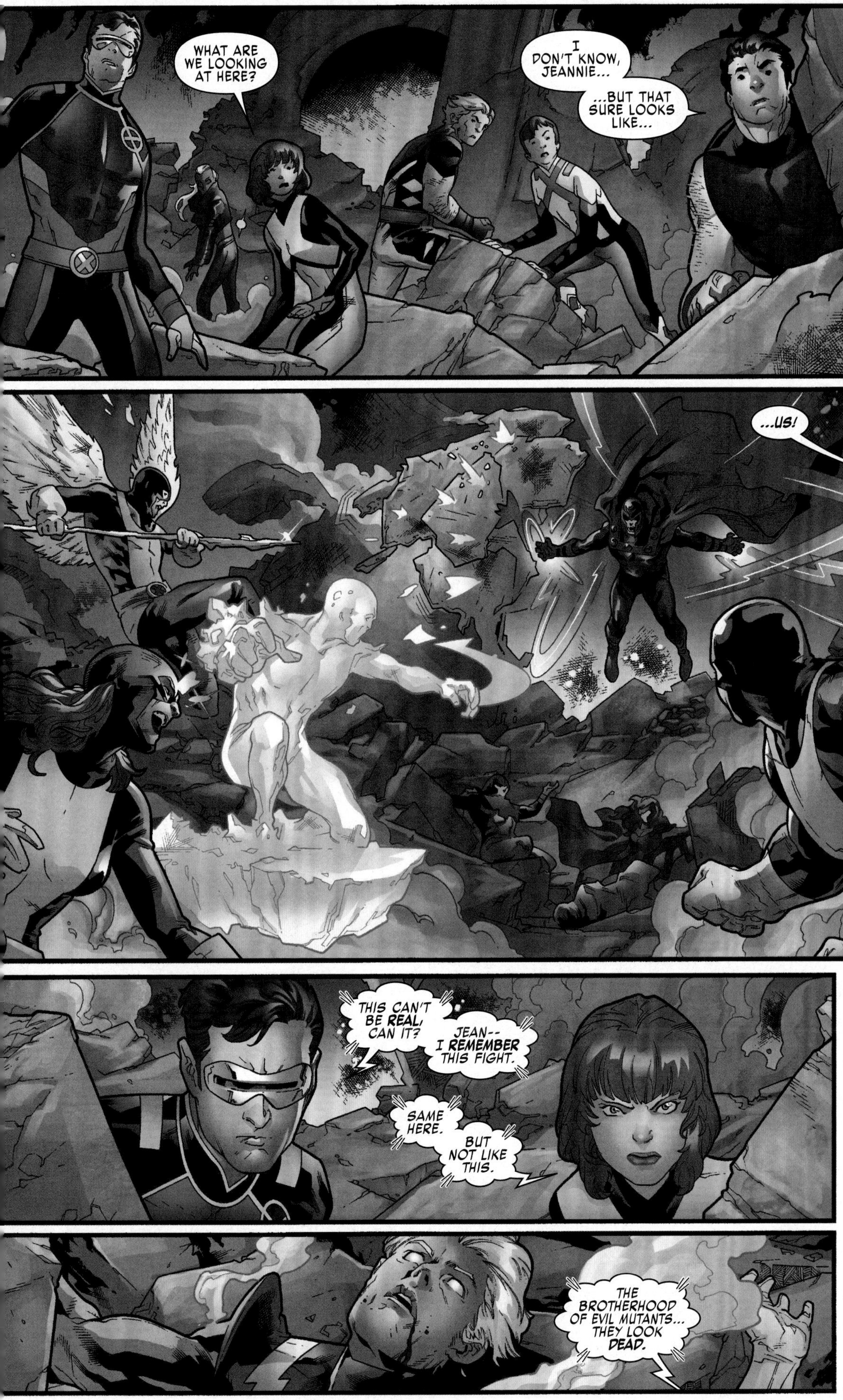
WHAT ARE WE LOOKING AT HERE?
I DON'T KNOW, JEANNIE...
...BUT THAT SURE LOOKS LIKE...
...US!
THIS CAN'T BE REAL, CAN IT?
JEAN-- I REMEMBER THIS FIGHT.
SAME HERE.
BUT NOT LIKE THIS.
THE BROTHERHOOD OF EVIL MUTANTS... THEY LOOK DEAD.

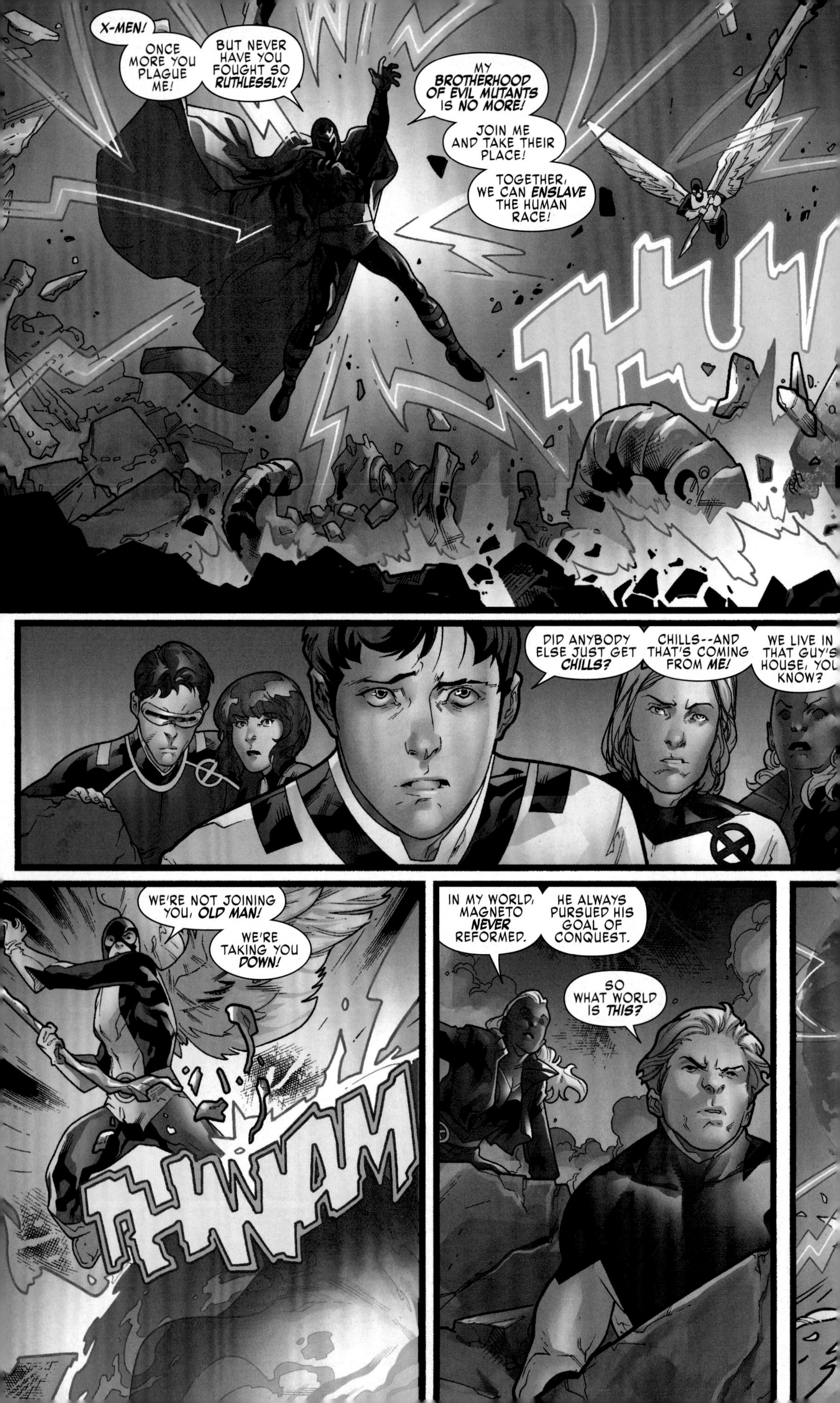
X-MEN!
ONCE MORE YOU PLAGUE ME!
BUT NEVER HAVE YOU FOUGHT SO RUTHLESSLY!
MY BROTHERHOOD OF EVIL MUTANTS IS NO MORE!
JOIN ME AND TAKE THEIR PLACE!
TOGETHER, WE CAN ENSLAVE THE HUMAN RACE!
THUM
DID ANYBODY ELSE JUST GET CHILLS?
CHILLS--AND THAT'S COMING FROM ME!
WE LIVE IN THAT GUY'S HOUSE, YOU KNOW?
WE'RE NOT JOINING YOU, OLD MAN!
WE'RE TAKING YOU DOWN!
THWAM
IN MY WORLD, MAGNETO NEVER REFORMED.
HE ALWAYS PURSUED HIS GOAL OF CONQUEST.
SO WHAT WORLD IS THIS?

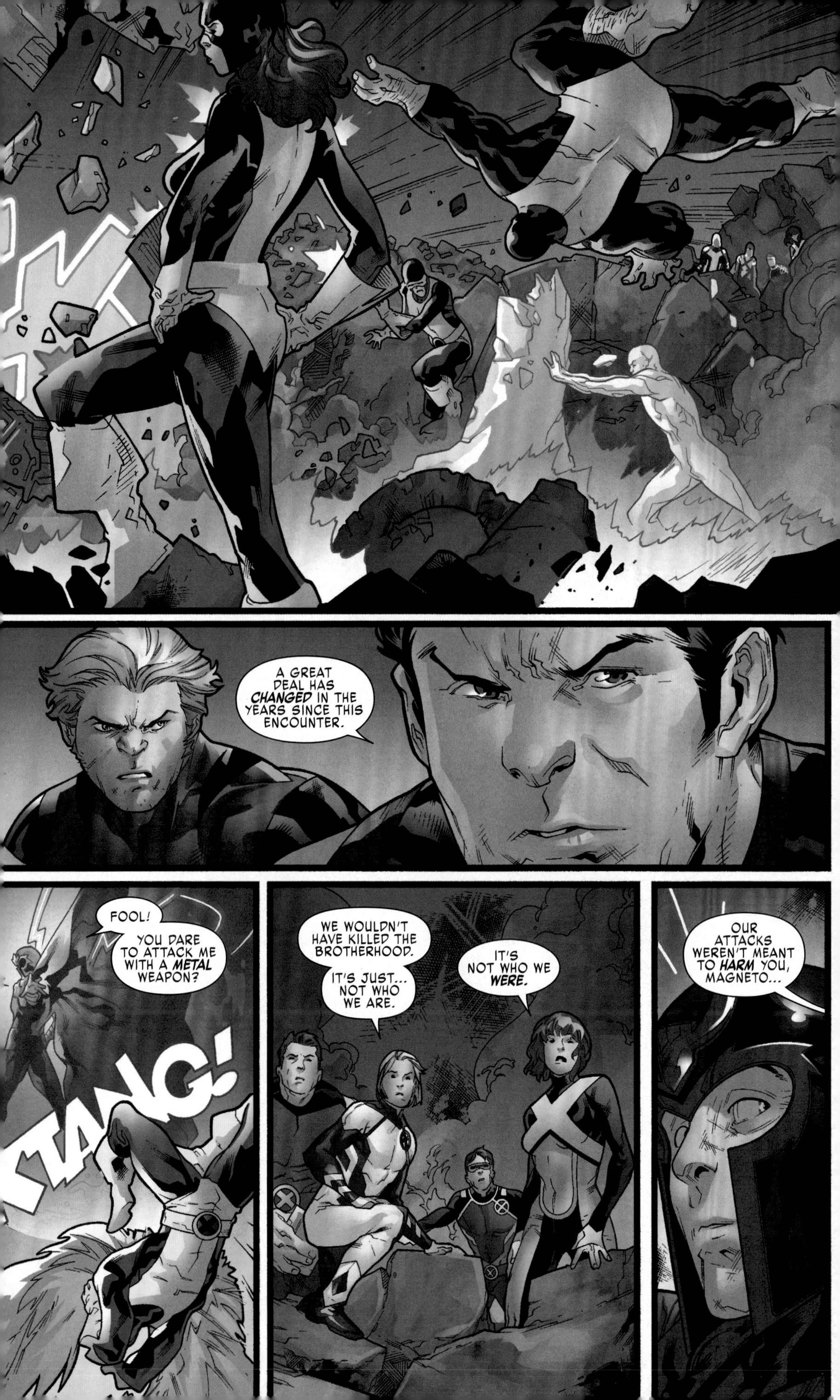
A GREAT DEAL HAS CHANGED IN THE YEARS SINCE THIS ENCOUNTER.
FOOL!
YOU DARE TO ATTACK ME WITH A METAL WEAPON?
TANG!
WE WOULDN'T HAVE KILLED THE BROTHERHOOD.
IT'S JUST... NOT WHO WE ARE.
IT'S NOT WHO WE WERE.
OUR ATTACKS WEREN'T MEANT TO HARM YOU, MAGNETO...

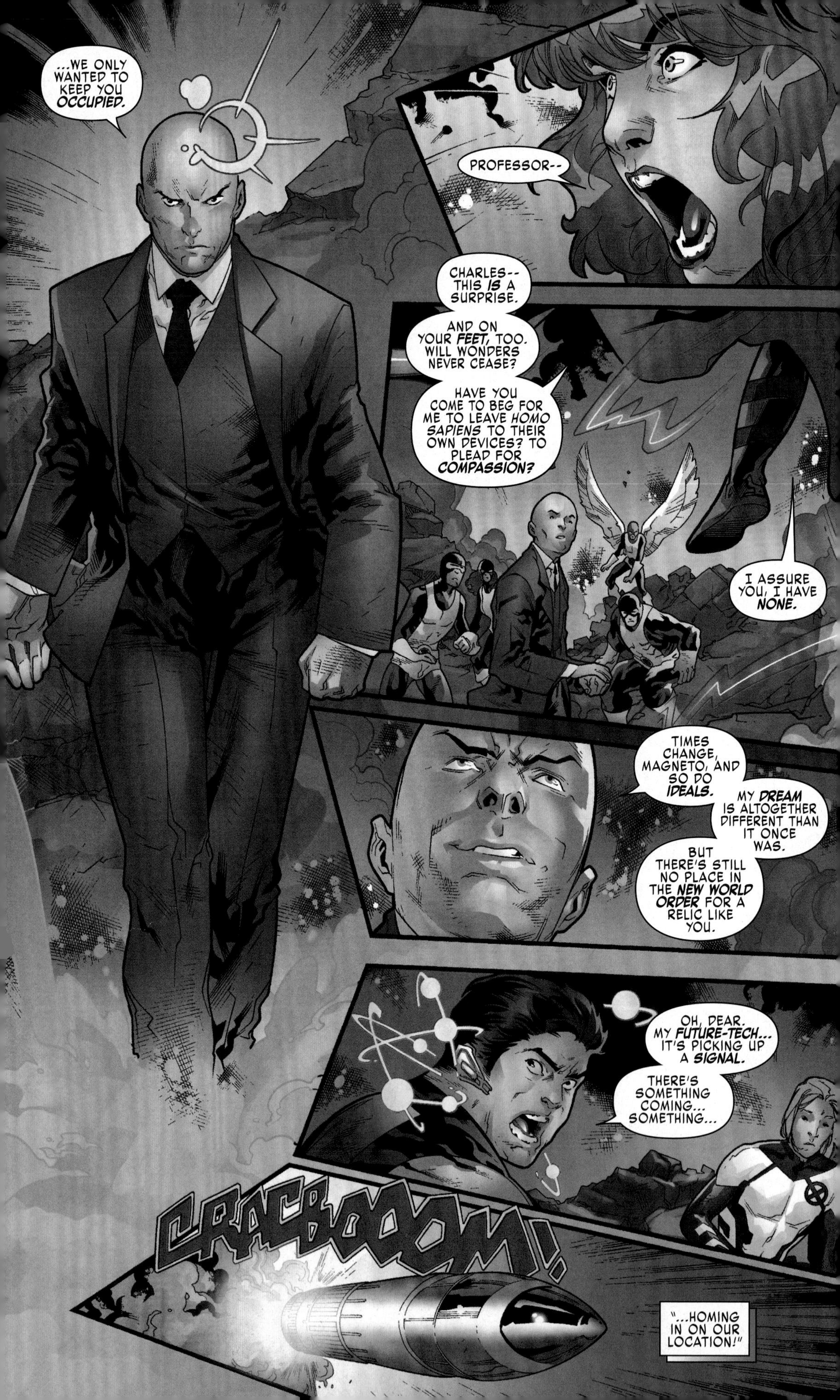

...WE ONLY WANTED TO KEEP YOU OCCUPIED.
PROFESSOR--
CHARLES-- THIS IS A SURPRISE.
AND ON YOUR FEET, TOO. WILL WONDERS NEVER CEASE?
HAVE YOU COME TO BEG FOR ME TO LEAVE HOMO SAPIENS TO THEIR OWN DEVICES? TO PLEAD FOR COMPASSION?
I ASSURE YOU, I HAVE NONE.
TIMES CHANGE, MAGNETO, AND SO DO IDEALS.
MY DREAM IS ALTOGETHER DIFFERENT THAN IT ONCE WAS.
BUT THERE'S STILL NO PLACE IN THE NEW WORLD ORDER FOR A RELIC LIKE YOU.
OH, DEAR. MY FUTURE-TECH... IT'S PICKING UP A SIGNAL.
THERE'S SOMETHING COMING... SOMETHING...
CRACBOOOM!
"...HOMING IN ON OUR LOCATION!"

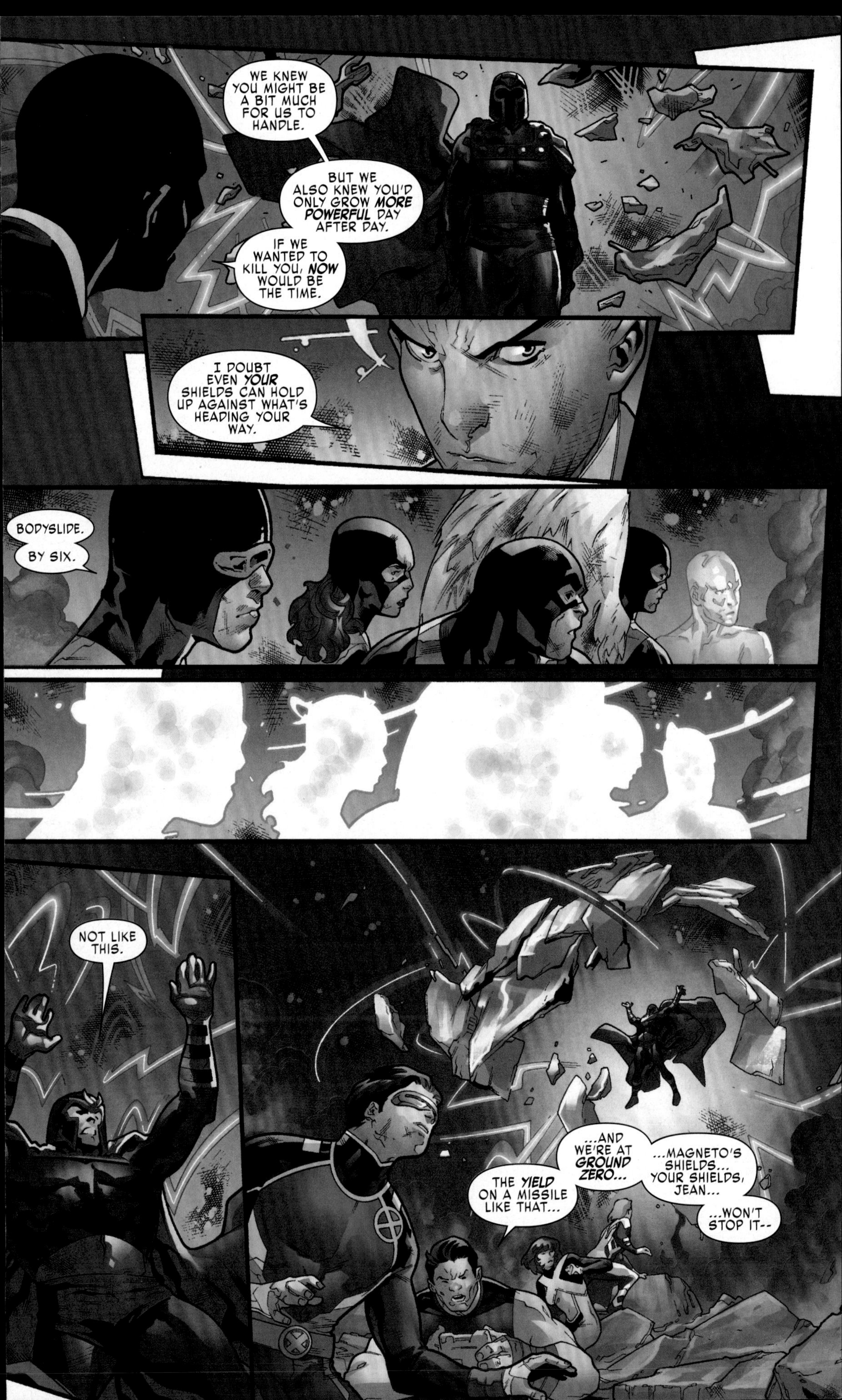
WE KNEW YOU MIGHT BE A BIT MUCH FOR US TO HANDLE.
BUT WE ALSO KNEW YOU'D ONLY GROW MORE POWERFUL DAY AFTER DAY.
IF WE WANTED TO KILL YOU, NOW WOULD BE THE TIME.
I DOUBT EVEN YOUR SHIELDS CAN HOLD UP AGAINST WHAT'S HEADING YOUR WAY.
BODYSLIDE.
BY SIX.
NOT LIKE THIS.
THE YIELD ON A MISSILE LIKE THAT...
...AND WE'RE AT GROUND ZERO...
...MAGNETO'S SHIELDS... YOUR SHIELDS, JEAN...
...WON'T STOP IT--

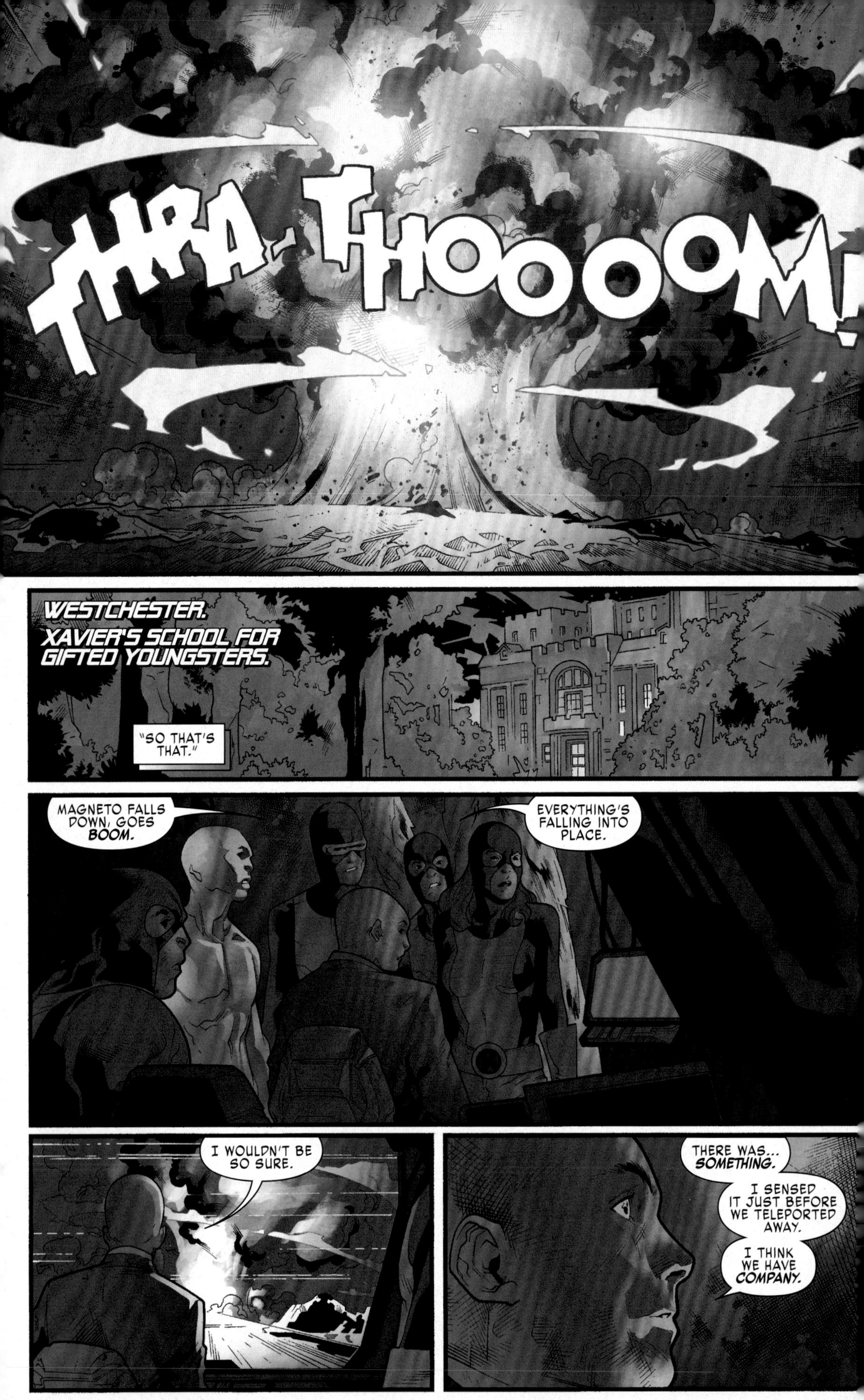
THRA-THOOOOM!
WESTCHESTER.
XAVIER'S SCHOOL FOR GIFTED YOUNGSTERS.
"SO THAT'S THAT."
MAGNETO FALLS DOWN, GOES BOOM.
EVERYTHING'S FALLING INTO PLACE.
I WOULDN'T BE SO SURE.
THERE WAS... SOMETHING.
I SENSED IT JUST BEFORE WE TELEPORTED AWAY.
I THINK WE HAVE COMPANY.

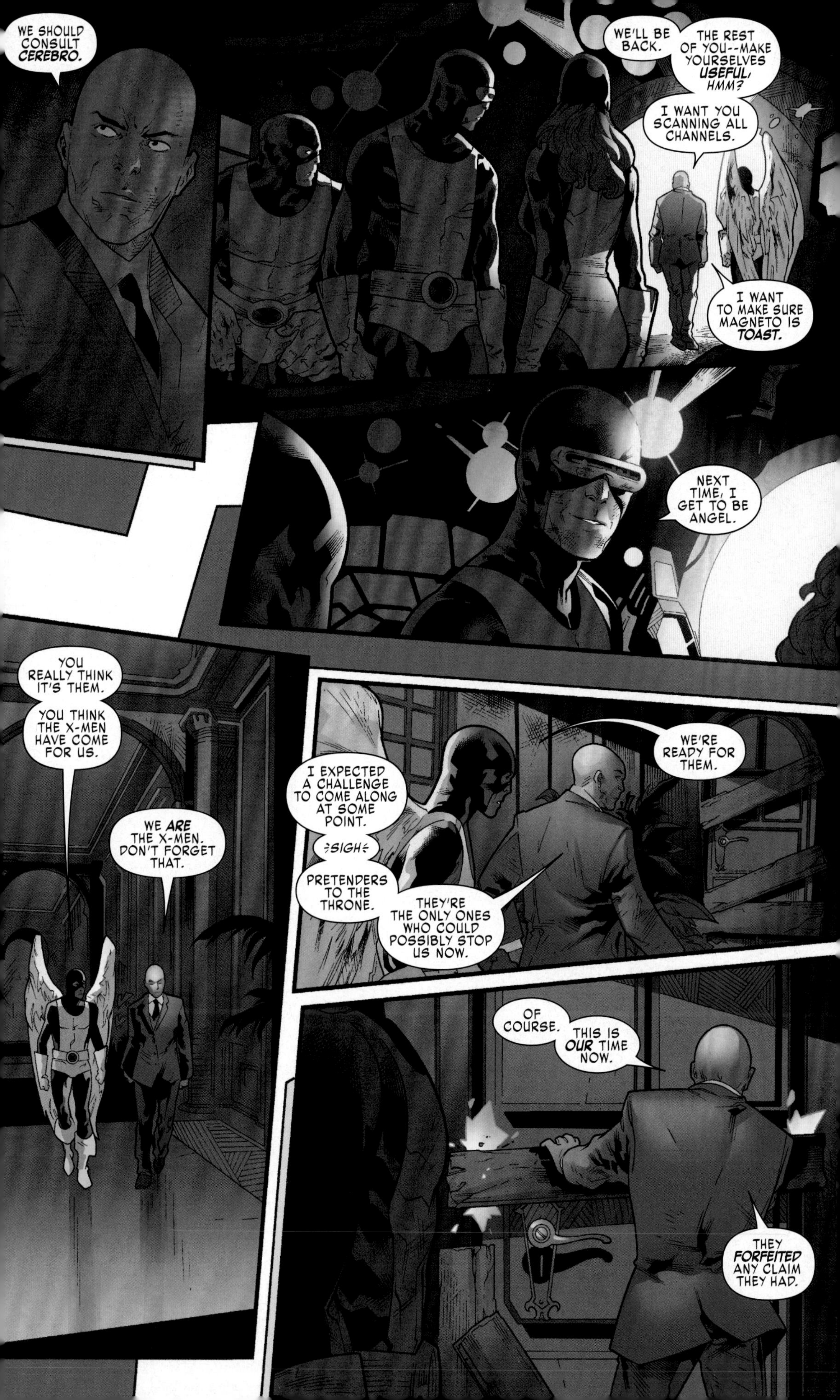

WE SHOULD CONSULT CEREBRO.
WE'LL BE BACK.
THE REST OF YOU--MAKE YOURSELVES USEFUL, HMM?
I WANT YOU SCANNING ALL CHANNELS.
I WANT TO MAKE SURE MAGNETO IS TOAST.
NEXT TIME, I GET TO BE ANGEL.
YOU REALLY THINK IT'S THEM.
YOU THINK THE X-MEN HAVE COME FOR US.
WE ARE THE X-MEN. DON'T FORGET THAT.
I EXPECTED A CHALLENGE TO COME ALONG AT SOME POINT.
SIGH
PRETENDERS TO THE THRONE.
WE'RE READY FOR THEM.
THEY'RE THE ONLY ONES WHO COULD POSSIBLY STOP US NOW.
OF COURSE.
THIS IS OUR TIME NOW.
THEY FORFEITED ANY CLAIM THEY HAD.

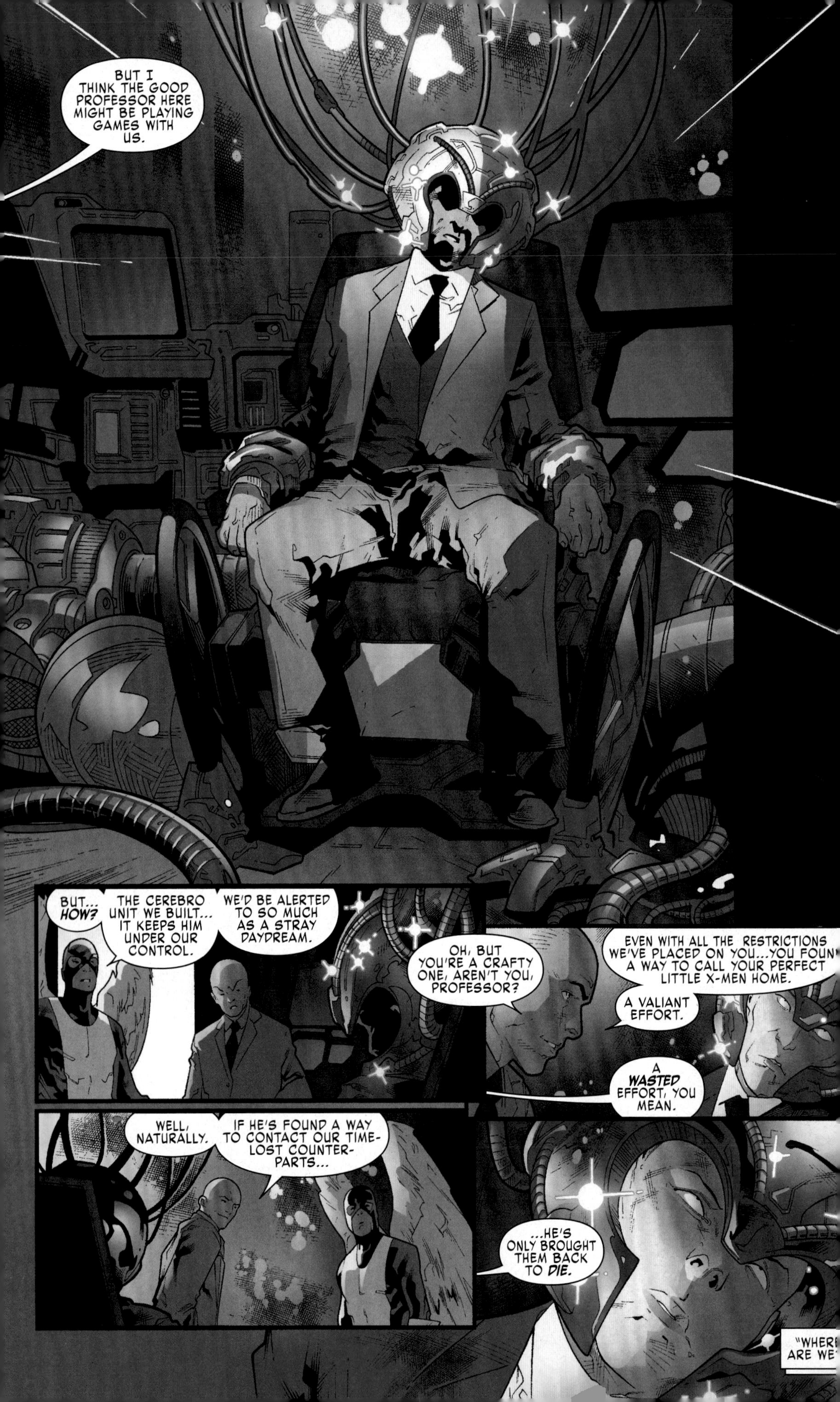
BUT I THINK THE GOOD PROFESSOR HERE MIGHT BE PLAYING GAMES WITH US.
BUT... HOW?
THE CEREBRO UNIT WE BUILT... IT KEEPS HIM UNDER OUR CONTROL.
WE'D BE ALERTED TO SO MUCH AS A STRAY DAYDREAM.
OH, BUT YOU'RE A CRAFTY ONE, AREN'T YOU, PROFESSOR?
EVEN WITH ALL THE RESTRICTIONS WE'VE PLACED ON YOU...YOU FOUN A WAY TO CALL YOUR PERFECT LITTLE X-MEN HOME.
A VALIANT EFFORT.
A WASTED EFFORT, YOU MEAN.
WELL, NATURALLY.
IF HE'S FOUND A WAY TO CONTACT OUR TIME-LOST COUNTER-PARTS...
...HE'S ONLY BROUGHT THEM BACK TO DIE.
"WHER ARE WE

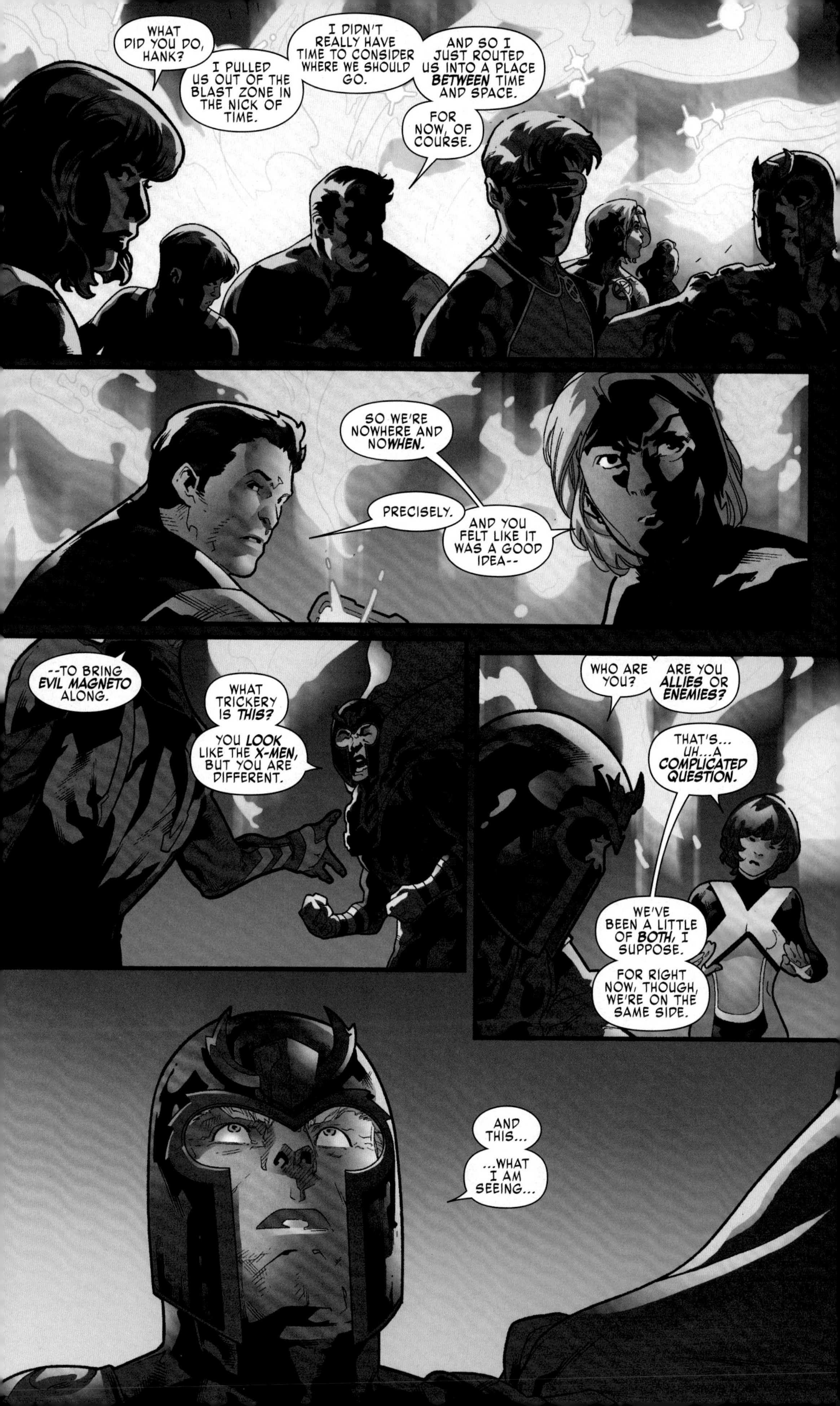
WHAT DID YOU DO, HANK?
I PULLED US OUT OF THE BLAST ZONE IN THE NICK OF TIME.
I DIDN'T REALLY HAVE TIME TO CONSIDER WHERE WE SHOULD GO.
AND SO I JUST ROUTED US INTO A PLACE BETWEEN TIME AND SPACE.
FOR NOW, OF COURSE.
SO WE'RE NOWHERE AND NOWHEN.
PRECISELY.
AND YOU FELT LIKE IT WAS A GOOD IDEA--
--TO BRING EVIL MAGNETO ALONG.
WHAT TRICKERY IS THIS?
YOU LOOK LIKE THE X-MEN, BUT YOU ARE DIFFERENT.
WHO ARE YOU?
ARE YOU ALLIES OR ENEMIES?
THAT'S... UH...A COMPLICATED QUESTION.
WE'VE BEEN A LITTLE OF BOTH, I SUPPOSE.
FOR RIGHT NOW, THOUGH, WE'RE ON THE SAME SIDE.
AND THIS...
...WHAT I AM SEEING...

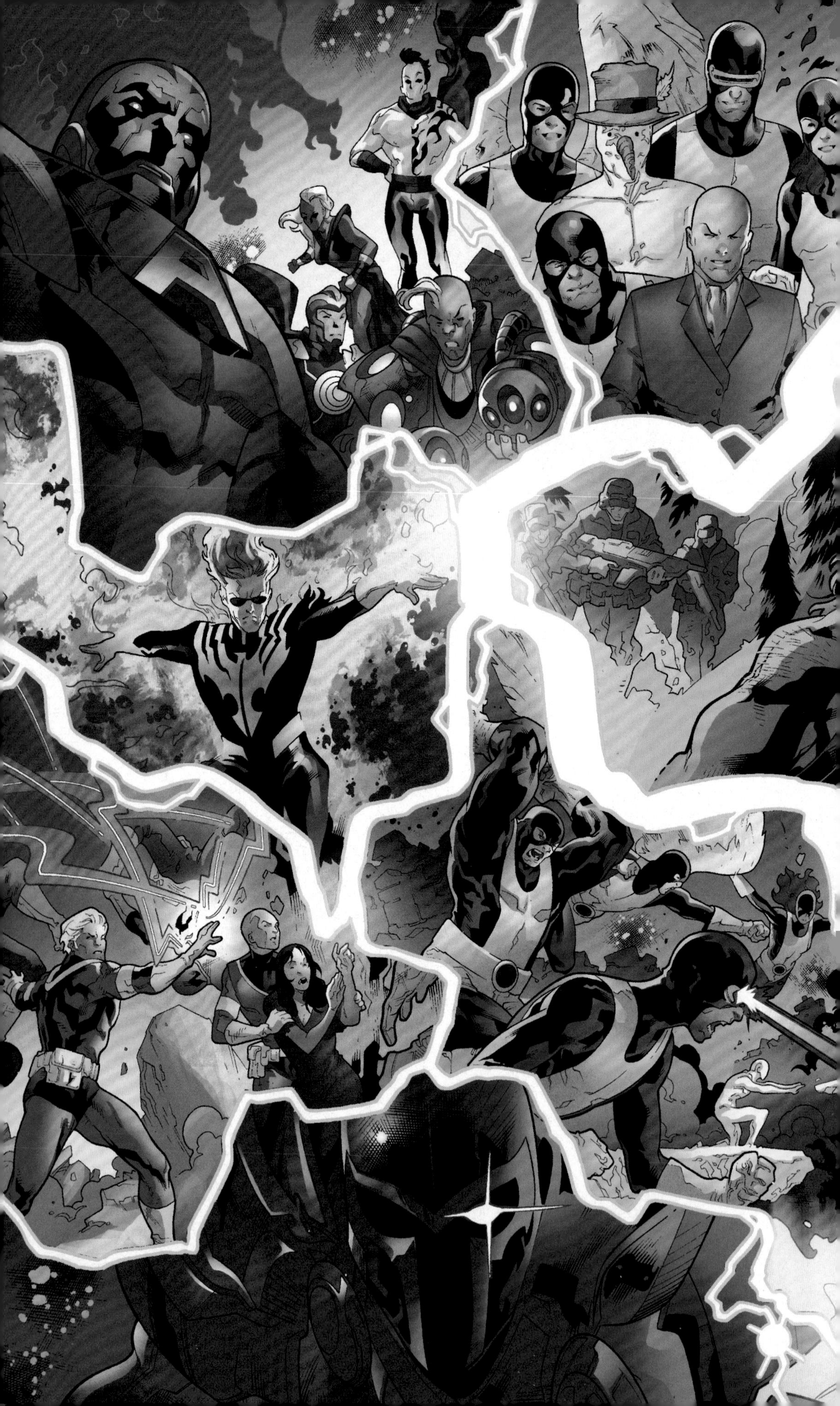

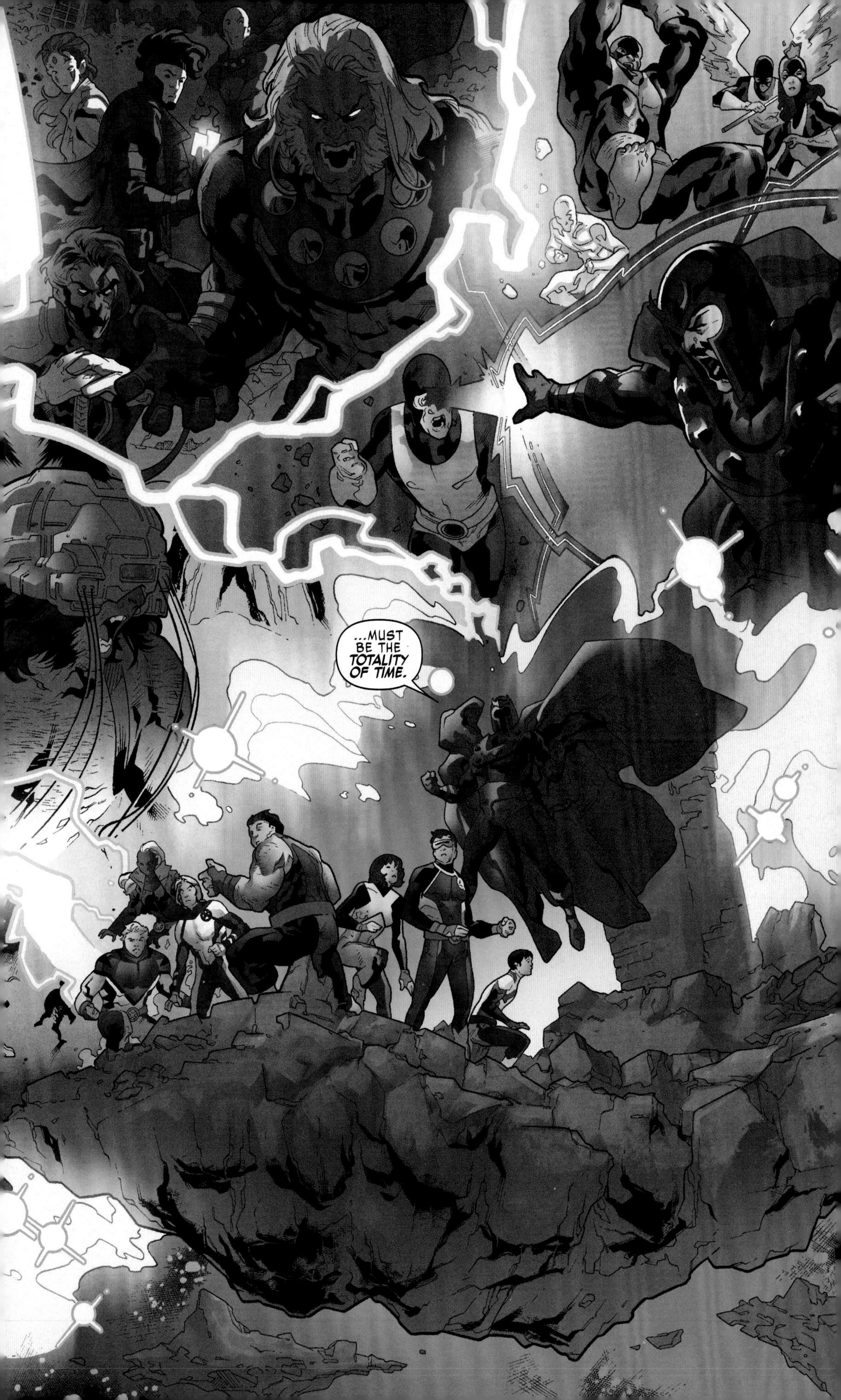
...MUST BE THE TOTALITY OF TIME.

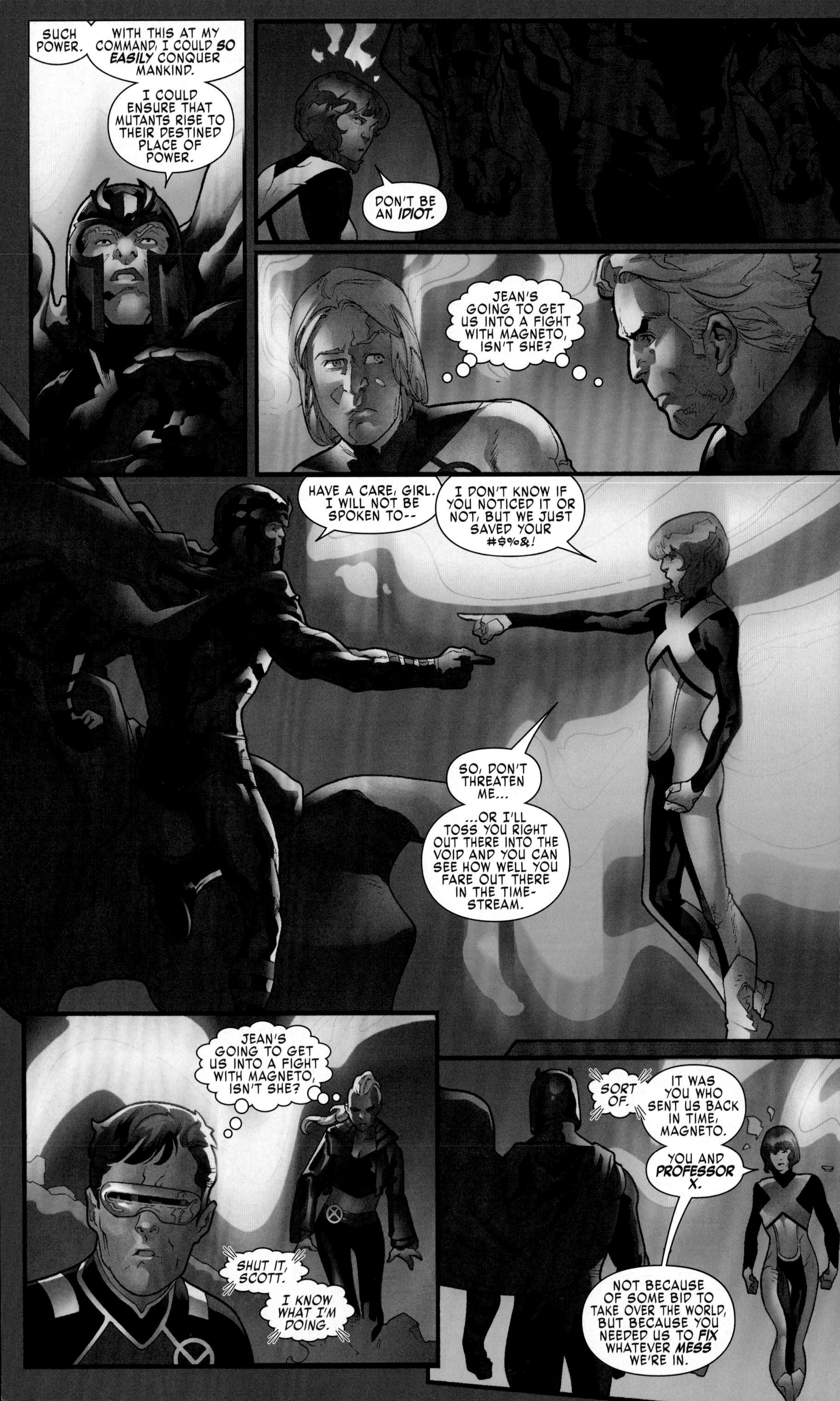
SUCH POWER.
WITH THIS AT MY COMMAND, I COULD SO EASILY CONQUER MANKIND.
I COULD ENSURE THAT MUTANTS RISE TO THEIR DESTINED PLACE OF POWER.
DON'T BE AN IDIOT.
JEAN'S GOING TO GET US INTO A FIGHT WITH MAGNETO, ISN'T SHE?
HAVE A CARE, GIRL. I WILL NOT BE SPOKEN TO--
I DON'T KNOW IF YOU NOTICED IT OR NOT, BUT WE JUST SAVED YOUR #$%&!
SO, DON'T THREATEN ME...
...OR I'LL TOSS YOU RIGHT OUT THERE INTO THE VOID AND YOU CAN SEE HOW WELL YOU FARE OUT THERE IN THE TIME-STREAM.
JEAN'S GOING TO GET US INTO A FIGHT WITH MAGNETO, ISN'T SHE?
SHUT IT, SCOTT.
I KNOW WHAT I'M DOING.
SORT OF.
IT WAS YOU WHO SENT US BACK IN TIME, MAGNETO.
YOU AND PROFESSOR X.
NOT BECAUSE OF SOME BID TO TAKE OVER THE WORLD, BUT BECAUSE YOU NEEDED US TO FIX WHATEVER MESS WE'RE IN.

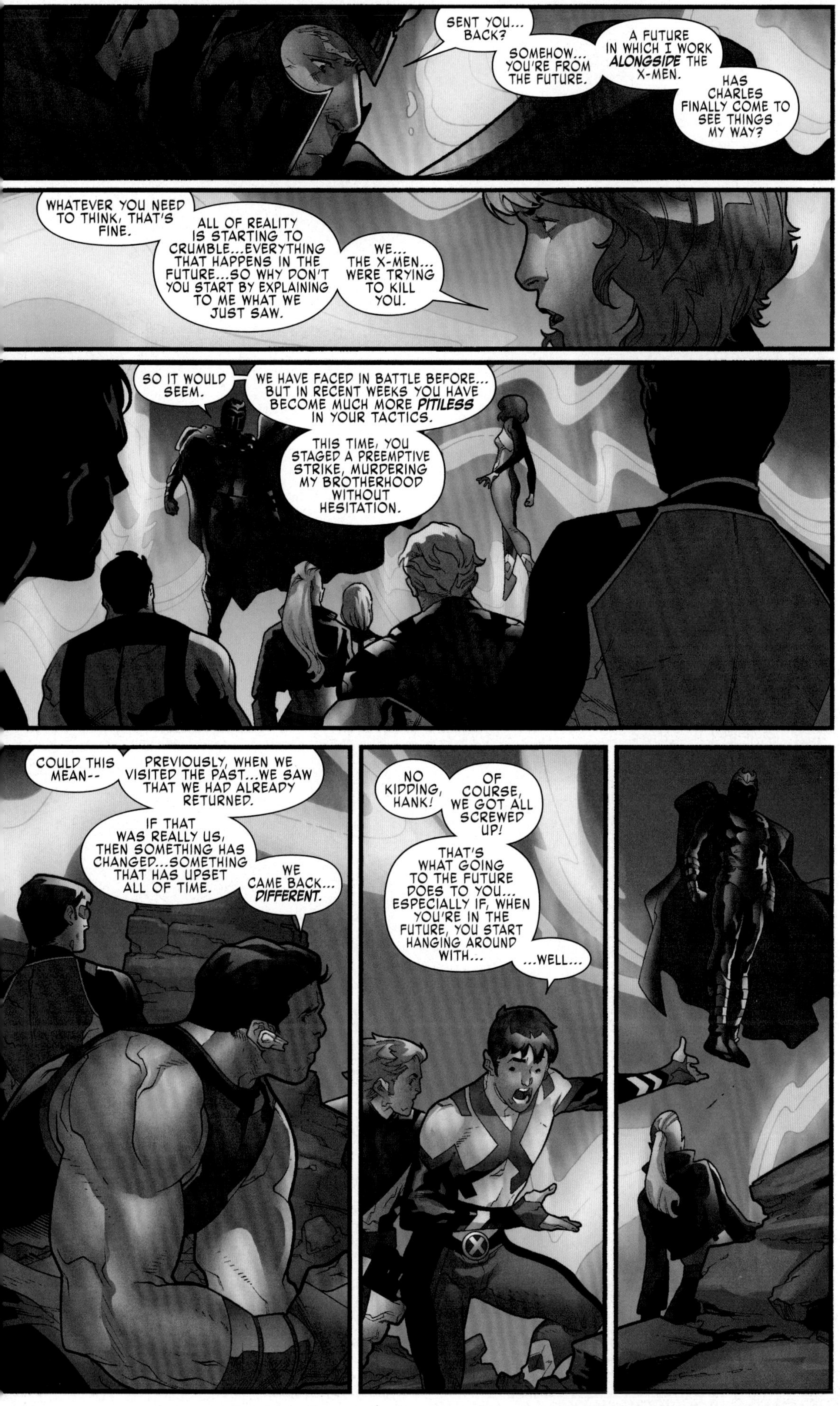
SENT YOU... BACK?
SOMEHOW... YOU'RE FROM THE FUTURE.
A FUTURE IN WHICH I WORK *ALONGSIDE* THE X-MEN.
HAS CHARLES FINALLY COME TO SEE THINGS MY WAY?
WHATEVER YOU NEED TO THINK, THAT'S FINE.
ALL OF REALITY IS STARTING TO CRUMBLE...EVERYTHING THAT HAPPENS IN THE FUTURE...SO WHY DON'T YOU START BY EXPLAINING TO ME WHAT WE JUST SAW.
WE... THE X-MEN... WERE TRYING TO KILL YOU.
SO IT WOULD SEEM.
WE HAVE FACED IN BATTLE BEFORE... BUT IN RECENT WEEKS YOU HAVE BECOME MUCH MORE *PITILESS* IN YOUR TACTICS.
THIS TIME, YOU STAGED A PREEMPTIVE STRIKE, MURDERING MY BROTHERHOOD WITHOUT HESITATION.
COULD THIS MEAN--
PREVIOUSLY, WHEN WE VISITED THE PAST...WE SAW THAT WE HAD ALREADY RETURNED.
IF THAT WAS REALLY US, THEN SOMETHING HAS CHANGED...SOMETHING THAT HAS UPSET ALL OF TIME.
WE CAME BACK... *DIFFERENT.*
NO KIDDING, HANK!
OF COURSE, WE GOT ALL SCREWED UP!
THAT'S WHAT GOING TO THE FUTURE DOES TO YOU... ESPECIALLY IF, WHEN YOU'RE IN THE FUTURE, YOU START HANGING AROUND WITH...
...WELL...

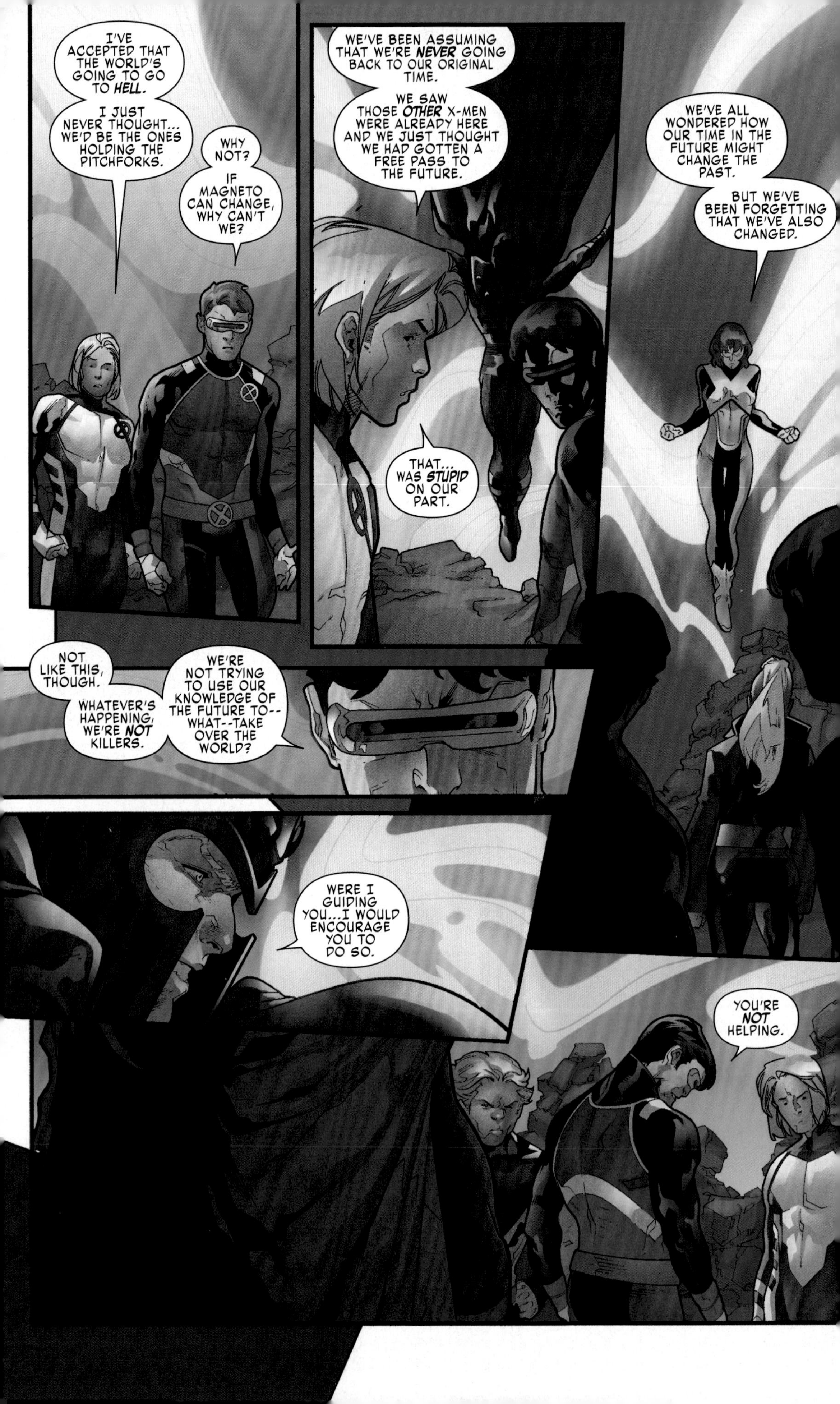
I'VE ACCEPTED THAT THE WORLD'S GOING TO GO TO *HELL.*
I JUST NEVER THOUGHT... WE'D BE THE ONES HOLDING THE PITCHFORKS.
WHY NOT?
IF MAGNETO CAN CHANGE, WHY CAN'T WE?
WE'VE BEEN ASSUMING THAT WE'RE *NEVER* GOING BACK TO OUR ORIGINAL TIME.
WE SAW THOSE *OTHER* X-MEN WERE ALREADY HERE AND WE JUST THOUGHT WE HAD GOTTEN A FREE PASS TO THE FUTURE.
THAT... WAS *STUPID* ON OUR PART.
WE'VE ALL WONDERED HOW OUR TIME IN THE FUTURE MIGHT CHANGE THE PAST.
BUT WE'VE BEEN FORGETTING THAT WE'VE ALSO CHANGED.
NOT LIKE THIS, THOUGH.
WHATEVER'S HAPPENING, WE'RE *NOT* KILLERS.
WE'RE NOT TRYING TO USE OUR KNOWLEDGE OF THE FUTURE TO-- WHAT--TAKE OVER THE WORLD?
WERE I GUIDING YOU...I WOULD ENCOURAGE YOU TO DO SO.
YOU'RE *NOT* HELPING.

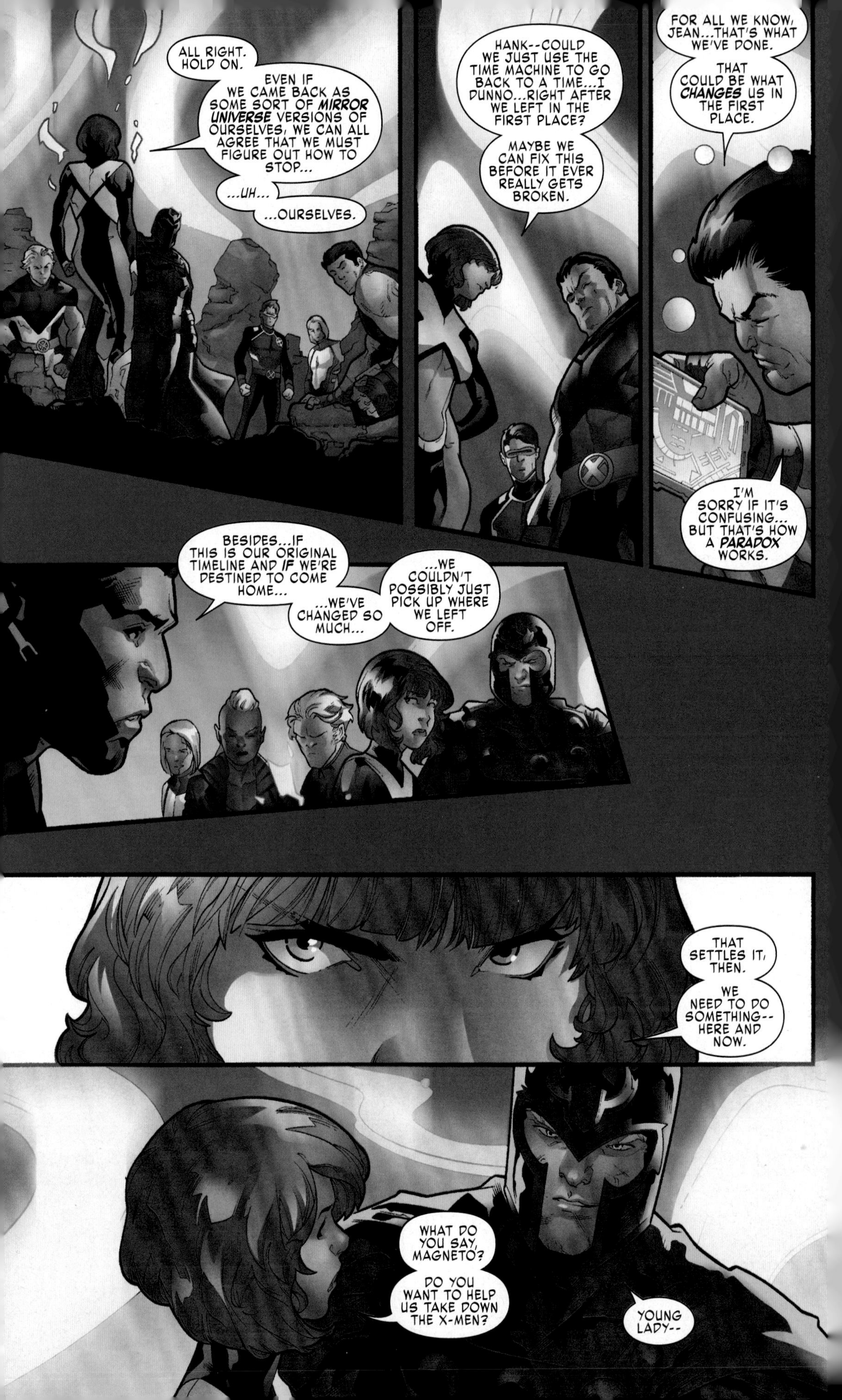
ALL RIGHT. HOLD ON.
EVEN IF WE CAME BACK AS SOME SORT OF MIRROR UNIVERSE VERSIONS OF OURSELVES, WE CAN ALL AGREE THAT WE MUST FIGURE OUT HOW TO STOP...
...UH...
...OURSELVES.
HANK--COULD WE JUST USE THE TIME MACHINE TO GO BACK TO A TIME...I DUNNO...RIGHT AFTER WE LEFT IN THE FIRST PLACE?
MAYBE WE CAN FIX THIS BEFORE IT EVER REALLY GETS BROKEN.
FOR ALL WE KNOW, JEAN...THAT'S WHAT WE'VE DONE.
THAT COULD BE WHAT CHANGES US IN THE FIRST PLACE.
I'M SORRY IF IT'S CONFUSING... BUT THAT'S HOW A PARADOX WORKS.
BESIDES...IF THIS IS OUR ORIGINAL TIMELINE AND IF WE'RE DESTINED TO COME HOME...
...WE'VE CHANGED SO MUCH...
...WE COULDN'T POSSIBLY JUST PICK UP WHERE WE LEFT OFF.
THAT SETTLES IT, THEN.
WE NEED TO DO SOMETHING-- HERE AND NOW.
WHAT DO YOU SAY, MAGNETO?
DO YOU WANT TO HELP US TAKE DOWN THE X-MEN?
YOUNG LADY--

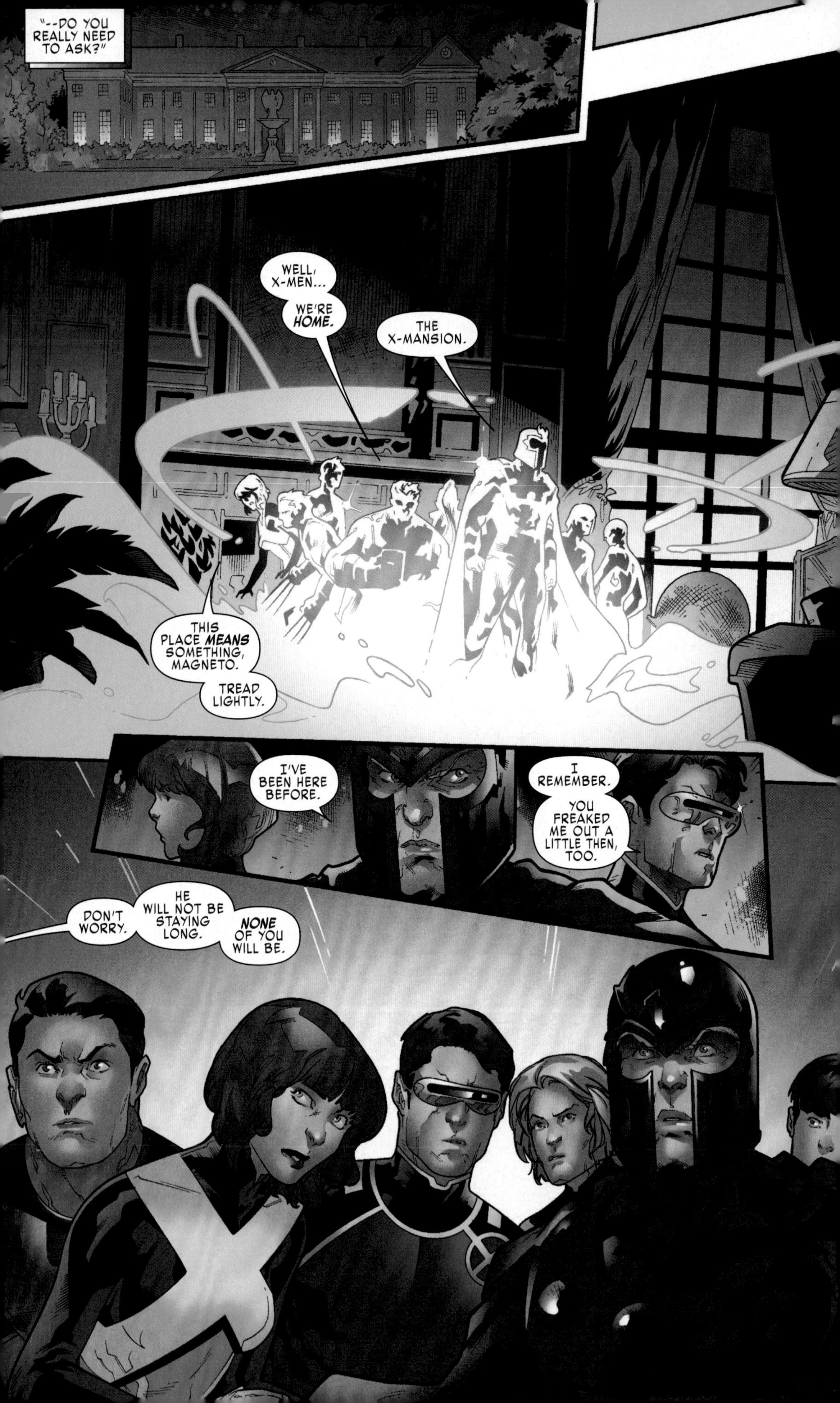
"--DO YOU REALLY NEED TO ASK?"
WELL, X-MEN...
WE'RE HOME.
THE X-MANSION.
THIS PLACE MEANS SOMETHING, MAGNETO.
TREAD LIGHTLY.
I'VE BEEN HERE BEFORE.
I REMEMBER.
YOU FREAKED ME OUT A LITTLE THEN, TOO.
DON'T WORRY.
HE WILL NOT BE STAYING LONG.
NONE OF YOU WILL BE.

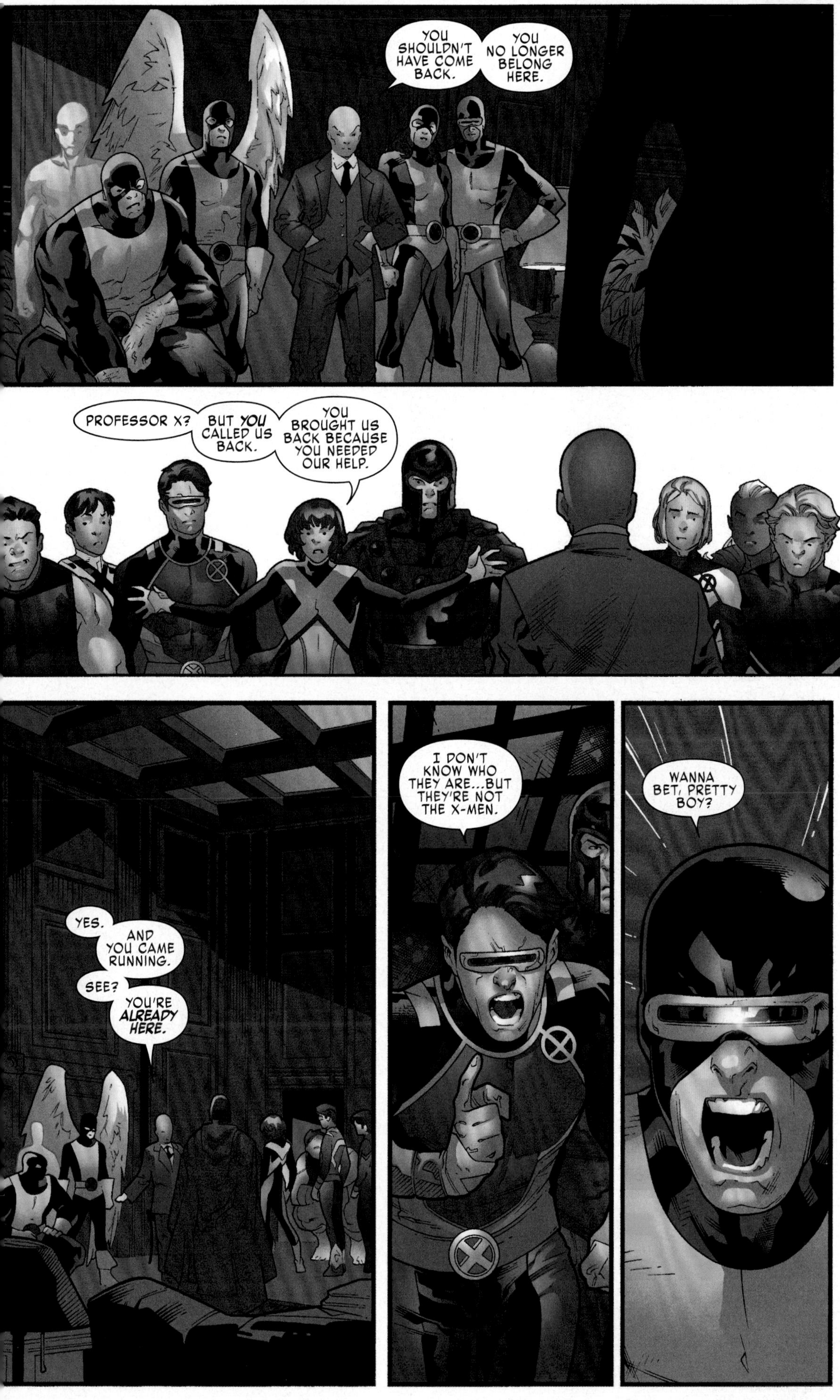
YOU SHOULDN'T HAVE COME BACK.
YOU NO LONGER BELONG HERE.
PROFESSOR X?
BUT YOU CALLED US BACK.
YOU BROUGHT US BACK BECAUSE YOU NEEDED OUR HELP.
YES.
AND YOU CAME RUNNING.
SEE?
YOU'RE ALREADY HERE.
I DON'T KNOW WHO THEY ARE...BUT THEY'RE NOT THE X-MEN.
WANNA BET, PRETTY BOY?

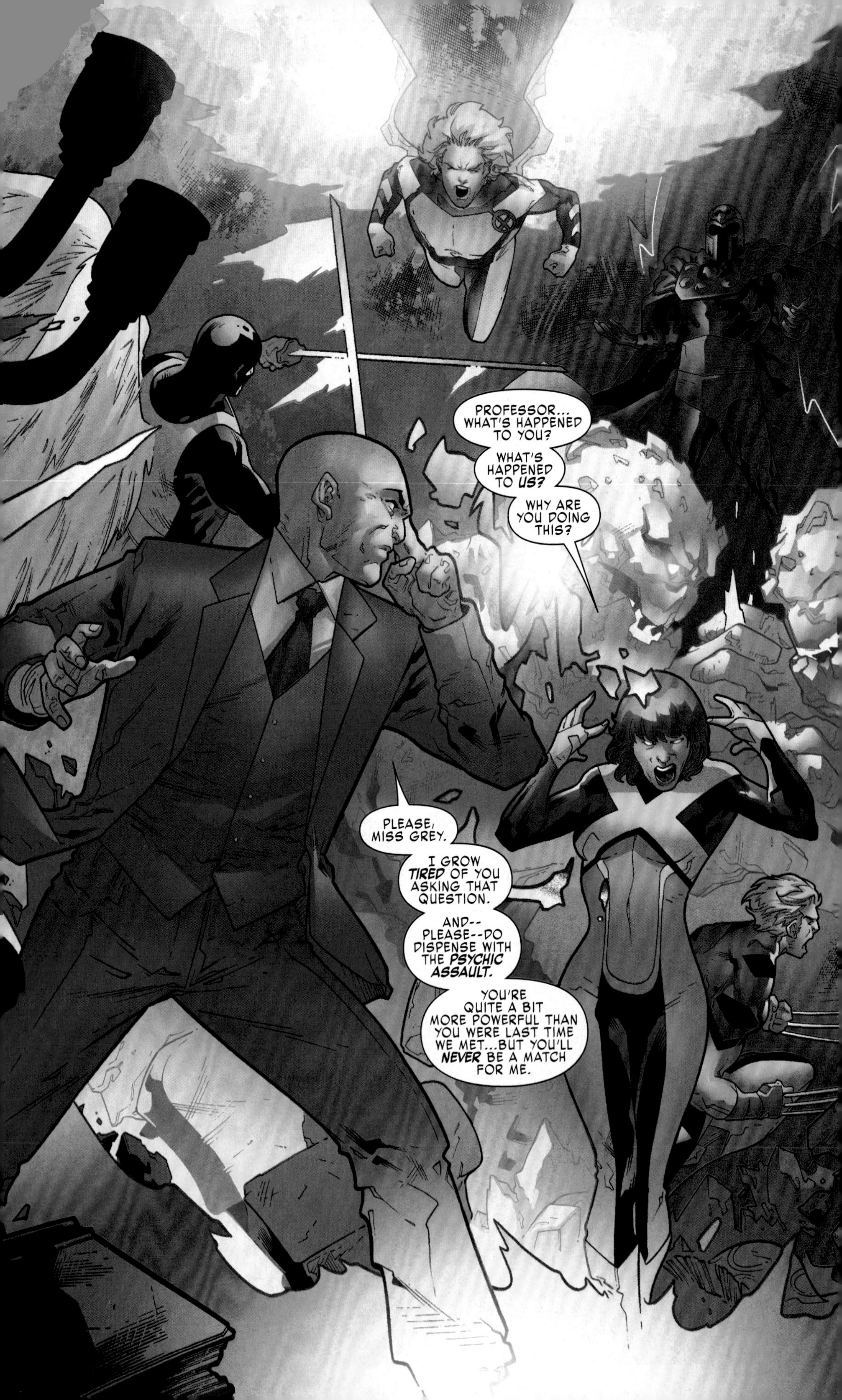
PROFESSOR... WHAT'S HAPPENED TO YOU?
WHAT'S HAPPENED TO US?
WHY ARE YOU DOING THIS?
PLEASE, MISS GREY.
I GROW TIRED OF YOU ASKING THAT QUESTION.
AND--PLEASE--DO DISPENSE WITH THE PSYCHIC ASSAULT.
YOU'RE QUITE A BIT MORE POWERFUL THAN YOU WERE LAST TIME WE MET...BUT YOU'LL NEVER BE A MATCH FOR ME.

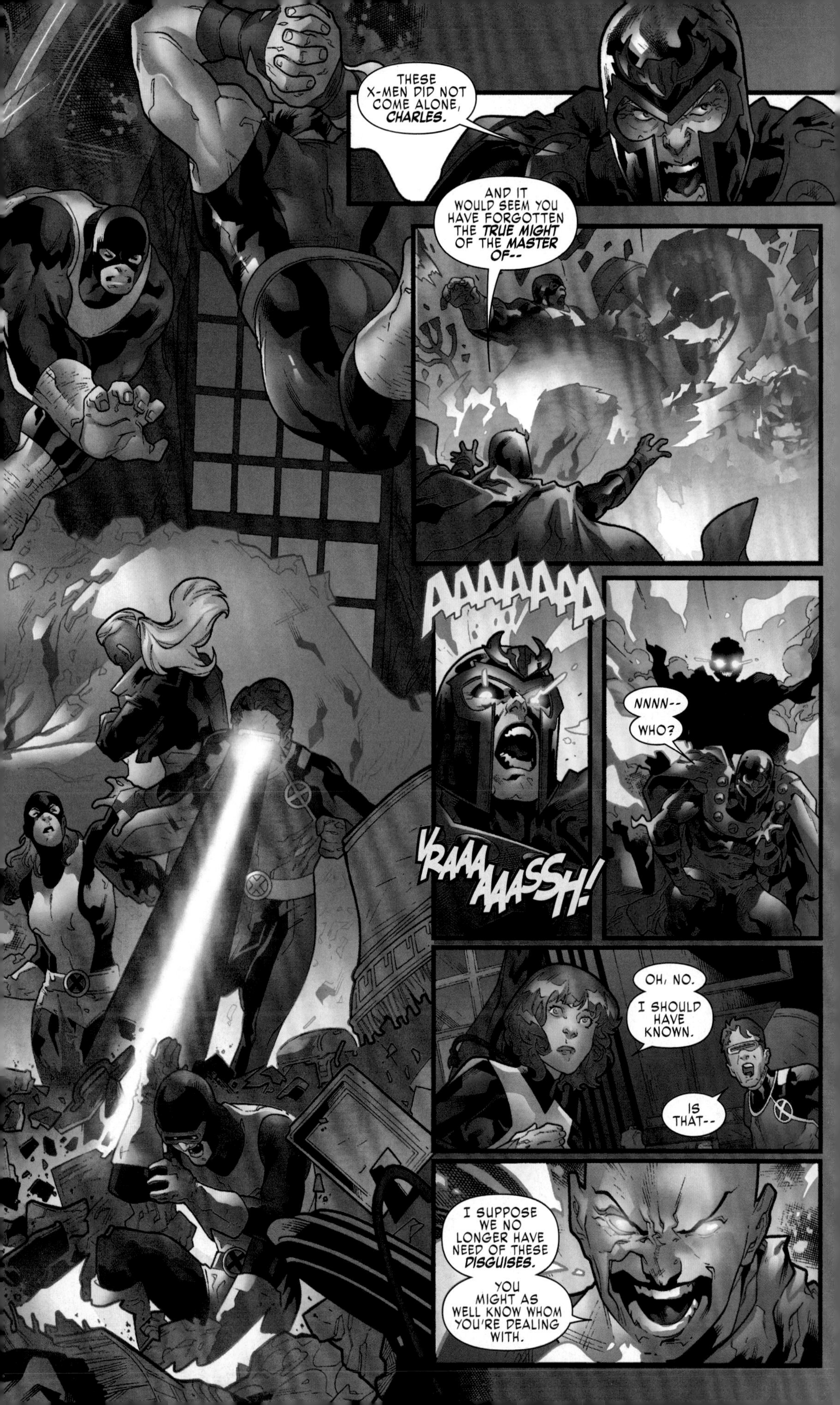
THESE X-MEN DID NOT COME ALONE, CHARLES.
AND IT WOULD SEEM YOU HAVE FORGOTTEN THE TRUE MIGHT OF THE MASTER OF--
AAAAAAA
VRAAAAAASSH!
NNNN--
WHO?
OH, NO.
I SHOULD HAVE KNOWN.
IS THAT--
I SUPPOSE WE NO LONGER HAVE NEED OF THESE DISGUISES.
YOU MIGHT AS WELL KNOW WHOM YOU'RE DEALING WITH.

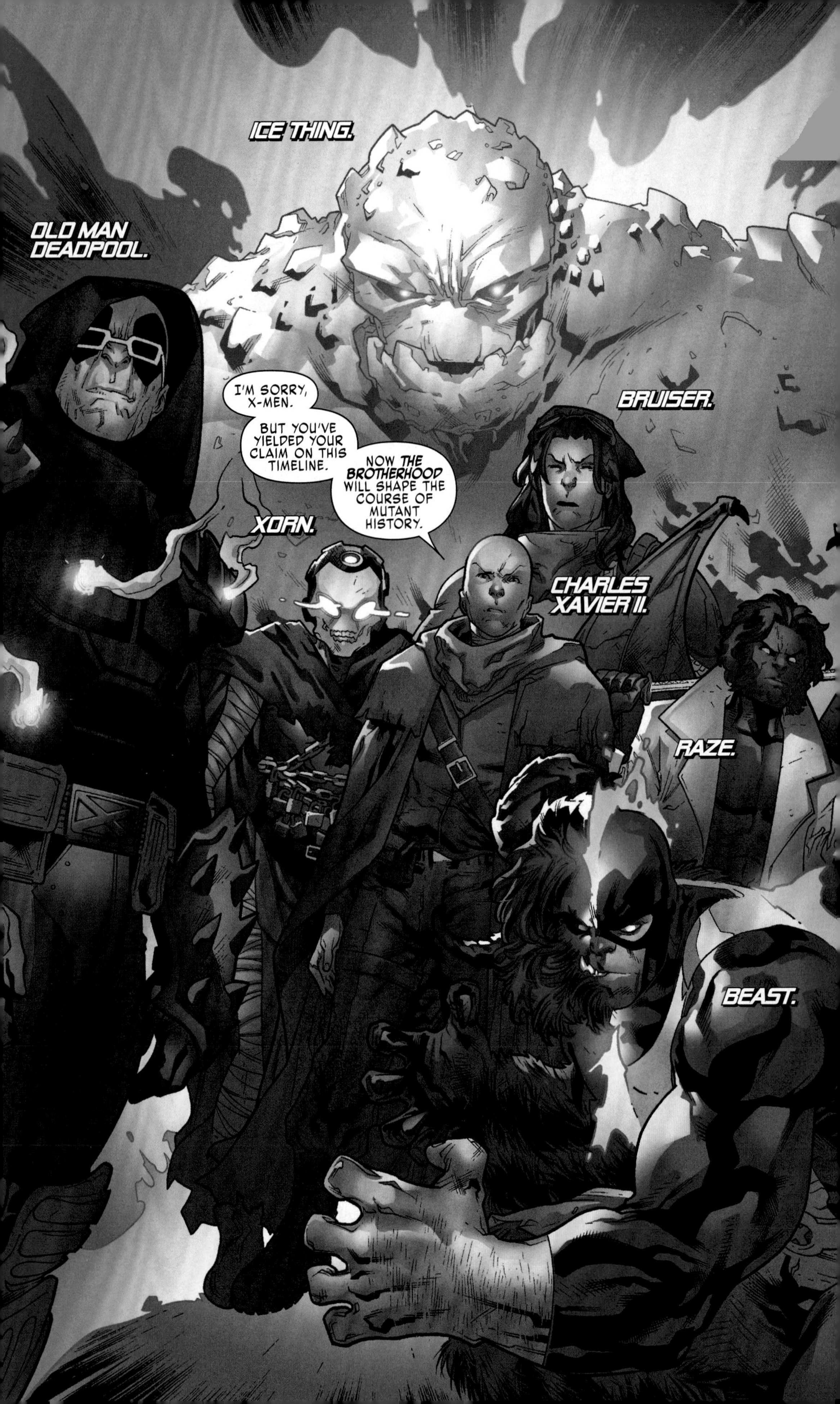
ICE THING.
OLD MAN DEADPOOL.
I'M SORRY, X-MEN.
BUT YOU'VE YIELDED YOUR CLAIM ON THIS TIMELINE.
NOW THE BROTHERHOOD WILL SHAPE THE COURSE OF MUTANT HISTORY.
BRUISER.
XORN.
CHARLES XAVIER II.
RAZE.
BEAST.

20

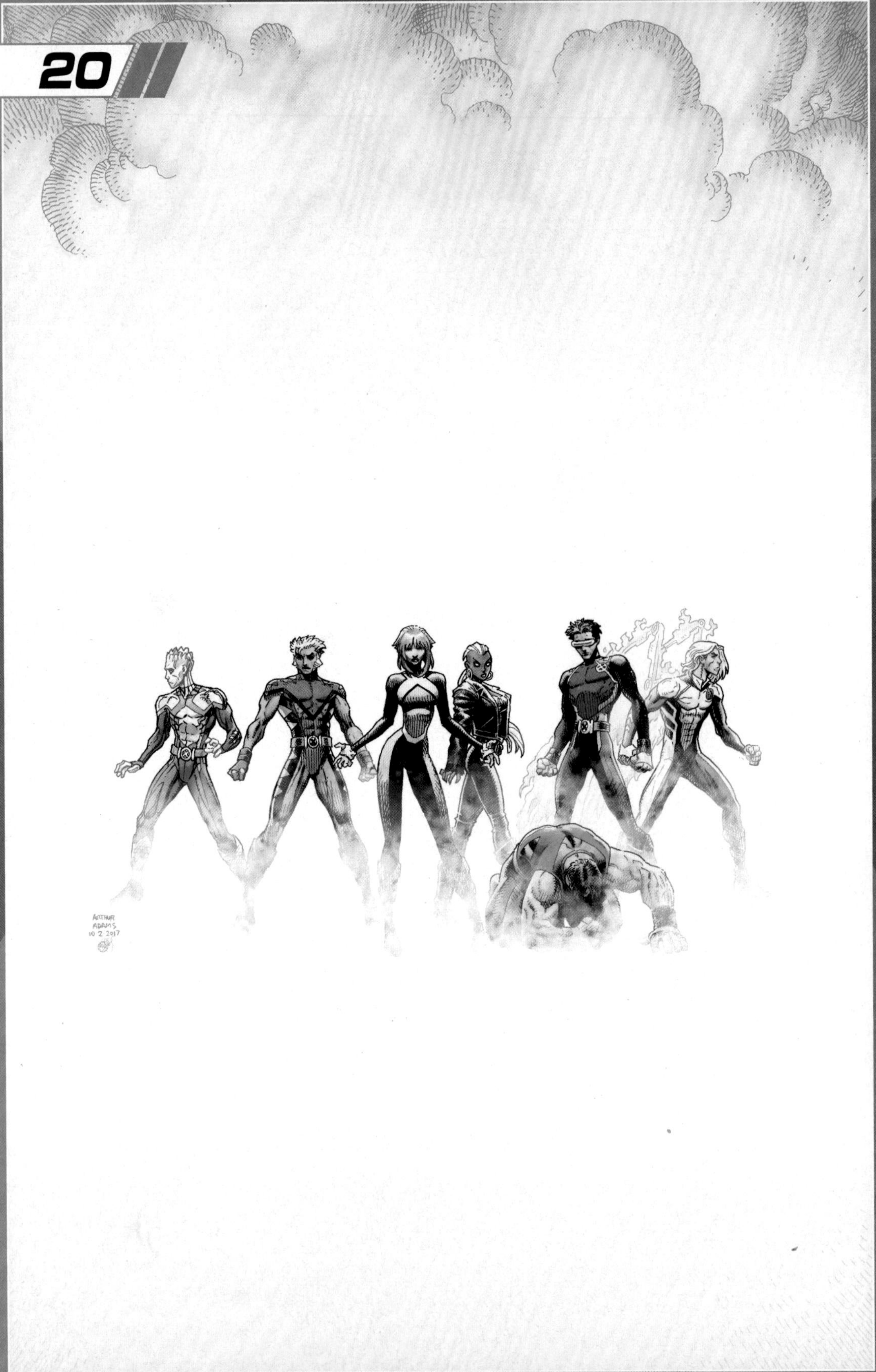
ARTHUR
ADAMS
10 2 2017

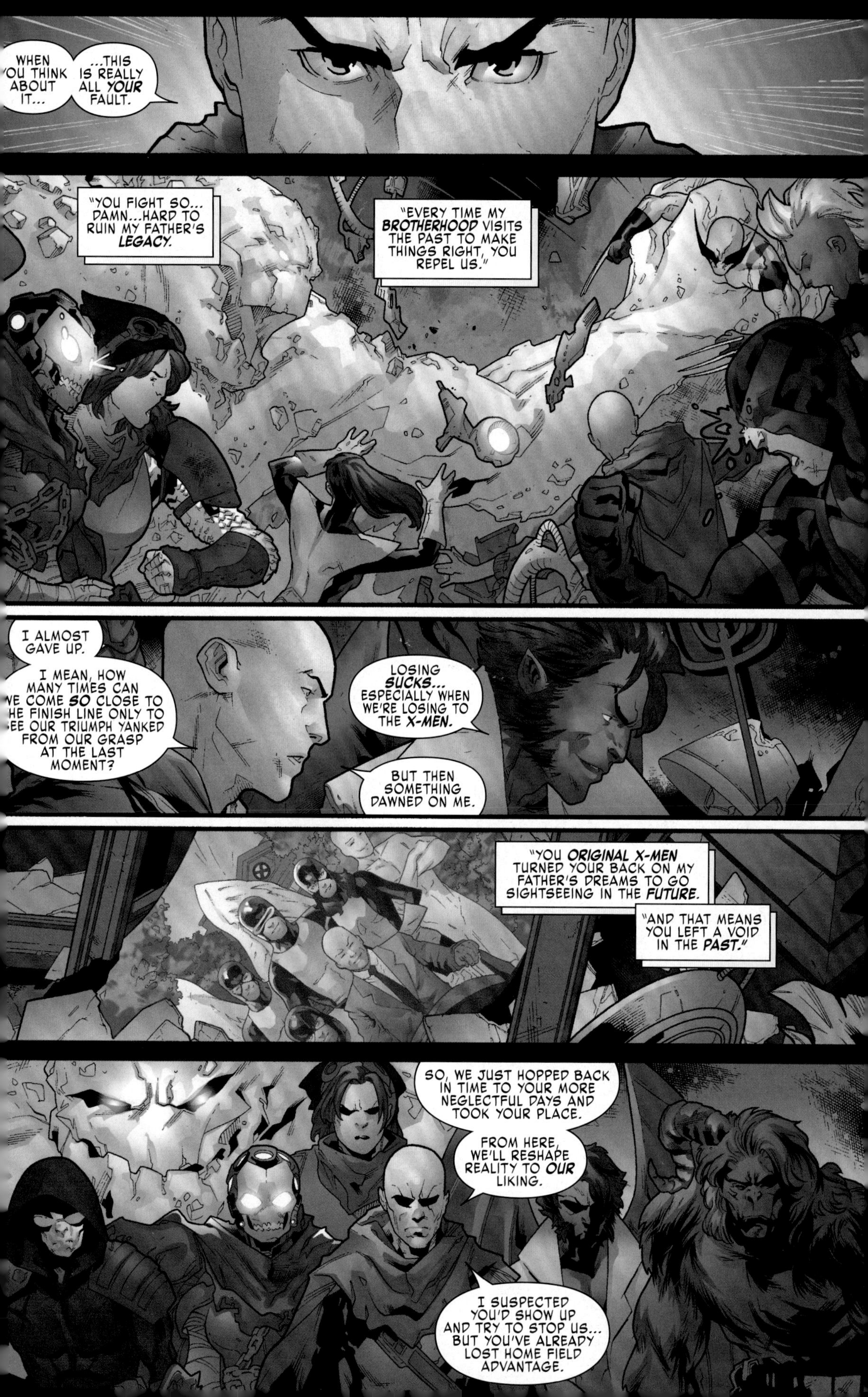

WHEN YOU THINK ABOUT IT...
...THIS IS REALLY ALL YOUR FAULT.
"YOU FIGHT SO... DAMN...HARD TO RUIN MY FATHER'S LEGACY.
"EVERY TIME MY BROTHERHOOD VISITS THE PAST TO MAKE THINGS RIGHT, YOU REPEL US."
I ALMOST GAVE UP.
I MEAN, HOW MANY TIMES CAN WE COME SO CLOSE TO THE FINISH LINE ONLY TO SEE OUR TRIUMPH YANKED FROM OUR GRASP AT THE LAST MOMENT?
LOSING SUCKS... ESPECIALLY WHEN WE'RE LOSING TO THE X-MEN.
BUT THEN SOMETHING DAWNED ON ME.
"YOU ORIGINAL X-MEN TURNED YOUR BACK ON MY FATHER'S DREAMS TO GO SIGHTSEEING IN THE FUTURE.
"AND THAT MEANS YOU LEFT A VOID IN THE PAST."
SO, WE JUST HOPPED BACK IN TIME TO YOUR MORE NEGLECTFUL DAYS AND TOOK YOUR PLACE.
FROM HERE, WE'LL RESHAPE REALITY TO OUR LIKING.
I SUSPECTED YOU'D SHOW UP AND TRY TO STOP US... BUT YOU'VE ALREADY LOST HOME FIELD ADVANTAGE.

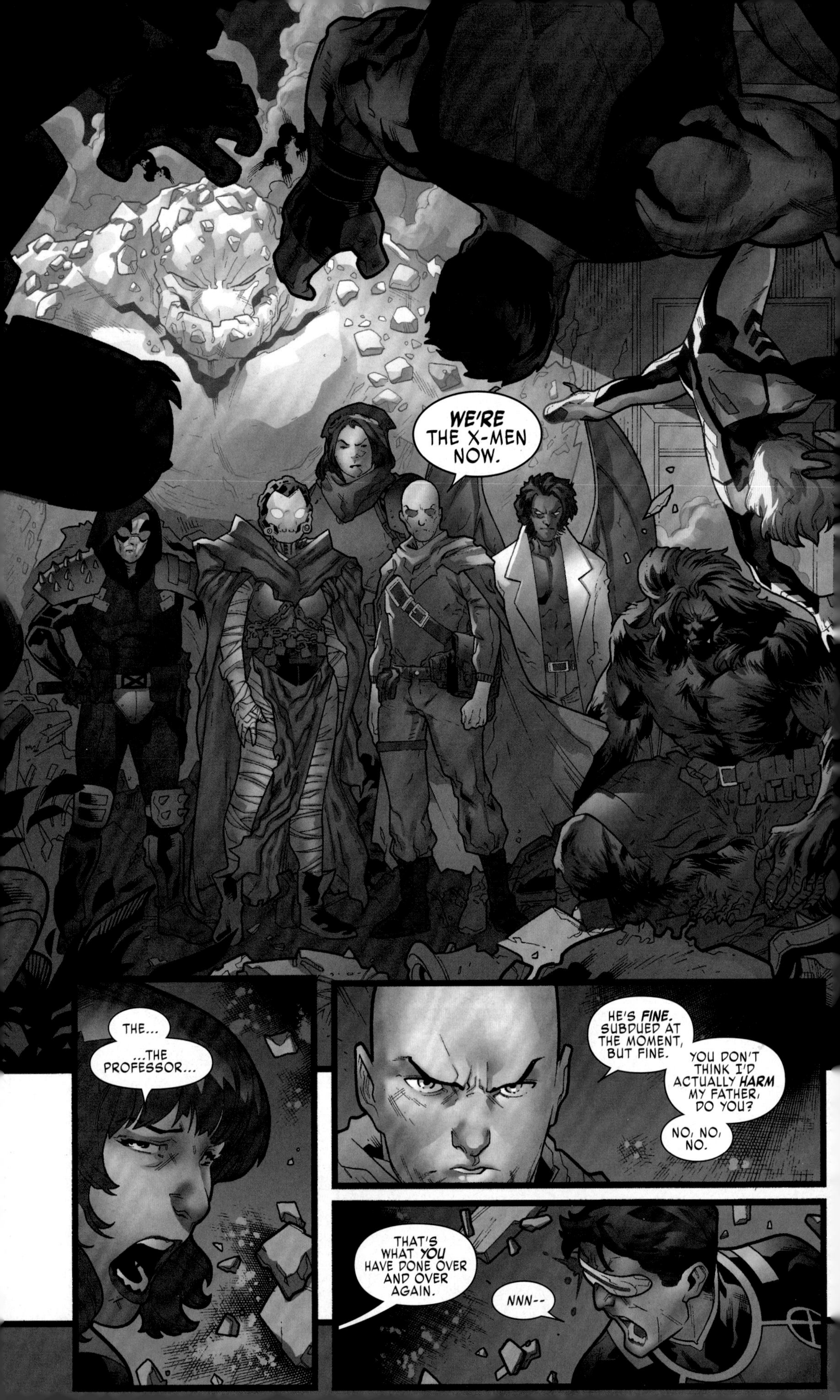
WE'RE THE X-MEN NOW.
THE...
...THE PROFESSOR...
HE'S FINE. SUBDUED AT THE MOMENT, BUT FINE.
YOU DON'T THINK I'D ACTUALLY HARM MY FATHER, DO YOU?
NO, NO, NO.
THAT'S WHAT YOU HAVE DONE OVER AND OVER AGAIN.
NNN--

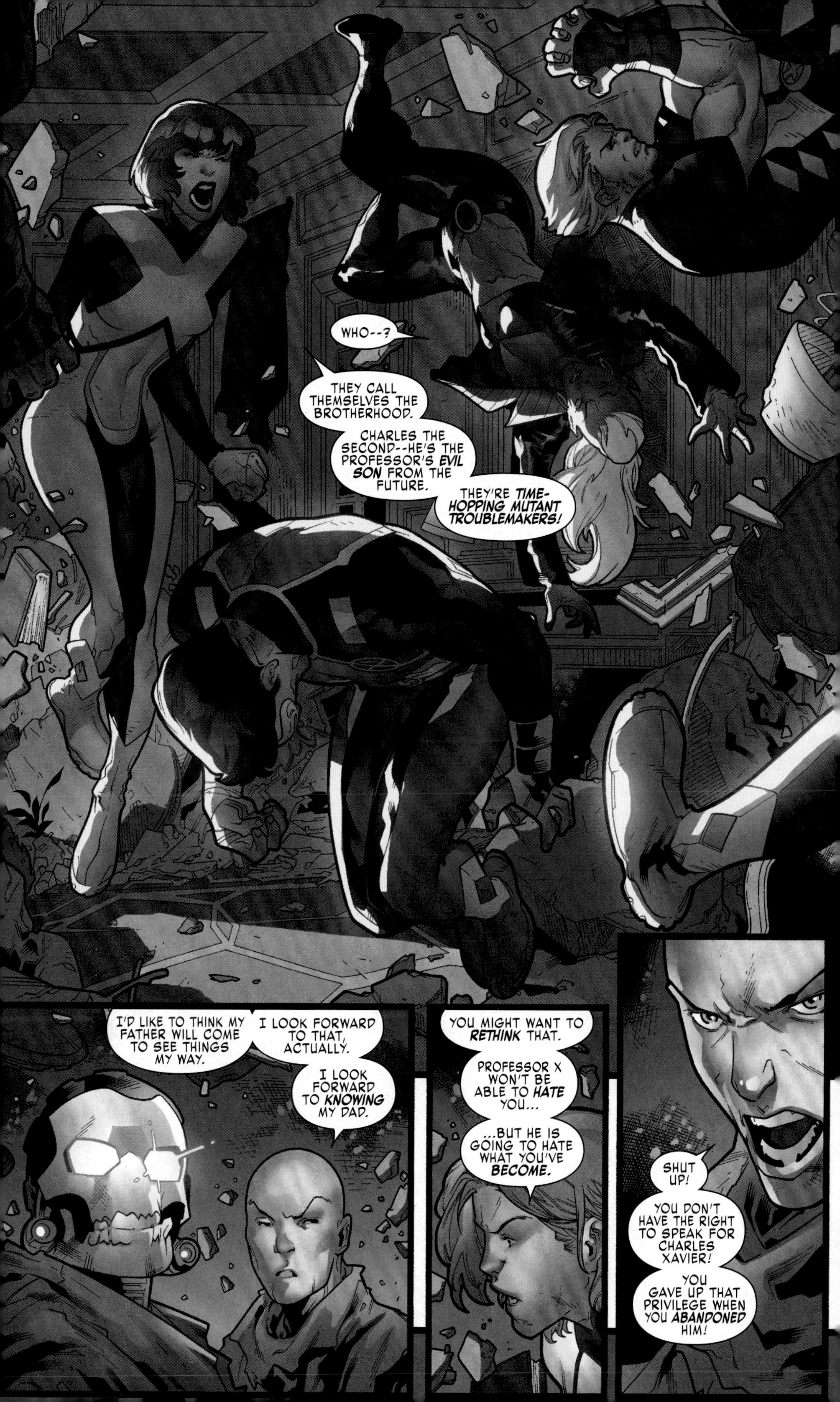
WHO--?
THEY CALL THEMSELVES THE BROTHERHOOD.
CHARLES THE SECOND--HE'S THE PROFESSOR'S EVIL SON FROM THE FUTURE.
THEY'RE TIME-HOPPING MUTANT TROUBLEMAKERS!
I'D LIKE TO THINK MY FATHER WILL COME TO SEE THINGS MY WAY.
I LOOK FORWARD TO THAT, ACTUALLY.
I LOOK FORWARD TO KNOWING MY DAD.
YOU MIGHT WANT TO RETHINK THAT.
PROFESSOR X WON'T BE ABLE TO HATE YOU...
...BUT HE IS GOING TO HATE WHAT YOU'VE BECOME.
SHUT UP!
YOU DON'T HAVE THE RIGHT TO SPEAK FOR CHARLES XAVIER!
YOU GAVE UP THAT PRIVILEGE WHEN YOU ABANDONED HIM!

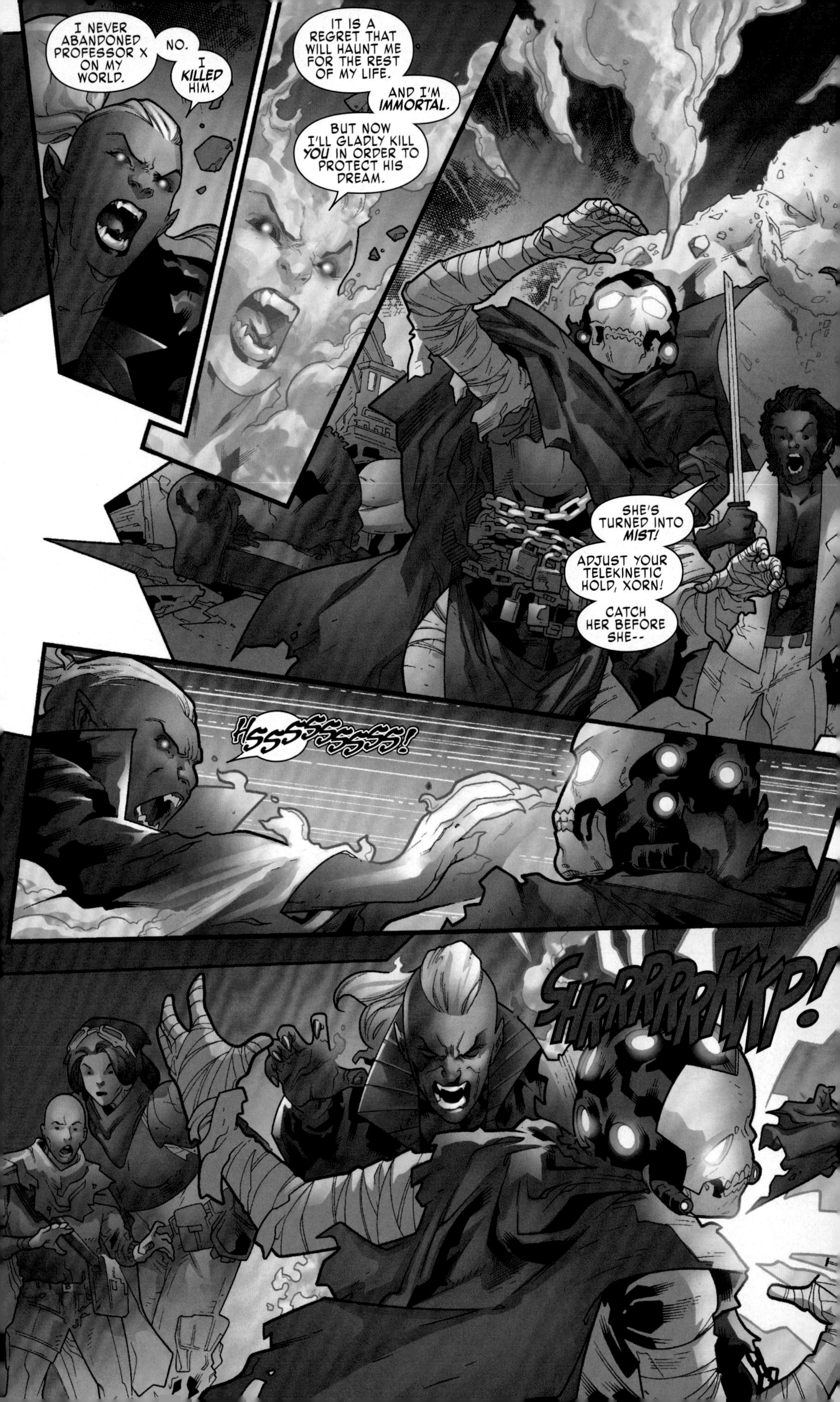
I NEVER ABANDONED PROFESSOR X ON MY WORLD.
NO.
I KILLED HIM.
IT IS A REGRET THAT WILL HAUNT ME FOR THE REST OF MY LIFE.
AND I'M IMMORTAL.
BUT NOW I'LL GLADLY KILL YOU IN ORDER TO PROTECT HIS DREAM.
SHE'S TURNED INTO MIST!
ADJUST YOUR TELEKINETIC HOLD, XORN!
CATCH HER BEFORE SHE--
HSSSSSSSSS!
SHRRRRRAKKP!

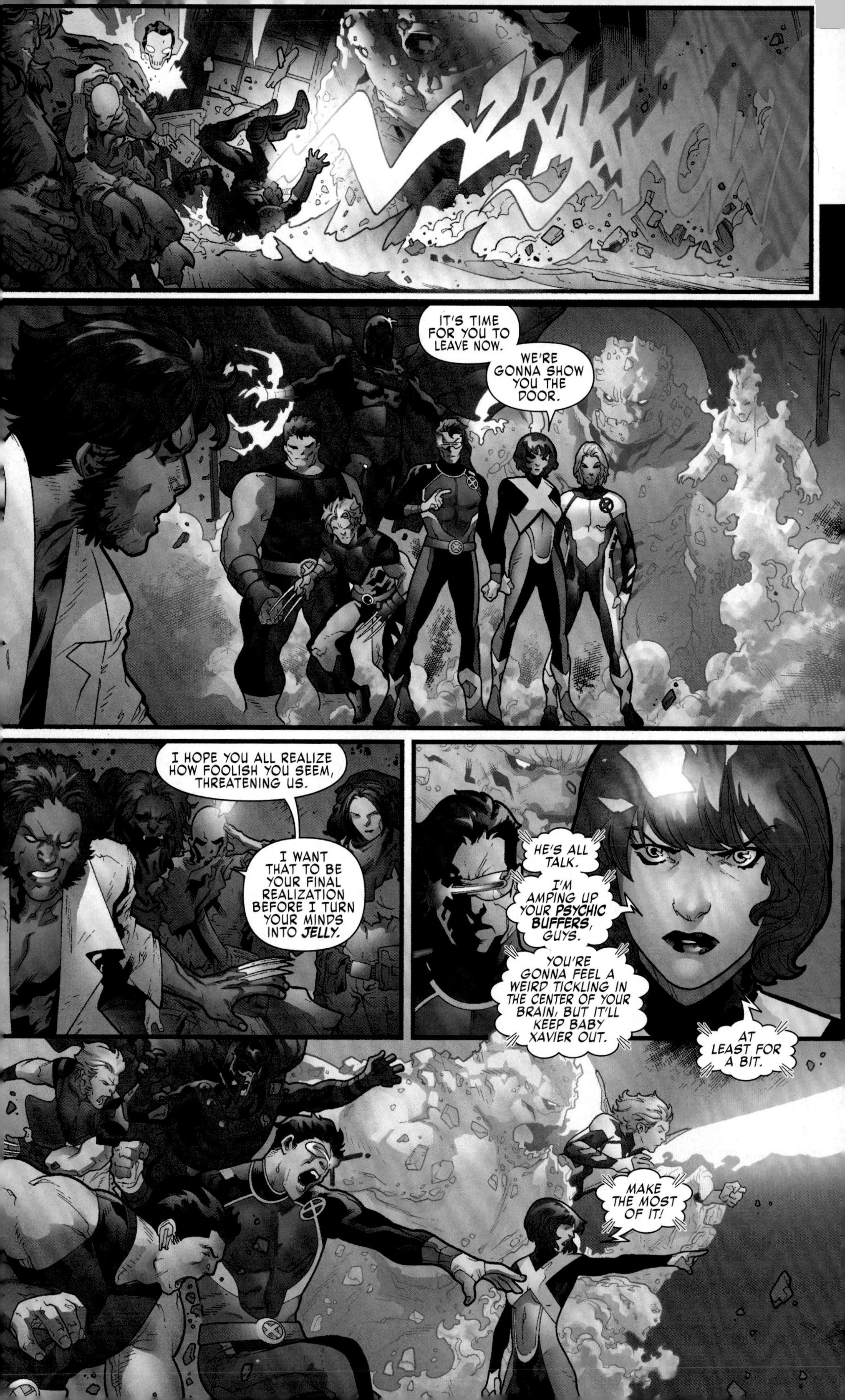
ZRAKA-KOOOW!
IT'S TIME FOR YOU TO LEAVE NOW.
WE'RE GONNA SHOW YOU THE DOOR.
I HOPE YOU ALL REALIZE HOW FOOLISH YOU SEEM, THREATENING US.
I WANT THAT TO BE YOUR FINAL REALIZATION BEFORE I TURN YOUR MINDS INTO JELLY.
HE'S ALL TALK.
I'M AMPING UP YOUR PSYCHIC BUFFERS, GUYS.
YOU'RE GONNA FEEL A WEIRD TICKLING IN THE CENTER OF YOUR BRAIN, BUT IT'LL KEEP BABY XAVIER OUT.
AT LEAST FOR A BIT.
MAKE THE MOST OF IT!

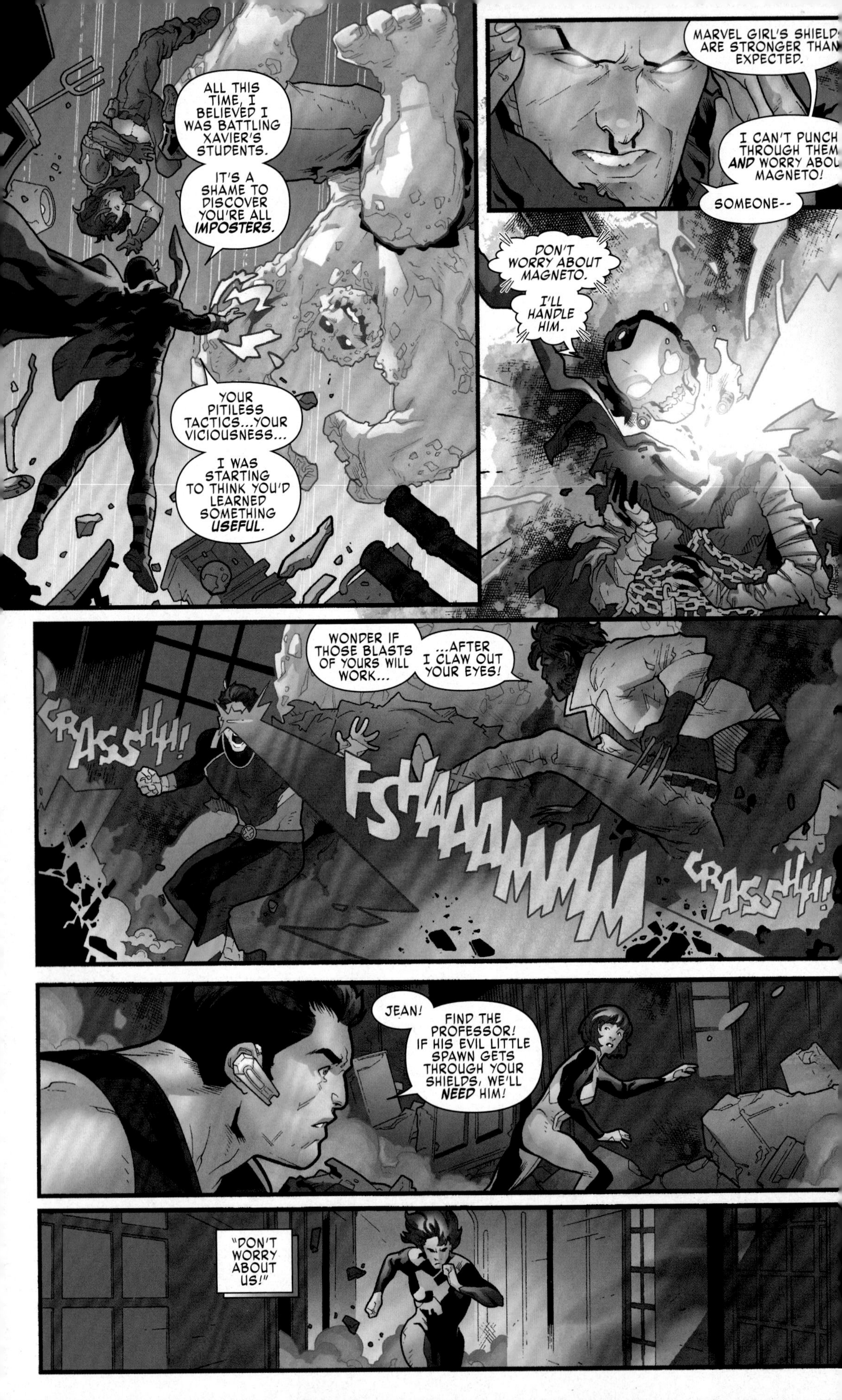

ALL THIS TIME, I BELIEVED I WAS BATTLING XAVIER'S STUDENTS.
IT'S A SHAME TO DISCOVER YOU'RE ALL *IMPOSTERS*.
YOUR PITILESS TACTICS...YOUR VICIOUSNESS...
I WAS STARTING TO THINK YOU'D LEARNED SOMETHING *USEFUL*.
MARVEL GIRL'S SHIELDS ARE STRONGER THAN EXPECTED.
I CAN'T PUNCH THROUGH THEM *AND* WORRY ABOUT MAGNETO!
SOMEONE--
DON'T WORRY ABOUT MAGNETO.
I'LL HANDLE HIM.
WONDER IF THOSE BLASTS OF YOURS WILL WORK...
...AFTER I CLAW OUT YOUR EYES!
CRASSHH!
FSHAAAMMM
CRASSHH!
JEAN!
FIND THE PROFESSOR! IF HIS EVIL LITTLE SPAWN GETS THROUGH YOUR SHIELDS, WE'LL *NEED* HIM!
"DON'T WORRY ABOUT US!"

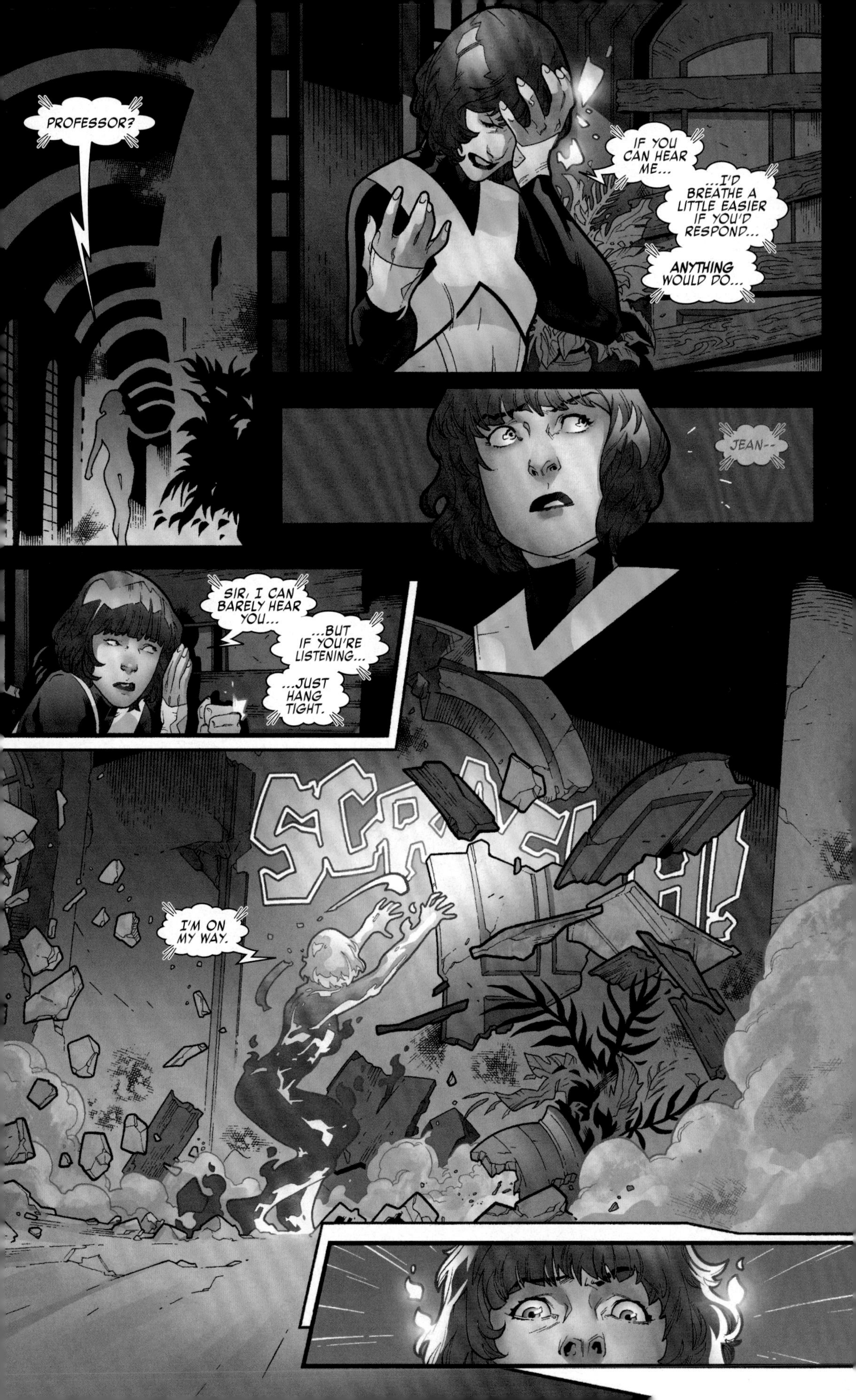
PROFESSOR?
IF YOU CAN HEAR ME...
...I'D BREATHE A LITTLE EASIER IF YOU'D RESPOND...
ANYTHING WOULD DO...
JEAN--
SIR, I CAN BARELY HEAR YOU...
...BUT IF YOU'RE LISTENING...
...JUST HANG TIGHT.
I'M ON MY WAY.

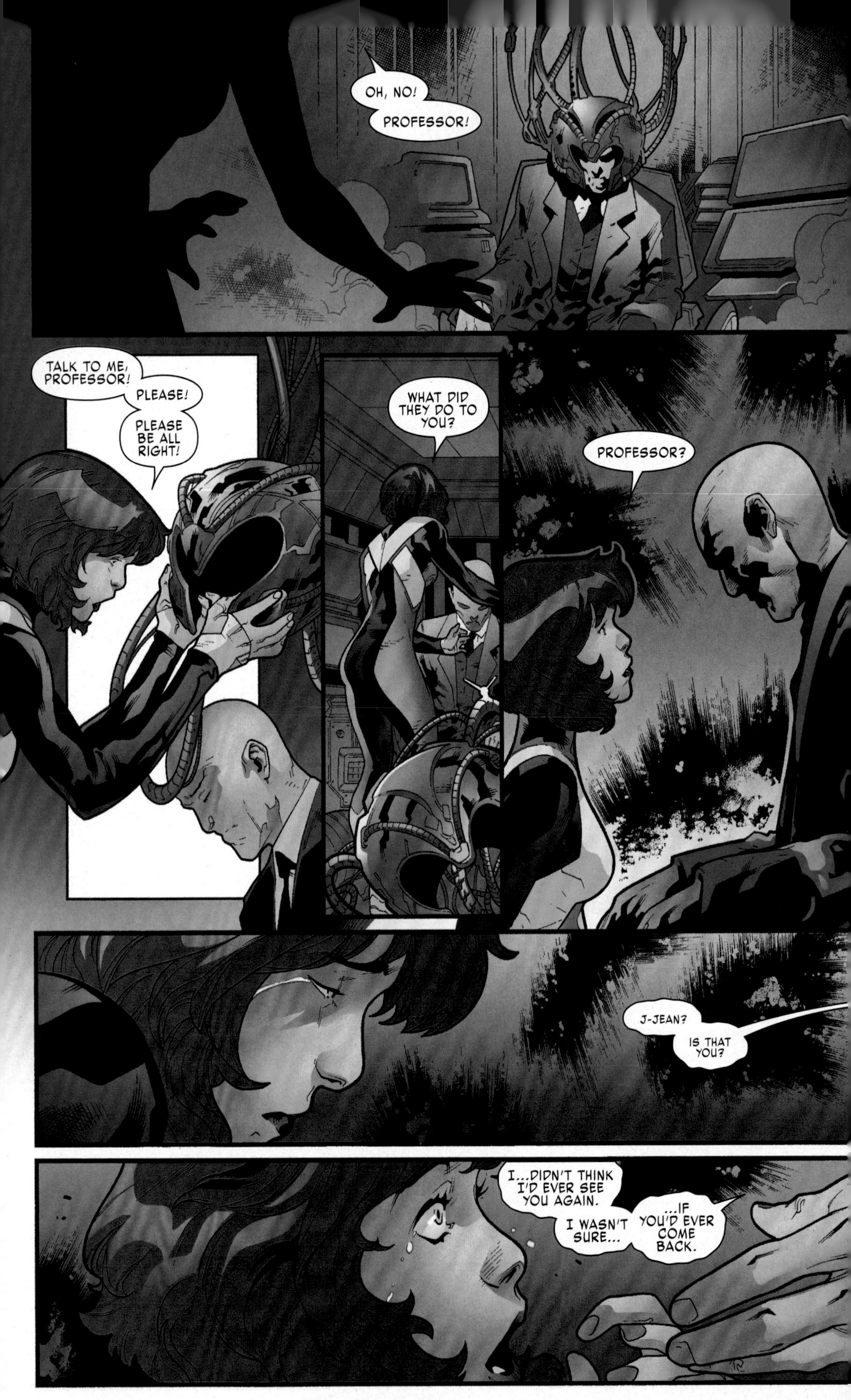

OH, NO!
PROFESSOR!
TALK TO ME, PROFESSOR!
PLEASE!
PLEASE BE ALL RIGHT!
WHAT DID THEY DO TO YOU?
PROFESSOR?
J-JEAN?
IS THAT YOU?
I...DIDN'T THINK I'D EVER SEE YOU AGAIN.
I WASN'T SURE...
...IF YOU'D EVER COME BACK.

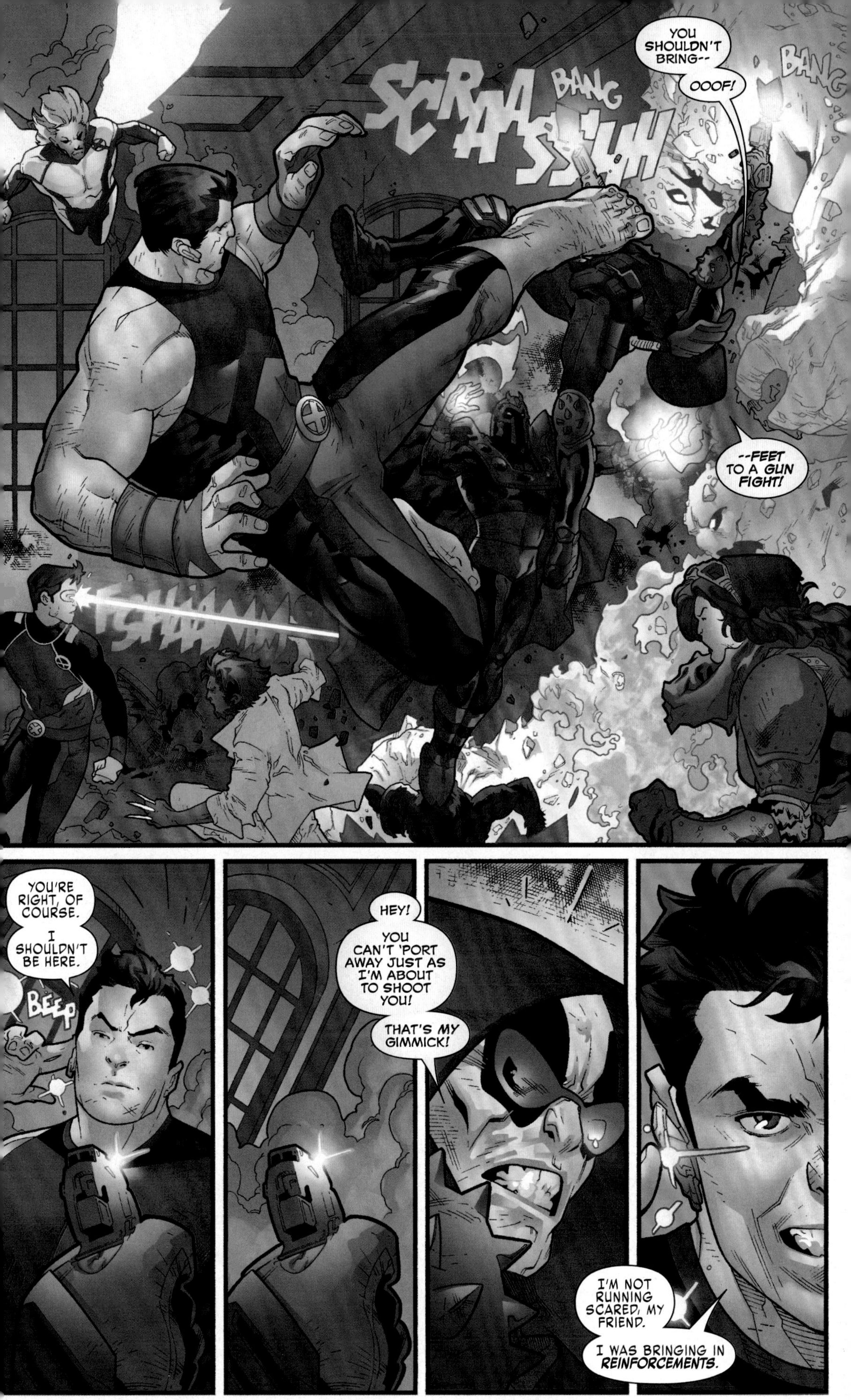
YOU SHOULDN'T BRING--
OOOF!
SCRAASSHH
BANG
BANG
--FEET TO A GUN FIGHT!
TSHAAMM
YOU'RE RIGHT, OF COURSE.
I SHOULDN'T BE HERE.
BEEP
HEY!
YOU CAN'T 'PORT AWAY JUST AS I'M ABOUT TO SHOOT YOU!
THAT'S MY GIMMICK!
I'M NOT RUNNING SCARED, MY FRIEND.
I WAS BRINGING IN REINFORCEMENTS.

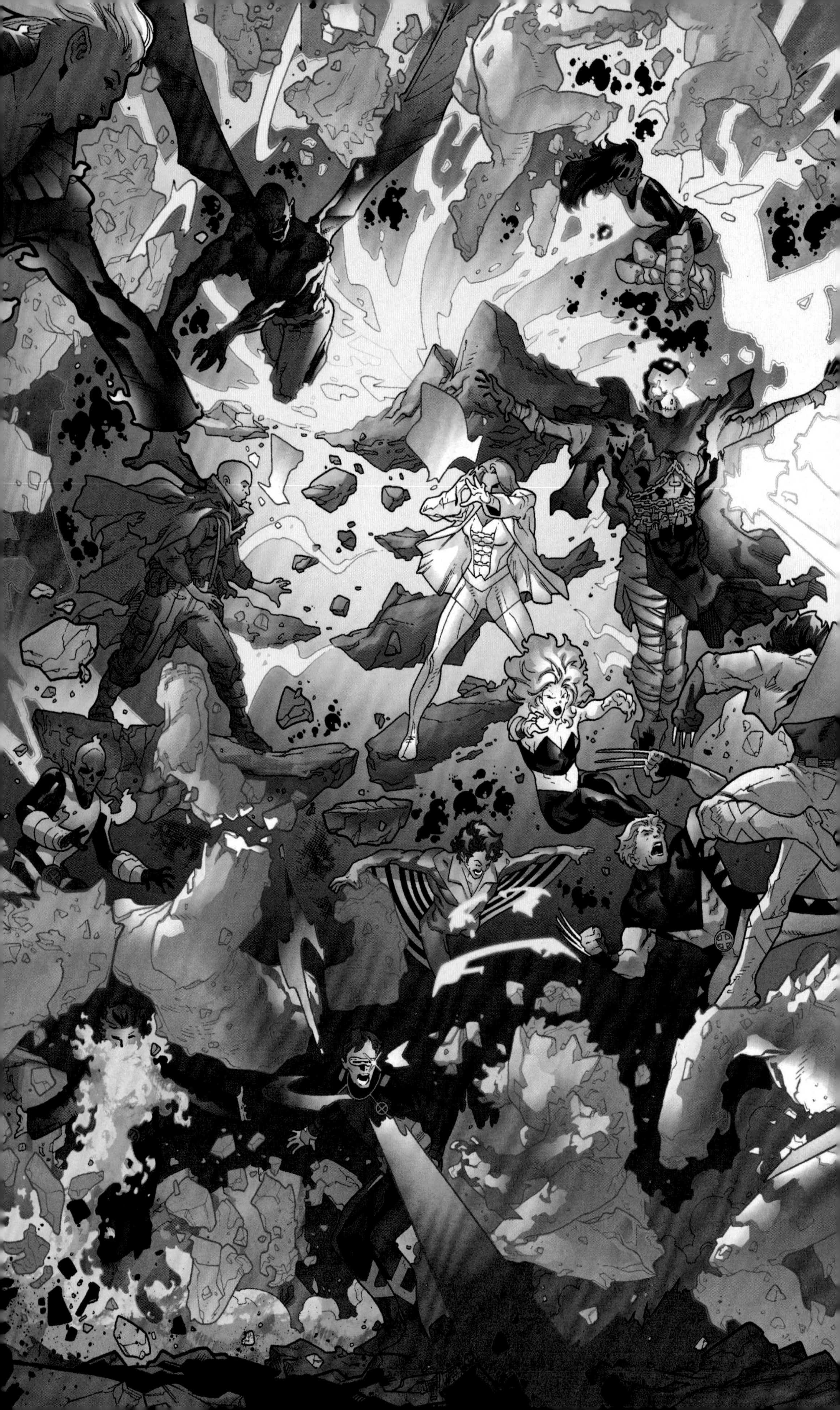

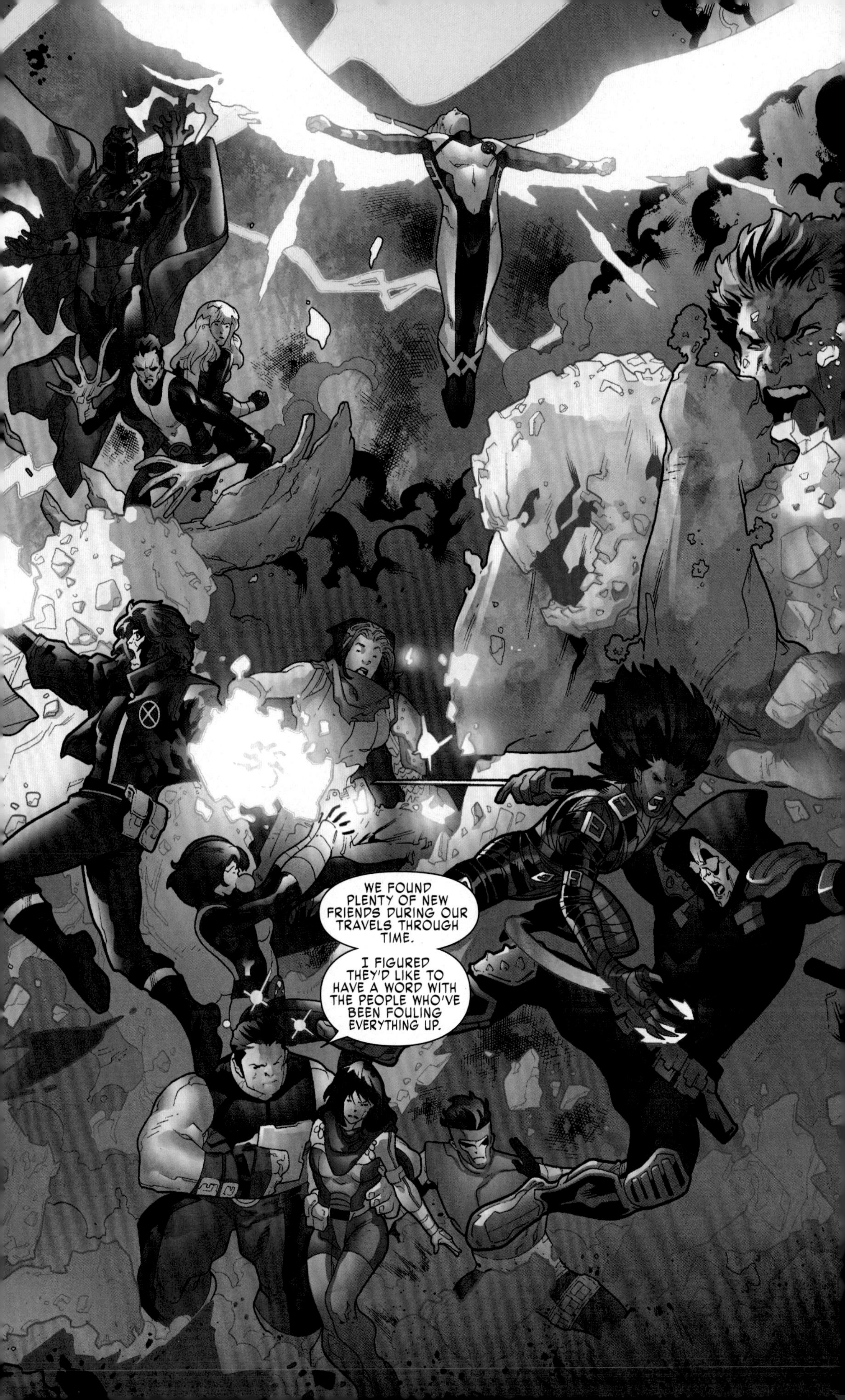
WE FOUND PLENTY OF NEW FRIENDS DURING OUR TRAVELS THROUGH TIME.
I FIGURED THEY'D LIKE TO HAVE A WORD WITH THE PEOPLE WHO'VE BEEN FOULING EVERYTHING UP.

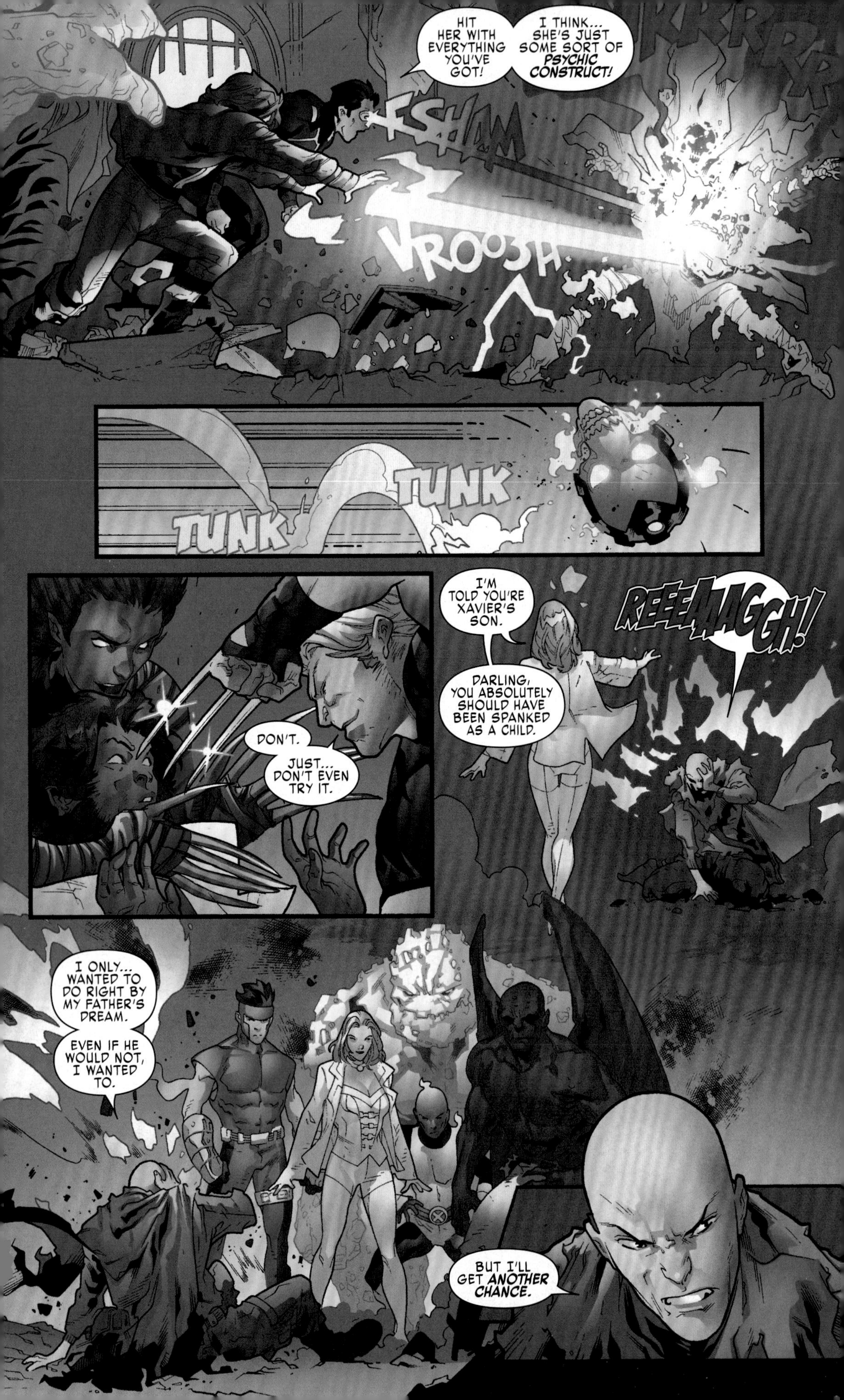
HIT HER WITH EVERYTHING YOU'VE GOT!
I THINK... SHE'S JUST SOME SORT OF PSYCHIC CONSTRUCT!
KRRRRR
FSHAM
VROOSH
TUNK
TUNK
DON'T.
JUST... DON'T EVEN TRY IT.
I'M TOLD YOU'RE XAVIER'S SON.
DARLING, YOU ABSOLUTELY SHOULD HAVE BEEN SPANKED AS A CHILD.
REEEAAAGGH!
I ONLY... WANTED TO DO RIGHT BY MY FATHER'S DREAM.
EVEN IF HE WOULD NOT, I WANTED TO.
BUT I'LL GET ANOTHER CHANCE.

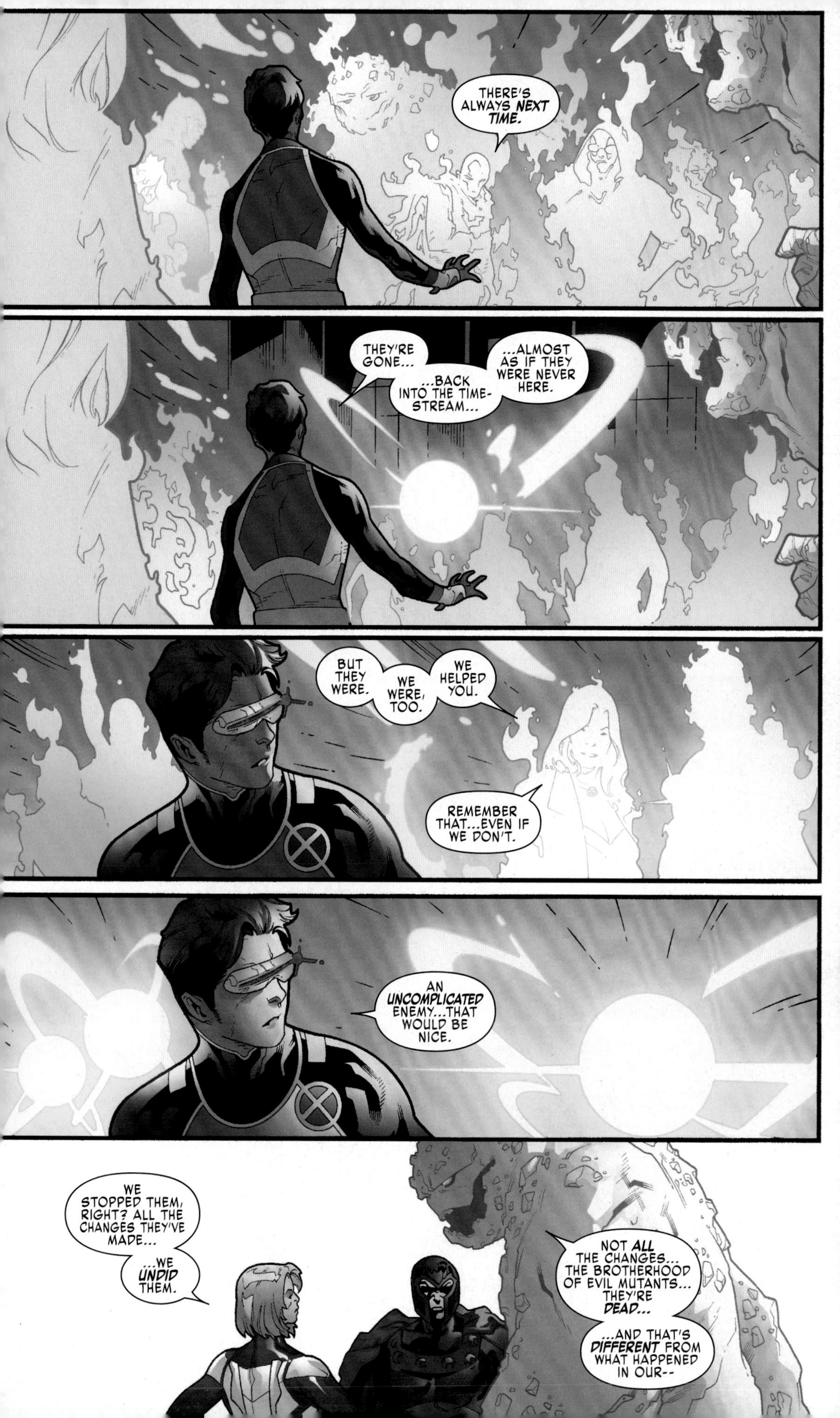

THERE'S ALWAYS NEXT TIME.
THEY'RE GONE...
...BACK INTO THE TIME-STREAM...
...ALMOST AS IF THEY WERE NEVER HERE.
BUT THEY WERE.
WE WERE, TOO.
WE HELPED YOU.
REMEMBER THAT...EVEN IF WE DON'T.
AN UNCOMPLICATED ENEMY...THAT WOULD BE NICE.
WE STOPPED THEM, RIGHT? ALL THE CHANGES THEY'VE MADE...
...WE UNDID THEM.
NOT ALL THE CHANGES... THE BROTHERHOOD OF EVIL MUTANTS... THEY'RE DEAD...
...AND THAT'S DIFFERENT FROM WHAT HAPPENED IN OUR--

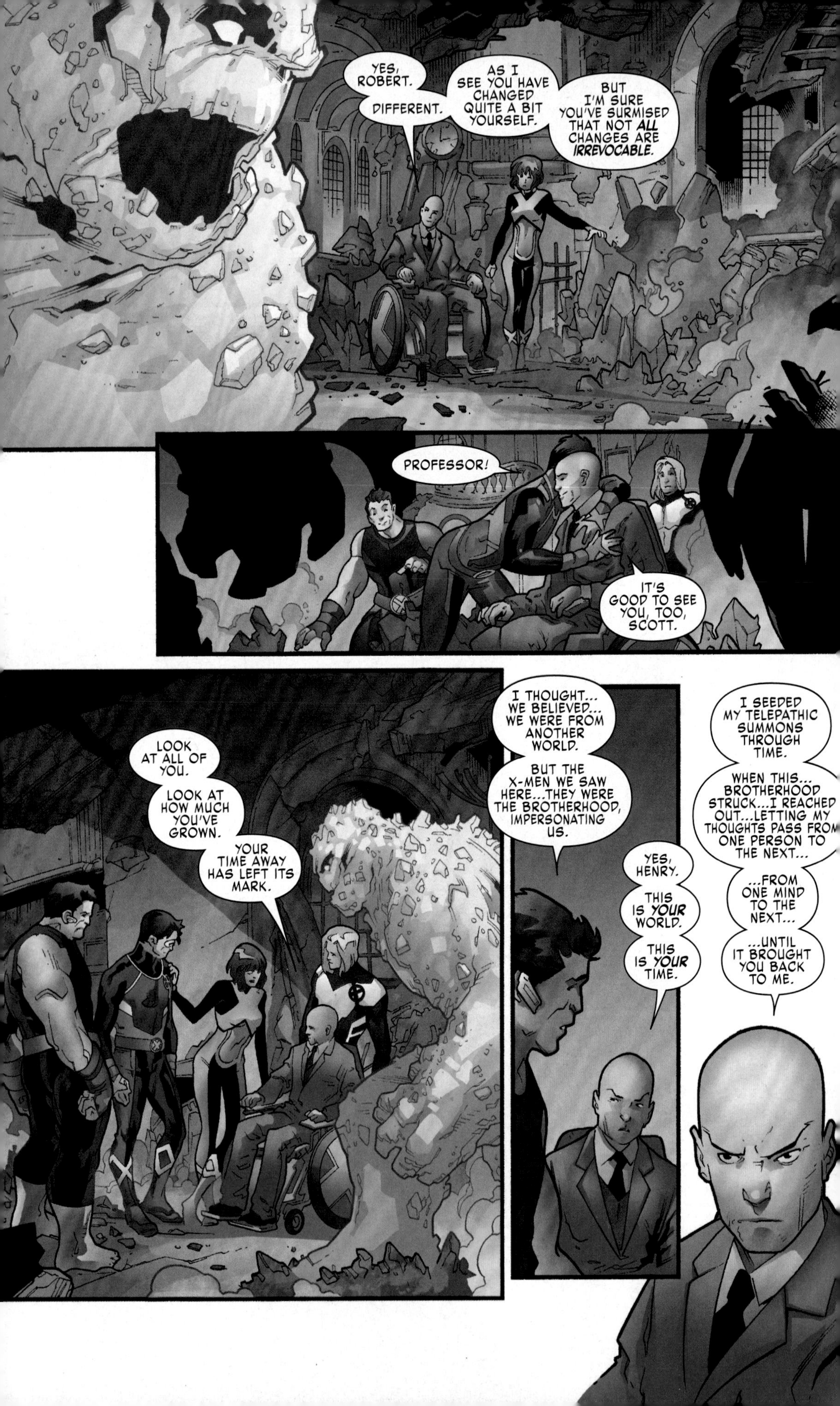

YES, ROBERT.
DIFFERENT.
AS I SEE YOU HAVE CHANGED QUITE A BIT YOURSELF.
BUT I'M SURE YOU'VE SURMISED THAT NOT ALL CHANGES ARE IRREVOCABLE.
PROFESSOR!
IT'S GOOD TO SEE YOU, TOO, SCOTT.
LOOK AT ALL OF YOU.
LOOK AT HOW MUCH YOU'VE GROWN.
YOUR TIME AWAY HAS LEFT ITS MARK.
I THOUGHT... WE BELIEVED... WE WERE FROM ANOTHER WORLD.
BUT THE X-MEN WE SAW HERE...THEY WERE THE BROTHERHOOD, IMPERSONATING US.
YES, HENRY.
THIS IS YOUR WORLD.
THIS IS YOUR TIME.
I SEEDED MY TELEPATHIC SUMMONS THROUGH TIME.
WHEN THIS... BROTHERHOOD STRUCK...I REACHED OUT...LETTING MY THOUGHTS PASS FROM ONE PERSON TO THE NEXT...
...FROM ONE MIND TO THE NEXT...
...UNTIL IT BROUGHT YOU BACK TO ME.

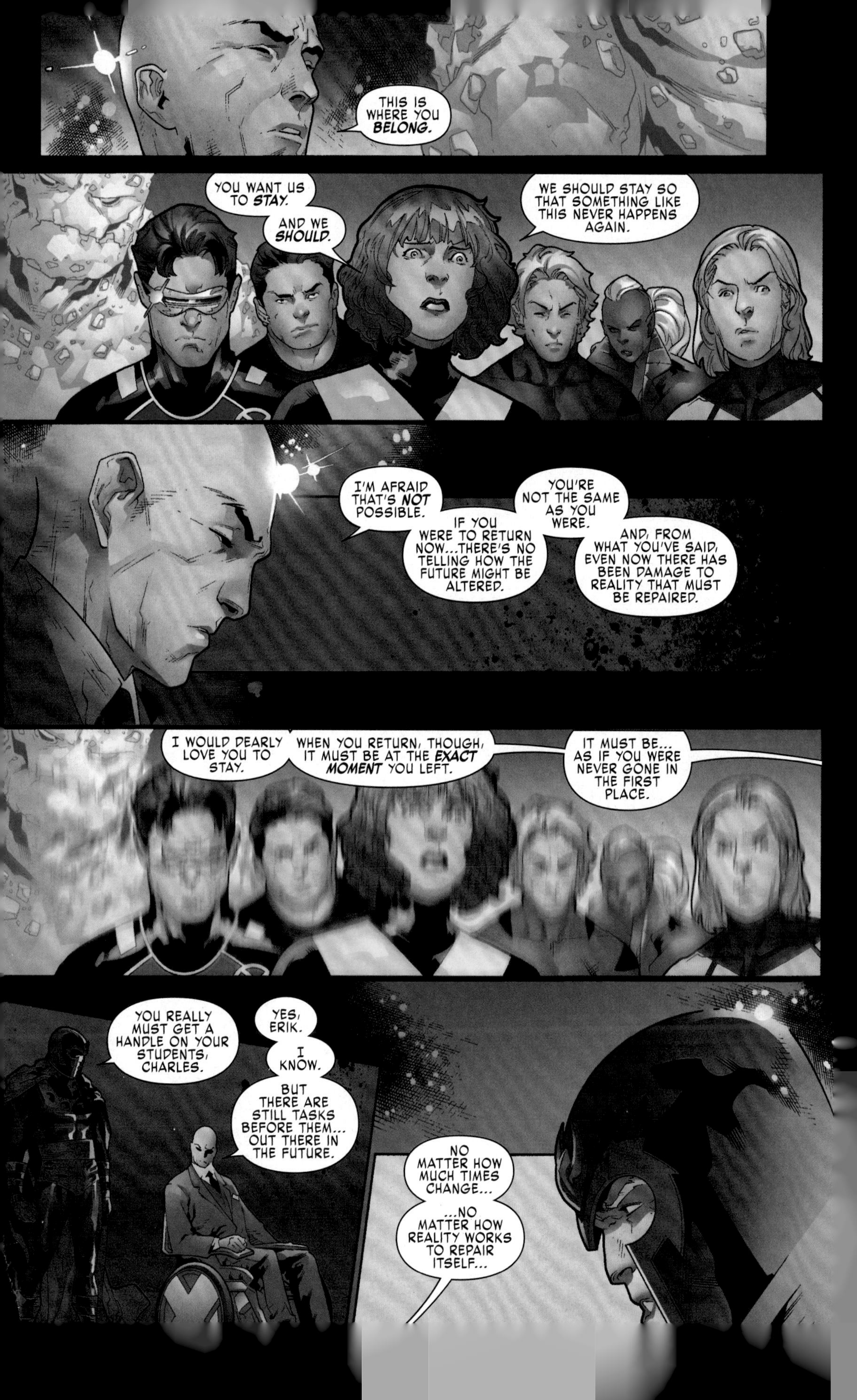
THIS IS WHERE YOU BELONG.
YOU WANT US TO STAY.
AND WE SHOULD.
WE SHOULD STAY SO THAT SOMETHING LIKE THIS NEVER HAPPENS AGAIN.
I'M AFRAID THAT'S NOT POSSIBLE.
IF YOU WERE TO RETURN NOW...THERE'S NO TELLING HOW THE FUTURE MIGHT BE ALTERED.
YOU'RE NOT THE SAME AS YOU WERE.
AND, FROM WHAT YOU'VE SAID, EVEN NOW THERE HAS BEEN DAMAGE TO REALITY THAT MUST BE REPAIRED.
I WOULD DEARLY LOVE YOU TO STAY.
WHEN YOU RETURN, THOUGH, IT MUST BE AT THE EXACT MOMENT YOU LEFT.
IT MUST BE... AS IF YOU WERE NEVER GONE IN THE FIRST PLACE.
YOU REALLY MUST GET A HANDLE ON YOUR STUDENTS, CHARLES.
YES, ERIK.
I KNOW.
BUT THERE ARE STILL TASKS BEFORE THEM... OUT THERE IN THE FUTURE.
NO MATTER HOW MUCH TIMES CHANGE...
...NO MATTER HOW REALITY WORKS TO REPAIR ITSELF...

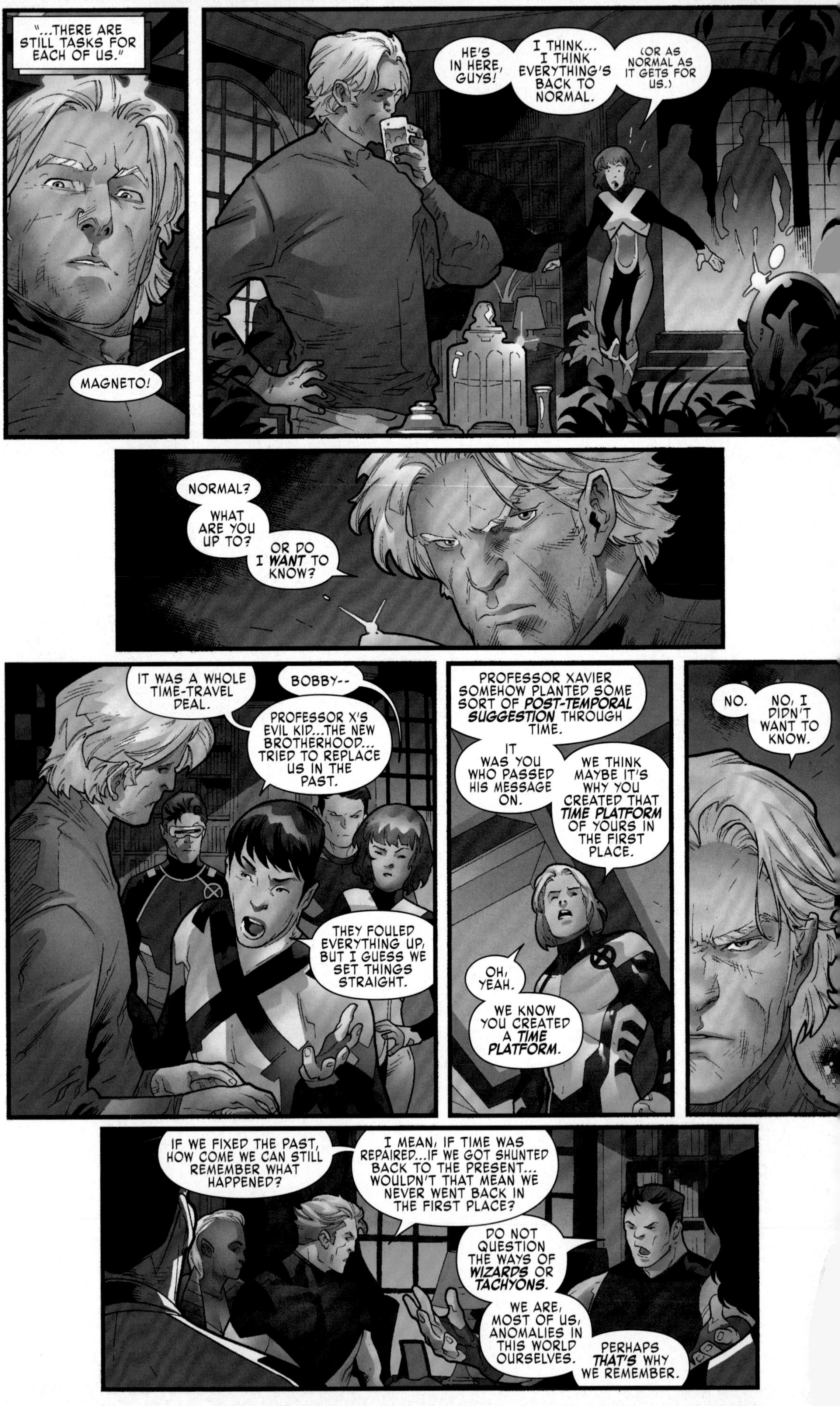
"...THERE ARE STILL TASKS FOR EACH OF US."
MAGNETO!
HE'S IN HERE, GUYS!
I THINK... I THINK EVERYTHING'S BACK TO NORMAL.
(OR AS NORMAL AS IT GETS FOR US.)
NORMAL? WHAT ARE YOU UP TO?
OR DO I WANT TO KNOW?
IT WAS A WHOLE TIME-TRAVEL DEAL.
BOBBY--
PROFESSOR X'S EVIL KID...THE NEW BROTHERHOOD... TRIED TO REPLACE US IN THE PAST.
THEY FOULED EVERYTHING UP, BUT I GUESS WE SET THINGS STRAIGHT.
PROFESSOR XAVIER SOMEHOW PLANTED SOME SORT OF POST-TEMPORAL SUGGESTION THROUGH TIME.
IT WAS YOU WHO PASSED HIS MESSAGE ON.
WE THINK MAYBE IT'S WHY YOU CREATED THAT TIME PLATFORM OF YOURS IN THE FIRST PLACE.
OH, YEAH.
WE KNOW YOU CREATED A TIME PLATFORM.
NO.
NO, I DIDN'T WANT TO KNOW.
IF WE FIXED THE PAST, HOW COME WE CAN STILL REMEMBER WHAT HAPPENED?
I MEAN, IF TIME WAS REPAIRED...IF WE GOT SHUNTED BACK TO THE PRESENT... WOULDN'T THAT MEAN WE NEVER WENT BACK IN THE FIRST PLACE?
DO NOT QUESTION THE WAYS OF WIZARDS OR TACHYONS.
WE ARE, MOST OF US, ANOMALIES IN THIS WORLD OURSELVES.
PERHAPS THAT'S WHY WE REMEMBER.

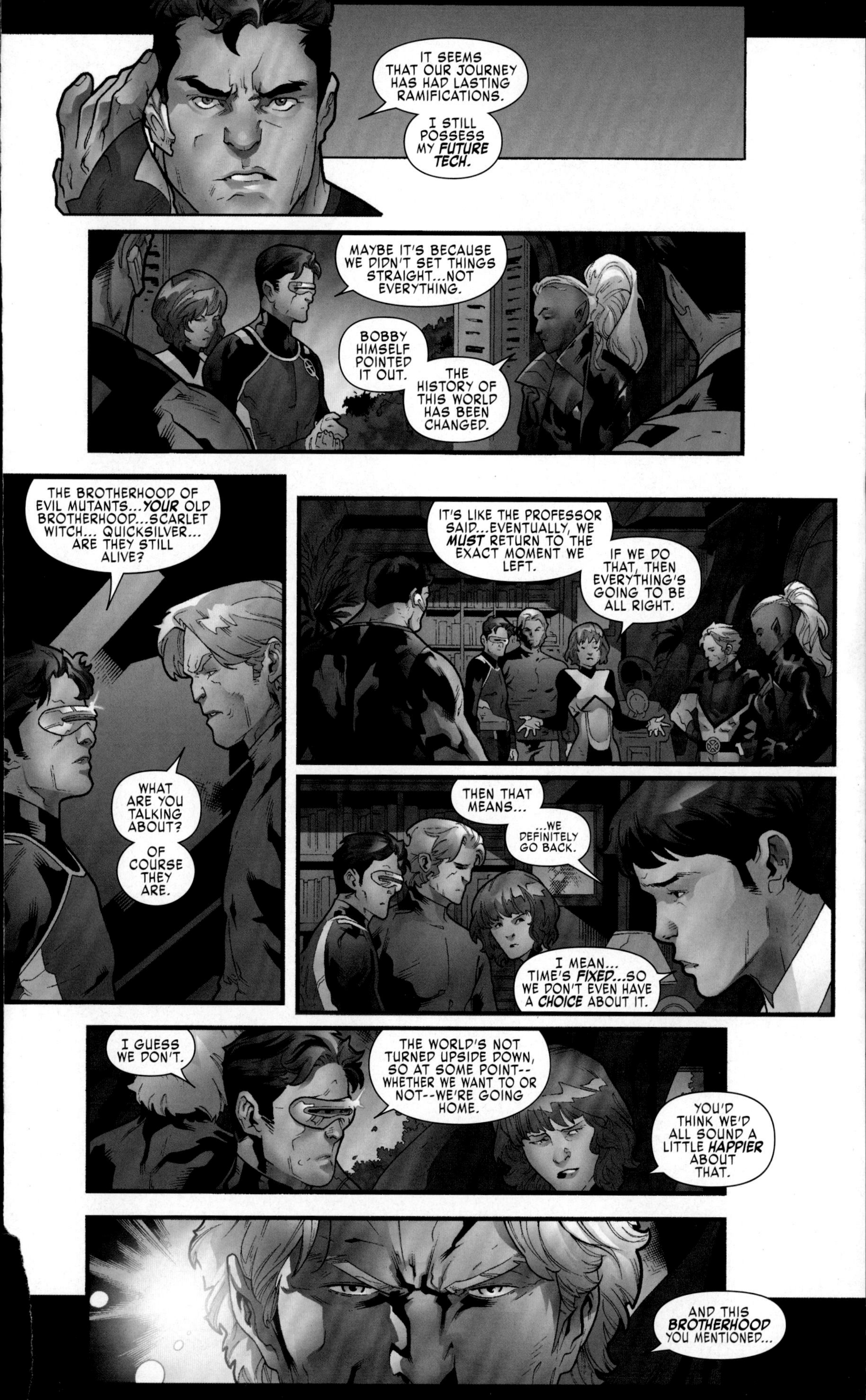
IT SEEMS THAT OUR JOURNEY HAS HAD LASTING RAMIFICATIONS.
I STILL POSSESS MY FUTURE TECH.
MAYBE IT'S BECAUSE WE DIDN'T SET THINGS STRAIGHT...NOT EVERYTHING.
BOBBY HIMSELF POINTED IT OUT.
THE HISTORY OF THIS WORLD HAS BEEN CHANGED.
THE BROTHERHOOD OF EVIL MUTANTS...YOUR OLD BROTHERHOOD...SCARLET WITCH... QUICKSILVER... ARE THEY STILL ALIVE?
WHAT ARE YOU TALKING ABOUT?
OF COURSE THEY ARE.
IT'S LIKE THE PROFESSOR SAID...EVENTUALLY, WE MUST RETURN TO THE EXACT MOMENT WE LEFT.
IF WE DO THAT, THEN EVERYTHING'S GOING TO BE ALL RIGHT.
THEN THAT MEANS...
...WE DEFINITELY GO BACK.
I MEAN... TIME'S FIXED...SO WE DON'T EVEN HAVE A CHOICE ABOUT IT.
I GUESS WE DON'T.
THE WORLD'S NOT TURNED UPSIDE DOWN, SO AT SOME POINT--WHETHER WE WANT TO OR NOT--WE'RE GOING HOME.
YOU'D THINK WE'D ALL SOUND A LITTLE HAPPIER ABOUT THAT.
AND THIS BROTHERHOOD YOU MENTIONED...

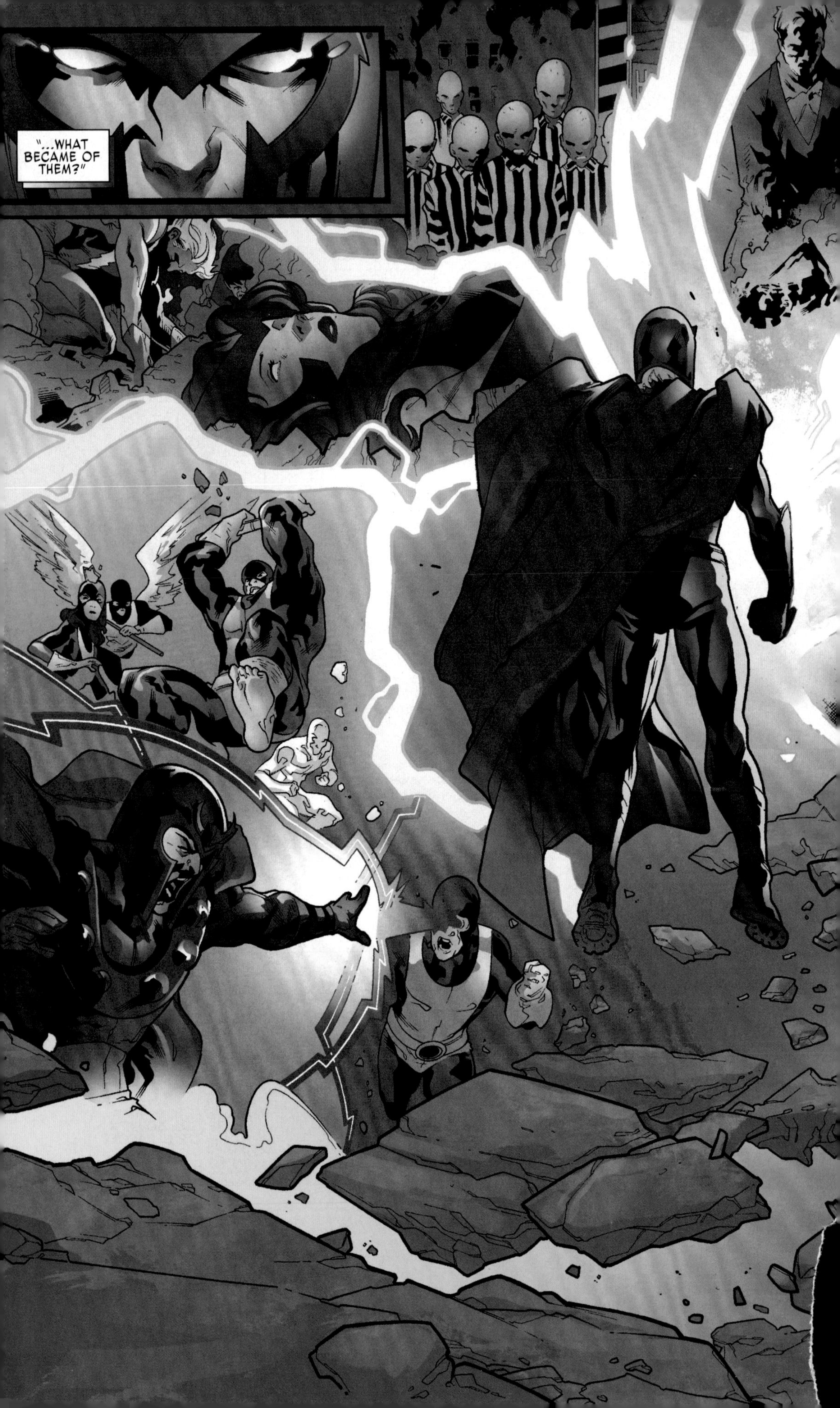
"...WHAT BECAME OF THEM?"

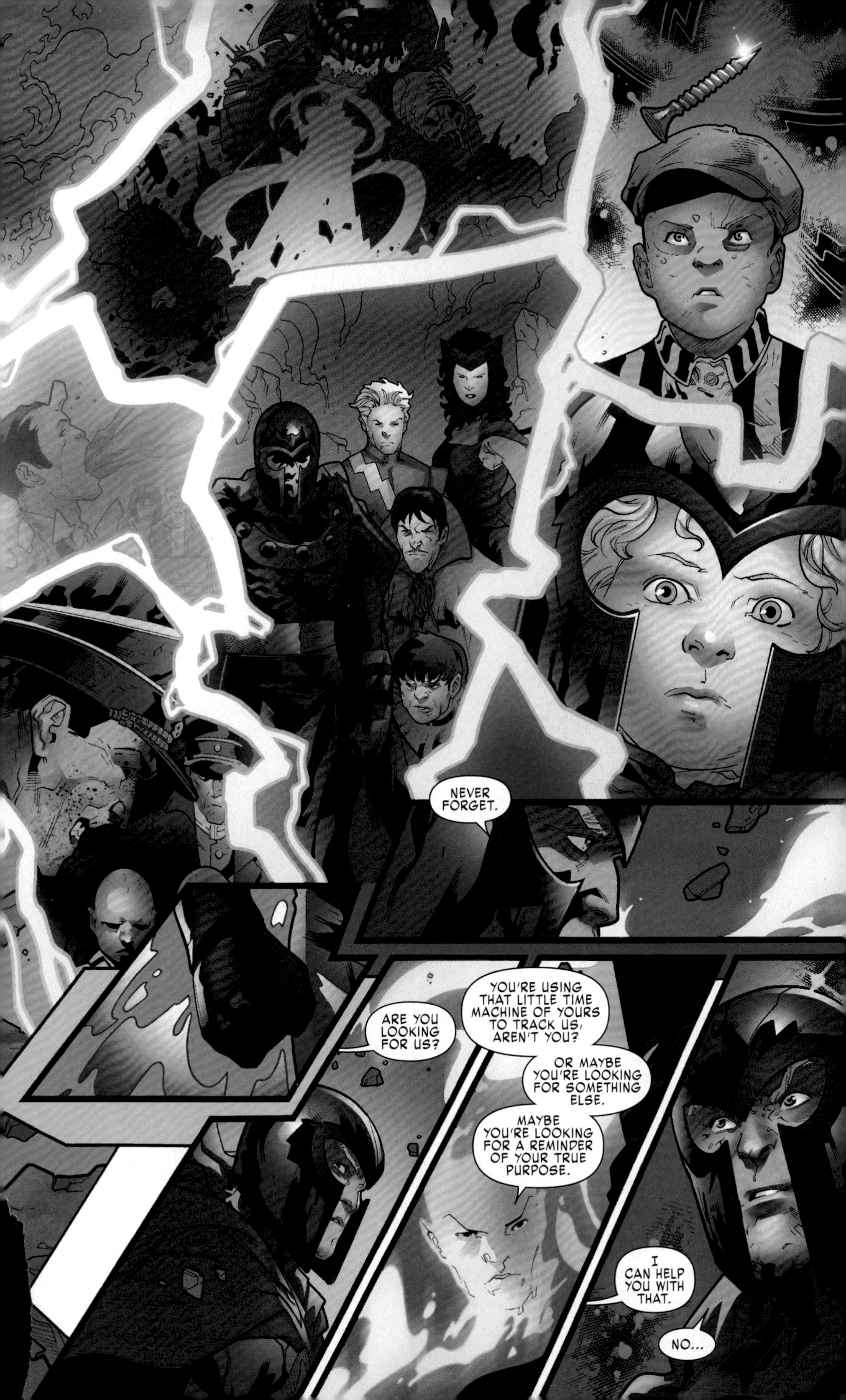
NEVER FORGET.
ARE YOU LOOKING FOR US?
YOU'RE USING THAT LITTLE TIME MACHINE OF YOURS TO TRACK US, AREN'T YOU?
OR MAYBE YOU'RE LOOKING FOR SOMETHING ELSE.
MAYBE YOU'RE LOOKING FOR A REMINDER OF YOUR TRUE PURPOSE.
I CAN HELP YOU WITH THAT.
NO...

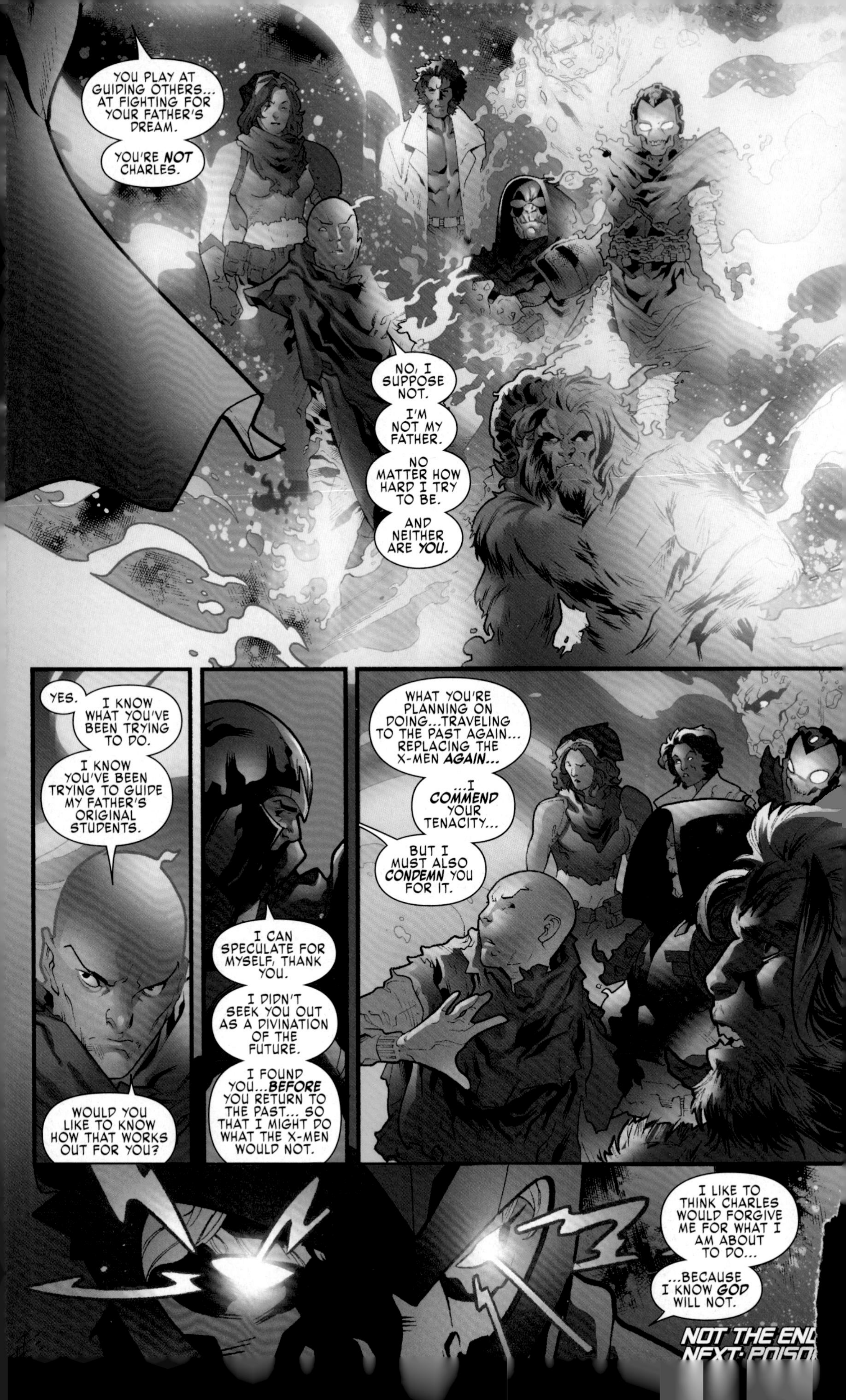
YOU PLAY AT GUIDING OTHERS... AT FIGHTING FOR YOUR FATHER'S DREAM.
YOU'RE NOT CHARLES.
NO, I SUPPOSE NOT.
I'M NOT MY FATHER.
NO MATTER HOW HARD I TRY TO BE.
AND NEITHER ARE YOU.
YES.
I KNOW WHAT YOU'VE BEEN TRYING TO DO.
I KNOW YOU'VE BEEN TRYING TO GUIDE MY FATHER'S ORIGINAL STUDENTS.
WOULD YOU LIKE TO KNOW HOW THAT WORKS OUT FOR YOU?
I CAN SPECULATE FOR MYSELF, THANK YOU.
I DIDN'T SEEK YOU OUT AS A DIVINATION OF THE FUTURE.
I FOUND YOU... BEFORE YOU RETURN TO THE PAST... SO THAT I MIGHT DO WHAT THE X-MEN WOULD NOT.
WHAT YOU'RE PLANNING ON DOING...TRAVELING TO THE PAST AGAIN... REPLACING THE X-MEN AGAIN...
...I COMMEND YOUR TENACITY...
BUT I MUST ALSO CONDEMN YOU FOR IT.
I LIKE TO THINK CHARLES WOULD FORGIVE ME FOR WHAT I AM ABOUT TO DO...
...BECAUSE I KNOW GOD WILL NOT.